IMISCOE Research Series

This series is the official book series of IMISCOE, the largest network of excellence on migration and diversity in the world. It comprises publications which present empirical and theoretical research on different aspects of international migration. The authors are all specialists, and the publications a rich source of information for researchers and others involved in international migration studies.

The series is published under the editorial supervision of the IMISCOE Editorial Committee which includes leading scholars from all over Europe. The series, which contains more than eighty titles already, is internationally peer reviewed which ensures that the book published in this series continue to present excellent academic standards and scholarly quality. Most of the books are available open access.

For information on how to submit a book proposal, please visit: http://www.imiscoe.org/publications/how-to-submit-a-book-proposal.

More information about this series at http://www.springer.com/series/13502

Sophie Hinger • Reinhard Schweitzer

Editors

Politics of (Dis)Integration

Editors
Sophie Hinger
Osnabrück University
Osnabrück, Germany

Reinhard Schweitzer
University of Vienna
Vienna, Austria

ISSN 2364-4087   ISSN 2364-4095   (electronic)
IMISCOE Research Series
ISBN 978-3-030-25088-1   ISBN 978-3-030-25089-8   (eBook)
https://doi.org/10.1007/978-3-030-25089-8

Acknowledgements

This book is the outcome of a collective endeavour to make sense of migration and integration processes and their management in contemporary Europe and beyond, which started within the framework of the Marie Skłodowska-Curie Initial Training Network (ITN) 'Integration and International Migration: Pathways and Integration Policies' (INTEGRIM). From the outset, this volume was primarily meant to constitute a project deliverable of the INTEGRIM network and, more precisely, of the working group on 'labour and social integration', in which several contributors to this volume were involved. However, we decided to put significantly more time and work into this book project than would have been necessary in order to tick a box on the deliverables list. We wanted to use the financial resources at our disposal and our existing network of both young and senior migration scholars to bring together insights from different European and other contexts in order to contribute to the heated debates around migration and integration.

Just after the *Brexit* decision, and in parallel with the ongoing conflict over refugee migration to and within Europe, we invited scholars from the INTEGRIM network to contribute to a collective volume under the working title '*Managing (Dis) Integration*'. We also extended the call to selected participants of the ITN 'Changing Employment', which brought together young scholars working on contemporary labour-market issues in Europe, some of whom were focusing on the intersection of employment and migration. In February 2017, we organised a first meeting at the Central European University (CEU) in Budapest, to which all potential contributors were invited. The CEU, which provided us with an excellent venue for exchanging our viewpoints and ideas, has recently been threatened with closure by the Hungarian government. It is with great concern that we follow the latest political developments in Hungary which, amongst other things, have led to the suspension of programmes for refugee education as well as crucial research on migration and migrant solidarity – an outcome which directly affects some of the contributors to this volume. The fact that we, as somewhat privileged young scholars, are also affected by the rise of nationalist and authoritarian forces in and beyond Europe in fact strengthens the very argument of this collective volume.

Our early discussions hugely benefited from the fact that each participant contributed specific knowledge and could draw on recent research experience in various landscapes of (dis)integration, both within and beyond Europe. Apart from varying geographical contexts, the proposed chapters also focus on a diverse range of groups or categories of people and scales of observation. A second meeting and dedicated workshop were held in April 2018 at the University of Sussex in conjunction with the Annual SCMR/JEMS and Graduate Migration conference. On this occasion, every author presented someone else's chapter in order to foster further engagement with and debates between the various contributions, arguments and perspectives.

The initial plan was to produce a truly collective publication, and to share the editing work between all contributors. Since this turned out to be impractical in terms of both internal and external communication as well as logistics, not least because the contributors were spread across many different countries and time zones, we ultimately took on the role as editors. This said, the whole process was still largely collaborative. For example, each author acted as a reviewer of at least two other chapters during the early stages of the writing process. Several rounds of reviews and discussions helped us to find a clear focus and solid collective argument to underpin the volume as a whole and to highlight and refine the connections between the individual chapters. Editing the book was a time-consuming and sometimes challenging task, but we are grateful to the author-collective for entrusting it to us. We certainly learned a lot in the process, especially because we could rely on the help and support of a whole range of other people.

We are grateful to all contributing authors for their dedication and collaboration. In particular, we want to thank Mike Collyer and Viola Zentai, who not only contributed to the volume but also accompanied the project from the very beginning to the very end and helped to organise and facilitate the two workshops.

We would also like to thank Prem Kumar Rajaram, Olena Fedyuk, Blanca Garcés-Mascareñas and all other workshop participants for their constructive feedback and helpful suggestions regarding many of the individual chapters as well as the overall arguments behind the book.

We feel especially indebted to Jenny Money, who not only took the greatest care of the language and copy-editing but who also, in so doing, provided crucial comments and advice on both the form and the content of the volume.

The whole book project was made possible through the financial support received from the European Union's Seventh Framework Programme (FP7/2007-2013). Some of the production costs as well as the research leading to the majority of the chapters (Chaps. 2, 3, 4, 7, 8 and 10) was funded under grant agreement no. 316796, the research underlying Chaps. 5 and 6 received funding under grant agreement no. 31732.

Last but not least, we want to thank the IMISCOE Editorial Committee for selecting our proposal as the Runner-Up for the 2017 IMISCOE Springer Competitive Call for Book Proposals and thus covering half of the Open Access Fees. Our thanks extend, in particular, to Evelien Bakker and Bernadette Deelen-Mans, who acted as our contact persons at Springer and, of course, to the two anonymous reviewers, whose constructive and detailed feedback has helped us to refine the overall argument of the book, and the contributing authors to highlight and strengthen their individual contributions to it.

Osnabrück, Germany   Sophie Hinger
Vienna, Austria   Reinhard Schweitzer

Contents

Contributors

Céline Cantat is a Marie Skłodowska-Curie Individual Fellow at the Centre for Policy Studies at the Central European University (CEU) in Budapest, working on 'MigSol: Migration Solidarity and Acts of Citizenship along the Balkan Route', a 24-month research project that examines solidarity with and by migrants and refugees along the Balkan route. Previously, Céline was Academic Programme Manager of CEU's OLIVe-UP, a university preparatory programme for refugee students, and a postdoctoral researcher on migration solidarity movements in Hungary. Before starting at CPS, Céline completed her PhD in Refugee Studies at the Centre for Research on Migration, Refugees and Belonging at the University of East London, and spent a year at Migrinter, Universite de Poitiers, as an INTEGRIM Marie Skłodowska-Curie Early Stage Researcher. Céline's research interests include globalisation and migration, migration solidarity, racism and exclusion in Europe, and the state formation and dynamics of mass displacement.

Michael Collyer is Professor of Geography at the University of Sussex. His research concerns the relationship between people on the move and state institutions. His recent research projects have looked at undocumented migrants and refugees in Morocco, the resettlement process as experienced by refugees arriving in the UK and migration into very poor urban areas in Colombo, Dhaka, Harare and Hargeisa. He is a member of the steering committee of Sanctuary on Sea, Brighton's City of Sanctuary group.

Amandine Desille is a Marie Skłodowska-Curie Individual Fellow at the Institute of Geography and Spatial Planning at the University of Lisbon, where she conducts a project entitled 'MigRural: Return Mobilities to Rural Portugal, an Assessment of the Production of Place'. Her research interests include return migration, local governance and small and mid-sized cities. She holds a PhD in geography from the University of Poitiers (France) and the University of Tel Aviv (Israel). In her doctoral research entitled 'Governing or Being Governed?', she adopted a scalar approach to the transformation of state power and authority through the case of the immigration and integration policies of four frontier towns in Israel. Previously, she has worked with NGOs and UN agencies on topics related to immigration, local economic development and urban planning.

Sophie Hinger is a PhD candidate at the Institute of Migration Research and Intercultural Studies (IMIS) and a teaching and research fellow in the Geography Department of the University of Osnabrück. In 2015–2016 she worked at the University of Sussex as a Marie Skłodowska-Curie Research Fellow within the INTEGRIM network. Her academic interests, as well as her political and social engagement, centre on questions of migration and asylum, transnational social movements and intercultural learning.

Mateusz Karolak is a postdoctoral research associate in the Institute of Sociology at the University of Wrocław (Poland). He is currently engaged in the 'PREWORK' research project ('Young Precarious Workers in Poland and Germany: A Comparative Sociological Study on Working and Living Conditions, Social Consciousness and Civic Engagement'). In his PhD research, Mateusz examined return migrants' inclusion and employment, focusing on the case of return migration to Poland from the UK. He studied philosophy and cultural anthropology in Poznań (AMU) and Berlin (HU). During 2013–2016 he was a Marie Skłodowska-Curie Research Fellow involved in the Initial Training Network 'Changing Employment'. His research interests include political economy, the reproduction of inequalities, the consequences of employment precarisation, and return migrations within the European Union. Mateusz is also a member of the editorial board of the journal *Praktyka Teoretyczna*.

Tina Magazzini is a research associate at the Robert Schuman Centre for Advanced Studies of the European University Institute, where she conducts research on religious diversity governance in Southern Europe. She holds a PhD in Human Rights from the University of Deusto, where she focused on Roma integration frameworks in Italy and Spain within the international research network INTEGRIM. She is interested in comparative politics, cultural identity and in the relationship between majorities, minorities and states. Her research was awarded the 2016 Ryoichi Sasakawa Young Leaders Fellowship and the 2018 Social Impact Award from the Marie Curie Alumni Association.

Sarah Nimführ is a DOC-Fellow of the Austrian Academy of Sciences at the Institute of European Ethnology at the University of Vienna. During her PhD studies she conducted field research on the impact of non-deportability on rejected asylum-seekers, particularly in the Mediterranean area. Since 2016, she has regularly held courses comprising ethics and methods in the field of flight, engaged anthropology as well as forced migration studies, with a focus on islands, at the Universities of Vienna and Bremen. Previously, Sarah worked as a researcher in a project on protest movements in asylum and deportation in the Institute of Political Science at the University of Vienna. She also worked and volunteered with a number of NGOs in the area of family reunification, educational counseling and advocacy in Austria,

Germany and Australia. She has worked and published together with (refugee) research partners several times in order to practise a collaborative approach towards knowledge production.

Laura Otto is a cultural anthropologist and a PhD candidate at the University of Bremen, where she is also a co-founder of the research group *Flight and Asylum: Transnational and Intersectional*. She has completed extensive field research with young refugees classified as unaccompanied minors in both Malta and Germany. Within her research, she understands the category of age as a field of tension in the context of forced migration to Europe, as this classification is both a legal and an everyday category. Currently a Lecturer at the Universities of Bremen and Vienna, as well as at the Humboldt University of Berlin, her teaching focuses on ethnographic border-regime analysis, transnationalism, intersectionality and processes of social negotiation through forms of research-based learning. Previously, she worked in extra-curricular youth education in heterogeneous and diversity-sensitive contexts.

Nina Sahraoui is currently affiliated to the GTM-CRESPPA, CNRS and the Collèges d'études mondiales, Fondation Maison des sciences de l'homme in Paris, where she co-coordinates the research project 'The (Un)deserving migrant?'. She was previously a postdoctoral research associate at the European University Institute within the ERC-funded 'EU Border Care' project. Nina completed a Marie Skłodowska-Curie Fellowship at London Metropolitan University. Her doctoral research focused on migrant workers' experiences of older-age care in London, Paris and Madrid, leading to a gendered political-economy analysis of the articulation of employment, care and migration regimes.

Gabriel Samateh grew up in the Gambia and has been living in Malta since 2014. The author has opted for a pseudonym, fearing that his co-authorship could jeopardise his status. Therefore, no further biographical information is given here. Gabriel has already published on the situation of non-arrival in the Maltese island state and is interested in different forms of the legal and social exclusion of refugees at Europe's external border.

Şahizer Samuk holds a PhD from the IMT Institute for Advanced Studies in Lucca, Italy. Her thesis is entitled 'Temporary Migration and Temporary Integration: Comparing the Cases of Canada and the UK'. She has been a postdoctoral researcher in the Department of Geography and Spatial Planning at the University of Luxembourg, working for the MOVE project for one and a half years. She also worked for IOM Ankara as a project assistant and, later, as a consultant on a project on supporting the development of harmonisation policies in Turkey. Besides her interest in temporary migration policies, and youth mobility policies in the EU, she also worked on Syrian children's educational integration in Turkey.

Reinhard Schweitzer is a postdoctoral researcher at the Department of Political Science at the University of Vienna, where he currently holds a Marie Skłodowska-Curie Individual Fellowship. As part of the INTEGRIM network he recently completed his PhD in Migration Studies at the University of Sussex and is associated with the Sussex Centre for Migration Research (SCMR) in Brighton, UK. His doctoral research focused on the contradictions underlying the public provision of healthcare, education and social assistance to migrants living irregularly in London and Barcelona. His current project 'REvolTURN' looks at the role and functioning of 'voluntariness' within the management of migrant return from Austria and the UK.

Violetta Zentai is Co-Director of the Center for Policy Studies and faculty member of the School of Public Policy and the Department of Sociology and Social Anthropology at the Central European University in Budapest. Her research focuses on ethnic and gender inequalities, post-socialist capitalist transformations, political and policy debates on social inequalities and pro-equality civil-society formations. She also worked for two decades as an expert with the Open Society Foundation on initiatives related to democratic local governance, equality mainstreaming and rights-based development.

Chapter 1
Politics of (Dis)Integration –
An Introduction

Michael Collyer, Sophie Hinger, and Reinhard Schweitzer

Public policies have always been concerned with the integration of specific migrant and non-migrant others, as well as with that of society as a whole. What is meant by integration has clearly changed over time and, with it, the precise nature of the policies designed to enact it, at both the individual and the societal level. Despite this shifting conceptual foundation, something called 'integration' has been an official policy goal for the last 50 years or more, at least in liberal democracies. As far as the integration of newcomers is concerned, this liberal consensus has begun to change in the last few years. Integration is used much more instrumentally, today, as a fixed and measurable set of requirements for the attainment of certain rights, including citizenship. While some migrants have always been excluded from integration policies, we can now also see a significant rise in the creation of barriers to their equal participation in social systems. In some cases, this even affects citizens who are either identified with specifically targeted migrant others – including black and minority-ethnic groups and national minorities – or who returned to their own country of origin after having lived abroad. The widespread anti-immigrant populism that provoked these developments started before 2014 but has become more pronounced since 2015 and 2016. The tensions that these changes create are exacerbated by the progressive withdrawal of government from practical support for integration over the last decade or so, and the corresponding increase in the role of market forces and the voluntary sector.

M. Collyer (✉)
University of Sussex, Brighton, UK
e-mail: M.Collyer@sussex.ac.uk

S. Hinger
Osnabrück University, Osnabrück, Germany
e-mail: sophie.hinger@uni-osnabrueck.de

R. Schweitzer
University of Vienna, Vienna, Austria
e-mail: reinhard.schweitzer@univie.ac.at

© The Author(s) 2020   1
S. Hinger, R. Schweitzer (eds.), *Politics of (Dis)Integration*,
IMISCOE Research Series, https://doi.org/10.1007/978-3-030-25089-8_1

We understand *integration* as a set of normative assumptions, practices, policies and discourses that are always embedded in specific contexts and directed at particular groups or categories of people. Integration is not a universal policy goal in the European Union or its member-states, particularly for migrants with uncertain or temporary status – including those in the asylum system. The context and perceived desirability of migrants' and minorities' integration ultimately depends on how they are categorised by the state in which they live. At one extreme, some migrants are *obliged* to fulfil certain criteria associated with integration in order to renew their visa, be reunited with their family or ultimately naturalise. For others, integration is temporarily *suspended* – for example until their asylum status has been determined – or simply not considered necessary, given their intended temporary residence or employment in the country. At the other extreme, integration efforts are explicitly *criminalised*, as in the case of those migrants whose presence in the country is deemed 'illegal'. Policies have begun to emerge which do not simply exclude groups from the potentially beneficial impact of integration policies, but which have the specific objective of undermining their integration or certain aspects of it.

This undermining of some integration processes is the basis for the conceptualisation of *disintegration* that is also central to this collection. In English, the word disintegration commonly denotes 'the process of losing cohesion or strength' or that of 'coming to pieces' (Oxford English Dictionary 2016). Within the social sciences it is thus employed to describe the character or composition of societies (as collectives) but not the actions of, or policies towards individual members (or those formally demarcated as non-members) of these societies. In German debates, the word *Desintegration* has been used more frequently, both in relation to a supposed coming apart of society and to the exclusion of certain individuals from society. Our use of this term builds on and adds to the work of German migration scholar Vicki Täubig. Studying the way in which the German state has put barriers into place to hinder asylum-seekers from participating in the various social systems, Täubig (2009) speaks of *organised disintegration*. Disintegration policies and practices do not only overlook settlement but also actively set out to do harm and discourage it, although they are sometimes justified within a broader integration framework. The notion that such harm should be a specific policy goal goes back no further than Theresa May's October 2013 call to 'create a really hostile environment for illegal immigrants' in the UK (Travis 2013). This was an important symbolic statement of intent, reinforced by the UK's two Immigration Acts of 2014 and 2016 that were brought into legislation while May was Home Secretary. Some policies thus explicitly pursue this goal, others lack such clear intentionality but still contribute to processes of disintegration or the undermining of integration. For example, policies denying asylum-seekers the right to work have long been criticised for undermining their long-term integration, although this has never been the policies' specific intention.

Yet, even in disintegration-focused policies, integration remains a central goal. Indeed, not only can 'one and the same social phenomenon have both integrative and disintegrative effects', as argued by Grimm (2013, cit. in Treibel 2015, p. 46), but also as policy objectives disintegration and integration are inherently connected. For example, the disintegration of some is routinely legitimised with the need to reserve capacities to accommodate and integrate others. That said, integration and disintegration are not a simple binary categorisation but are intertwined in that the logic of one is always present in the other. This connection is sometimes explicit, often implicit but ever present in migrant lives. We use the notation *(dis)integration* to describe this intertwining.

With this notion, we hope to contribute to the debate around the usefulness of integration as an analytical concept. In the eyes of some critical observers, the explicit use of integration as a policy category makes it entirely irredeemable as a tool of analysis (Hess et al. 2015; Favell 2019). Indeed, integration is a politically and emotionally loaded concept, which in its daily usage mostly serves to mark otherness. Those targeted by integration measures are furthermore relegated to a position of passivity, obscuring the historical struggles of migrants for equal rights (Bojadzijev 2008). Although we share this criticism, we do not believe that simply abandoning integration as an analytical concept (and thus leaving its use and definition entirely to policy-makers) is the right answer. First, this would mean to forego a broader debate and institutionalisation of integration (cf. Treibel 2015). From a broader socio-theoretical perspective, integration connotes a problem and process, which society as a whole and all of its members individually must face. From such a perspective, no individual can ever be entirely integrated (Bommes 2013). Second, we argue that a critical and conscientious analysis that always examines integration in explicit relation to its ever-present opposite – disintegration – and vice versa, constitutes a fruitful scholarly undertaking. We also do not agree that all struggles of migrants have been absorbed through the integration paradigm (Bojadzijev 2008), because as stated above, not everyone is supposed to integrate. Rather, we hope that the notion of (dis)integration will help to bring migrant agency back into this debate.

In addition to being inherently connected, integration and disintegration are also highly stratified processes. Although the procedural nature of integration is now increasingly recognised, it is still typically measured in terms of outcomes (eg. Garcés-Mascareñas and Penninx 2016). The contributions to this volume attempt to reverse this approach, emphasising the procedural elements and the dynamic nature of the processes of (dis)integration. A concern with integration and disintegration processes rather than outcomes also highlights the fragility of the distinctions on which the corresponding policies are based. For example, the disintegration of illegalised migrants helps to foster a climate of intolerance and racism which undermines the inclusion of citizens with migration backgrounds. Official state hostility that is focused on certain groups (illegalised migrants) can thereby weaken public support for the integration of those recognised by the same state as rightfully present. A focus on procedures rather than outcomes also helps, highlighting the implicit assumptions behind particular outcomes – for example, that migrants will be employed in certain low-skilled sectors of the labour market simply because that is where migrant workers are already significantly concentrated.

Viewing (dis)integration as a process also draws attention to the variety of actors involved, which leads to our concern with the politics of this process. The *politics* of (dis)integration provides a conceptual tool with which to analyse the role of numerous actors – including migrants and ethnically defined others, policy-makers, the media, public and private institutions and civil-society associations. A focus on politics means that we seek to reveal processes of negotiation around (dis)integration, taking into account different actors with their various interests, strategies and power positions. It also means that we take a reflexive stance towards our own participation as researchers in these negotiations (Hess 2012), as we seek to define, measure and represent (dis)integration. This perspective highlights how different individual and institutional actors not only take radically different stances on the same issue but also have varying capacities and opportunities to influence outcomes. These power asymmetries reinforce the stratification of (dis)integration processes.

1.1   Situating (Dis)Integration in the Existing Literature

Our concept of (dis)integration overlaps with but is distinct from three related frames of analysis which we build on and contribute to: civic stratification, inclusion/exclusion, and critical citizenship. We consider these in turn. '*Civic stratification*', highlights the variety of statuses that may be occupied by the foreign-born (Morris 2002), ranging from full citizen to undocumented migrant. With regard to the UK, Lydia Morris has identified 25 distinct packages of rights and restrictions, each associated with a different legal status. She did not include undocumented migrants who, despite becoming the target of disintegration policies in many countries, still retain some fundamental rights. According to Morris (2003), civic stratification allows for the management of certain contradictions that unavoidably arise from government policies. As many of the contributions to this volume show, also the politics of (dis)integration is usually aimed at consolidating conflicts between different policy objectives or between official discourses and actual practice. The key difference is that, whereas civic stratification considers a static picture of differentiated rights as the outcome of official categorisation, (dis)integration analyses the processes through which those rights are acquired or lost. In addition to that, civic stratification is based around a continuum whereas (dis)integration concerns the intertwining of two apparently contradictory processes.

In this, (dis)integration has much in common with the established analysis of differential inclusion/exclusion (e.g. Portes and Zhou 1993; Castles 1995), particularly in its concern with the specifics of precarity. Analysis of precarity tends to focus on its socio-economic aspects (Standing 2014) but there is a clear overlap with precarity of legal status. This may extend to any individual whose legal status is not fully secure, an ever larger group given recent changes in legislation in many liberal democracies to remove nationality. (Dis)integration on the basis of legal and/or economic precarity also affects groups that Ngai (2004) characterised as 'alien citizens'. These hold formal citizenship status but because at least one of their parents was born elsewhere are nonetheless perceived and treated as 'permanently foreign and unassimilable to the nation' (*ibid.*, p. 8). More-recent research has specifically focused on the complex relationship between exclusion and inclusion (eg. Andrijasevic 2009; Ataç and Rosenberger 2013). Such work often challenges the assumption that inclusion is the opposite of exclusion, highlighting the differential ways in which they operate and particularly how one may even be directly produced by the other (Dua 2007). For example, the disproportionate *inclusion* of migrant workers in particular sections of the labour market – such as domestic or night work – may make their *exclusion* from various other domains of social and everyday life more likely.

Current research in this area highlights the barriers faced by many migrants to their achievement of any kind of equal access to the benefits that come with living in wealthier countries. This results in significant disadvantage and inequality, even for those whose integration is officially supported by state institutions. Policies which effectively bring the state's border onto the state's territory reinforce legal precariousness and further undermine integration efforts and processes. Since this territorialisation of national borders relies on various forms of 'everyday bordering' (Yuval-Davis et al. 2018), the unequal effects of such policies go far beyond the people and situations they explicitly target. Mezzadra and Neilson's (2013) 'Border as Method' approach connects this proliferation of practices of border control within society to the dynamic of inclusion/exclusion. By focussing on the reproduction of forms of inclusion and exclusion that transcend national borders and their control, this analysis already points at the broader connections between integration and disintegration processes, which this collection sets out to expand on. Like inclusion/exclusion, (dis)integration considers the complex interrelations between apparently contradictory processes, in relation to certain individuals or groups, but also society as a whole.

Apart from top-down attempts to control or 'manage' migration and the effects it has on receiving societies, (dis)integration always also involves migrant-led efforts and processes. In this respect, our analysis of the politics of (dis)integration has much in common with *critical citizenship* studies, the third area of work which we draw from and aim to contribute to. The notion of 'acts of citizenship' (Isin and Nielsen 2008) captures the agency of migrants, especially those with precarious or no status. This allows a better engagement with processes of negotiation which are not necessarily state-led. In a similar vein, we speak of 'acts of integration' to recognise efforts that are made by migrants with uncertain status to achieve equality of access or inclusion. In some cases, these acts of integration are recognised or even required by state institutions. In others, recognition and solidarity comes from NGOs, migrant support groups and/or individual citizens.

As already noted above, this book makes use of a terminology which, in German, unlike in English academic and public debates, has been quite common. Besides the more recent use by migration scholars, there has been an ongoing debate among German sociologists about 'social disintegration'. Wilhelm Heitmeyer, in fact, coined this notion in his studies of racist and xenophobic violence. He found that social disintegration, understood as an increasing lack of social cohesion, paired with increasing experiences of individual exclusion, furthered tendencies towards violent behaviour and conflict (Heitmeyer 1994). Similar to our endeavour, Heitmeyer makes a link between individual and collective (dis)integration processes, underlining that experiences of disintegration are not a problem experienced by a few individuals but a phenomenon of mainstream society and its institutions (*Ibid.*).

In this book, however, we look at the relationship between integration and disintegration at both the individual and the collective level from a slightly different angle, by highlighting instances where the disintegration of certain individuals is not just a side-effect of broader societal changes (globalisation, individualisation, etc.) but is produced by law, policy and/or everyday practice. Moreover, we do not suppose that a certain 'disintegration' of society can be avoided altogether but, rather, see such developments as a fundamental characteristic of functionally differentiated societies (Nassehi 1999).

1.2   The Three Central Contributions of this Volume

As a whole, this book thus explicitly sets out to analyse a wide range of aspects of the politics of (dis)integration, the longer-term trends which produced them and their likely future implications. It thereby makes three important contributions to the literature discussed above. First, it explores how integration is framed in terms of limited capacity, thus requiring accompanying measures of disintegration. Second, it highlights how individuals engage in 'acts of integration', which range from adapting to the constraints of disintegration measures to migrant activism and solidarity with identified others. Third, it shows that the (dis)integration of some is inherently connected to the (dis)integration of society as a whole.

1.2.1   The Limited Capacity Argument

Several contributions in this volume show that integration policies and discourses often build on the assumption that not everyone can be integrated because the resources, facilities or simply public acceptance that is necessary for the integration of newcomers is limited. In other words, the successful integration of some is linked to the disintegration of others. The limited capacity argument rests on the notion of society as a container or finite space and it is often but not necessarily linked with ethno-nationalist conceptions of belonging. It furthermore entails calls for a limitation of (certain kinds of) immigration and a selection of who may stay and integrate and who may not.

Against the background of supposedly limited integration capacities, decision-makers take an interest in *selecting* only those persons for the 'integration track', who are 'likely to stay' (Samuk and Hinger in this volume), 'who really need it'

(Hinger and Schweitzer, in this volume) and/ or 'who really deserve it' because of their supposed economic utility (Desille, in this volume). Such selection criteria are, however, not only difficult to implement but also in themselves contradictory. What Sébastien Chauvin and Blanca Garcés-Mascareñas (2014) have observed with regard to deservingness frames mobilised in negotiations of migrant (il)legality, also holds true for negotiations of (dis)integration – they are characterised by several tensions: e.g. between claims based on vulnerability versus civic performance, universal versus particular claims, and economic versus cultural deservingness. While a differentiation based on deservingness frames does not correspond to legal statuses, it may affect both informal and formal practices of (dis)integration (Chauvin and Garcés-Mascareñas 2014). For example, Sophie Hinger shows in her chapter in this volume that asylum applicants in Germany, even though they formally share the same legal status, are increasingly differentiated upon arrival and registration according to their supposed need for protection. This early selection then translates into differential access to various social systems. In a similar vein, undocumented migrants do not only participate in informal, clandestine ways in the social systems of their host societies, but their participation often actually becomes part of an official pathway towards more recognition (Chauvin and Garcés-Mascareñas 2012).

Precisely because states create possibilities for immigrants with insecure residence status to prove their deservingness, they also try to prevent immigrants from becoming 'too integrated' or too deserving (ibid, 2014, p. 422) and thus implement a range of disintegration measures. These may be general measures, such as the enforcement of internal border controls. The chapter by Reinhard Schweitzer for example demonstrates how measures are taken to render the access to welfare institutions more difficult for undocumented migrants. Again, such measures are routinely justified with a limited capacity argument, that is, the supposed need to protect the welfare state against (undeserving) immigrants. Disintegration measures may also target a specific group such as proclaimed 'bogus refugees'. In the German case cited above, those asylum claimants deemed 'undeserving', are excluded from accessing the labour market and from participating in language and integration courses; in some cases, they are even spatially set apart until the end of their asylum procedure (Hinger, in this volume). Another example presented in this volume by Sahizer Samuk is the undermining of some immigrants' equal participation in social systems by framing their stay as 'temporary'. Temporary labour migrants are supposed to contribute to their host countries' economies but their efforts are not necessarily rewarded with more rights and possibilities to stay in the long term, as Samuk shows. We consider the creation of such barriers to integration as *intentional disintegration*.

In addition to prompting the adoption of (intentional) disintegration measures for some, and thus turning integration into a privilege, the limited capacity argument also helps to transform integration into a duty for others. This means that integration is increasingly framed as an individual responsibility – with a strong focus on successful labour-market integration and independence from social benefits. This can be considered part of a broader neoliberal conception of individuals being responsible for their own sustenance, paired with diminishing state intervention and public budgets. It also reflects the influence of the idea of 'workfare' – namely, that social benefits are made dependant on continuous training and contributions to society in the form of voluntary or low-paid work – which has penetrated public welfare systems in many countries. While these developments affect many of those who are unemployed or considered not sufficiently integrated into the labour market, they affect immigrants in particular and, more specifically, persons without a secure residence status. These people's access to legal security and thus social and political rights is often made dependent on their economic performance. This becomes apparent, for example, in debates on whether persons with insecure residence status, who have a job or are engaged in a training, should be protected from deportation. Even the protection of recognised refugees is increasingly linked with their economic performance (Hinger, in this volume). Those who quickly learn the language and succeed in sustaining themselves are rewarded with faster access to legal security and more rights, for example to decide where they want to live within the country. In addition, those who choose professions where their labour is the most needed (i.e. they engage in an apprenticeship instead of enrolling at university) are rewarded with more security, as they are protected from deportation throughout their job training.

While the life chances of persons with an insecure residence status are especially affected by the neoliberal take on integration, also some citizens increasingly have to prove their deservingness, this concerns especially those who are living on social welfare and share certain characteristics with migrant others. Tina Magazzini, in her chapter, shows how, in Italy, for example, policy-makers frame the socio-economic deprivation of a significant part of the country's Roma population as a cultural or behavioural problem, thereby obscuring discriminatory patterns and the lack of institutional support granted to Roma. An understanding of integration as an individual duty and not as one that requires an effort on behalf of state institutions, may effectively lead to disintegration. Moreover, it implies that the blame for distributive inequalities or unequal participation is put on the individual, who is perceived and presented as 'unwilling' or 'unable to integrate'. This also comes to the fore Mateusz Karolak's study of return-migrants in this volume. Karolak shows how Polish citizens struggle to re-integrate into the labour market of their home country at a level that fits their qualifications, after having lived and worked in the UK.

At first sight, and in the context of a broader trend of diminishing public welfare spending, the conception of integration as a duty seems inclusive in the sense that it is applied to both citizens and non-citizens, to the established as well as to newcomers. However, the idea of integration as a duty has not replaced discrimination on the basis of legal status and/or ethnicity. The case of Jewish immigrants in Israel, presented in this book by Amandine Desille, is another case in point. Whereas all Jews may immigrate to Israel and are entitled to citizenship, their prescribed integration paths and access to rights depend on their perceived economic deservingness which, in turn, is linked to their ethnicity and/or country of origin. Seen as part of the politics of (dis)integration, the limited capacity argument provides one important link between the integration of some and the disintegration of others. On the one hand, it implies that those who can have to manage on their own; on the other hand, it means that some are not even given a chance to participate equally because, it is argued, the integration capacities have to be spared for those who really need (or really deserve) it.

1.2.2   Acts of Integration and Solidarity

The second major contribution of this collection is to highlight the central involvement of individuals who are themselves the focus of any form of integration in its enactment. Despite the significant role of individuals that is inherent in the obligations put on individuals, considered above, there is still a tendency to frame this obligation in terms that deny any agency. Since these are demands made of migrants, in a way that cannot be demanded of citizens, migrants are placed in the role of guardians of good citizenship. This suggests that integration is something that is 'done to' individuals. Yet the history of public policies to shape integration highlights how difficult it is to consciously shape a process as dynamic and complex as the progressive and relatively equal involvement of newcomers in a collective. Integration is a process in which those newcomers are actively involved, either as willing participants or to actively contest its normative assumptions. This active and often critical involvement is entirely constitutive of what integration actually is. The most that policy approaches can do is to shape or incentivise certain elements of that engagement. We explore how the engagement and activism of individuals shapes the integration process.

These forms of engagement and activism should be understood as *acts of integration* along the lines of the literature on 'acts of citizenship' (Isin and Nielsen 2008). We draw on Isin and Nielsen's pioneering reorientation of the study of citizenship to encompass forms of civic behaviour, democratic participation and protest by non-citizens. The authors demonstrate that civic behaviour is common to those who are denied the privilege of citizenship. The increasingly common policy framing of integration as a privilege creates a similar group who are denied the benefits of integration yet who, nonetheless, actively engage in acts of integration and therefore help to constitute the integration process.

In some cases, acts of integration are restricted, in others they are explicitly criminalised. Sahizer Samuk considers in her chapter a situation where these restrictions are explicit. In the case of temporary workers, all avenues for integration are officially closed off, yet through research in Canada and the UK, Samuk suggests that temporary workers nonetheless take steps to develop elements of longer-term integration. These acts of integration include familiarity with conditions of work, language development and awareness of social and cultural norms, yet rights are limited as access to more genuine integration is an increasingly restricted privilege. In a related investigation, Nina Saharoui investigates the experiences of workers in the care sector in London, Paris and Madrid. Her study includes migrants with limited rights to integration as well as racialised minorities with full access to citizenship. As racism changes form, becoming less overt, both groups face barriers in achieving redress and their equality of treatment continues to be blocked by barriers that, as Saharoui demonstrates, form an evolving type of institutional racism.

It is increasingly common for participation in certain elements of the integration process to be explicitly criminalised, as in the case for illegalised migrants. Reinhard Schweitzer's chapter considers the ways in which this exclusion is enacted in key institutions which have traditionally been central to supporting integration, health, education and social services. Yet, he shows that acts of integration are widespread and, in some cases, are supported by representatives of the institutions concerned. Despite official restrictions, even illegalised migrants retain certain rights which are central to the wider functioning of society. The institutionalised restrictions of these rights may therefore set up internalised contradictions within these institutions which have to be managed through particular, dedicated sectors. In some cases, institutional actors have a degree of flexibility around obligations to investigate report and act on discoveries of illegalised status.

Acts of integration, performed by those who are typically the subject of integration processes, thus have a corollary in acts of solidarity. Solidarity with those affected by integration measures arises immediately amongst those with similar experiences though it may also encompass those who are not the individual subject of integration processes but have a wider concern for social equality. Schweitzer's chapter demonstrates how acts of solidarity may arise from individuals within the institutions who have been tasked with implementing much greater hostility. These institutions are fundamental to the liberal welfare state and were established to systematise solidarity, so it is not altogether surprising that they continue to attract individuals with a concern for equality. This highlights an additional barrier that policies of disintegration must inevitably overcome.

Solidarity can also emerge within sub-state and non-state organisations. Sophie Hinger's chapter considers the tensions between national- and local-level integration policies in Germany. At the national level, there is a clear distinction between 'genuine refugees' and others whereas local-level responses to integration have much greater interest in blurring these categorisations in the broader contexts of contribution to urban solidarity. Amongst the explicitly anti-migration politics of contemporary Hungary, Céline Cantat highlights the attempts of state institutions to clearly identify a desirable Hungarian public. This is achieved at least in part through the enactment of highly publicised border policies, the 'border spectacular'. Within this extremely hostile context, solidarity emerges within civil society collectives. Even though their room for manoeuvre is severely constrained, Cantat shows that acts of solidarity also contribute to the normative challenge to official policies of disintegration. This is especially the case in countries like Hungary, where acts of integration are repressed or criminalised and the flexibility that both Hinger and Schweitzer identify within state institutions at the local and national levels is absent.

1.2.3   The (Dis)Integration of Certain Groups or Individuals Is Linked to that of Society as a Whole

As mentioned above, we understand integration and disintegration as two inherently connected processes, even though the policies and practices that help to produce them apparently pursue opposite goals. In addition to that, we also contend that both concepts – and the corresponding efforts, practices, discourses or policies – can (and should) be analysed in relation to individuals as well as collectives. Like integration and disintegration, also the latter (individual – collective) do not constitute a simple dichotomy but are usually intertwined, with a range of institutions and various organisational forms constituting crucial links between the two levels.

The combination of both pairs of concepts results in the two-dimensional framework shown in Fig. 1.

As already indicated, in its everyday use the term 'integration' is usually employed to describe the integration of a particular individual (or group of individuals) *into* society, but as an analytical concept it can also mean the integration *of* that same society as a whole (cf. Treibel 2015). In (social) policy language, the latter is usually referred to as social or community 'cohesion' or the 'inclusiveness' of a society or its institutions. Particularly when related to immigration, this kind of integration is often taken for granted and/or portrayed as being threatened by the arrival of newcomers, especially those accused of being 'reluctant to integrate *themselves*'. Much of the existing scholarship on migrant integration has been criticised for the implicit assumption that the society into which individual newcomers are (supposed to be) integrating is itself not only homogenous but also inherently integrated (Imbusch and Heitmeyer 2012). From a systems theoretical perspective, too, which sees modern societies as necessarily consisting of various functionally differentiated sub-systems, the idea of an 'integrated society' appears problematic (Nassehi 1999).

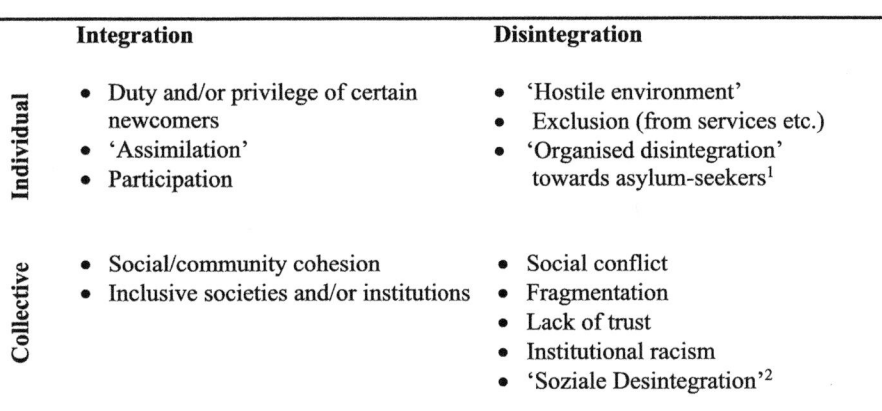

	Integration	Disintegration
Individual	• Duty and/or privilege of certain newcomers • 'Assimilation' • Participation	• 'Hostile environment' • Exclusion (from services etc.) • 'Organised disintegration' towards asylum-seekers[1]
Collective	• Social/community cohesion • Inclusive societies and/or institutions	• Social conflict • Fragmentation • Lack of trust • Institutional racism • 'Soziale Desintegration'[2]

Note: [1] Täubig (2009); [2] Heitmeyer (1994).

Fig. 1 Two-dimensional framework of concepts

That said, however, a certain relationship between the integration of individuals and that of society is usually recognised and many grassroots initiatives, as well as research projects focusing on the local level are explicitly trying to build on this conceptual but also practical overlap. Arguably, both an individual's integration *into* society, and that *of* society as a whole, thereby hinge on the same connections and interactions between people (and institutions), which also means that the two cannot be regulated as if they were entirely separate processes (Schweitzer 2017). By building and maintaining social relations with others, individuals thus always also contribute to a (more) integrated collective.

A related argument (e.g. by Brubaker 1992) is that the perception and practices of integration depend on the dominant perception of nationhood. As the contributions to this volume of Magazzini and Desille suggest, this also works the other way around – integration policies that officially target only specific groups or individuals often serve as an arena in which the broader issue of belonging (or not) to the nation is renegotiated. From this perspective, also discourses and everyday practices that rather contribute to, or even aim at, the disintegration of certain foreigners or minorities must be seen as means of nation-building.

With this book, we thus want to highlight that an inherent connection between the individual and the collective level not only exits in relation to integration, but also with regard to what we describe as disintegration policies and practices. These can have a great variety of forms and intended as well as unintended consequences, as several of the contributions to this volume demonstrate. The above-mentioned 'hostile environment' approach of the British government towards irregular migrants (Schweitzer, in this volume) is just one example but similar policies or mechanisms also target other categories of people, including temporary migrants (Samuk, in this volume), those who returned to their country of citizenship (Karolak, in this volume) or ethnic/national minorities (Magazzini, in this volume). Notably, such policies are never directed against integration in its collective sense (i.e. against 'social cohesion') but do aim – in more or less explicit ways – to circumvent or undermine the integration of certain individuals or groups who are identified as undeserving or unwanted.

We argue that, in analysing such policies and the related processes of (dis)integration, much more attention has to be paid to the issue of how they also (potentially) affect the rest of society. For example, Schweitzer's contribution to this volume shows that the increasing exclusion of irregular residents from public welfare affects not only the excluded but also the institutions and individuals providing such services and, ultimately, society as a whole, since it requires critical changes in the logic of public service provision more broadly. The fact that immigration control – including the corresponding restrictions in terms of access and rights – is becoming more and more internalised and thus reliant on various local actors such as employers, welfare bureaucrats and private landlords, ultimately undermines the necessary trust that migrant and other disadvantaged communities have in the state and its institutions.

The explicitly negative portrayal of immigrants and/or refugees in public and political discourse thereby also challenges existing networks of solidarity, as Cantat as well as Sarah Nimführ, Laura Otto and Gabriel Samateh discuss in their chapters on the current situation in Hungary and Malta, respectively. Institutionalised racism and everyday discrimination, including in the workplace – which is the focus of Nina Sahraoui's chapter in this book – are also phenomena that can be related to policies and discourses that target certain migrant others. The (negative) effects of such policies and/or related practices are thereby often particularly visible at the local level, as both Hinger and Desille show in their contributions to this volume.

Our aim in this regard is to not only highlight the various links and contradictions between integration and disintegration but also the far-reaching consequences that these can have at both the individual and the collective level. The widespread effects of the politics of (dis)integration also explain the significant diversity of the contributions to this volume (in terms of methodology as well as geographical and analytical focus), which the remainder of this introduction will briefly consider, before introducing each chapter in detail.

1.3 (Dis)Integration across Scales and Contexts: The Chapters in this Volume

In this book we were interested in the relationship between integration and disintegration at three different scales, in a variety of different empirical contexts. The tools of qualitative research rather than survey methodologies are most appropriate for this purpose, but even within the range of qualitative approaches there is considerable methodological diversity, from ethnography to structured interviews with key informants. This mix of approaches is one of the strengths of this edited volume and justified by the variety of scales in play. First, the micro scale, considers impacts on and the role of individuals in (dis)integration. Second, the meso scale provides an account at the level of organisations, such as municipal councils or NGOs. Finally, the macro scale explores the ways in which (dis)integration is an essential nation-building process, carefully policing the borders of membership. By combining these levels of analysis, we are interested in highlighting instances where the (dis)integration of certain individuals is produced by law, policy and/or everyday practice.

In addition, we wish to highlight the various ways in which (dis)integration processes are intertwined across different social systems. Some contributions in this volume primarily focus on one such system – like the labour market or welfare institutions – and show how policies designed to prevent certain groups from participating in these systems may negatively affect the functioning of relevant institutions and have implications for their involvement in other spheres of life. Other contributions examine categorisation processes in policymaking and their effects across various social systems.

Rather than limiting the book's geographical focus strictly to Europe, we decided to also include chapters that look at Israel and Canada. The former presents a unique case that allows highlighting the crucial role that the politics of (dis)integration can play in relation to ongoing processes of nation-building. The Canadian case delivers a transatlantic comparative insight as it is juxtaposed with an analysis of policies in the UK.

Turning to the chapters themselves, first, **Sophie Hinger**'s chapter 'Integration through disintegration?' enquires into the meanings of local and national integration policies in Germany which target asylum-seekers. The core argument is that there is a difference between the logics underlying the policies at both the national and the local level. The national integration law is mainly marked by an ethno-national framing of integration, which contributes, through the introduction of the notion of '(not) being likely to stay', to a further fractioning of the refugee label and thus the deterioration of rights of asylum claimants. While it posits integration as a privilege and duty for 'genuine' refugees, it aims to undermine the integration of those not deemed to be genuine refugees, following the logic that the disintegration of the latter is necessary in order to successfully integrate the former. At the local level, on the other hand, asylum-seekers are increasingly viewed as a potential resource for and part of a heterogeneous urban society, where participation rather than legal status matters. Yet, also at the local level, integration is ultimately tied to disintegration, as local authorities try to select who becomes part of the urban population in the first place.

Tina Magazzini's chapter on Roma integration picks up on the framework set out in this introduction to consider 'integration' as 'a set of normative assumptions, practices, policies and discourses that are always embedded in specific context'. Her chapter examines the context of integration policies and practices addressed at a specific minority, the Roma, in two Southern European countries – Italy and Spain – which share many characteristics and yet have adopted very different understandings of 'Roma integration'. Roma integration strategies are examined as a way of contributing to an understanding of how policies that are officially aimed at 'integrating' others can, in practice, be used to compartmentalise and exclude a group from the national imagined community. This chapter relates to the idea of integration as a stratified process (how the very concept of 'Roma integration' is the result of layers of meaning attributed by different European directives and national governments) and draws attention to the actors involved (the policy-makers in charge of integration policies). The main point is to show how the regimes of (dis)integration apply not only to migrants but also to ethnic minorities who are narrated and treated as similarly 'foreign' to the mainstream's imagined community. In this sense, Roma-specific integration measures do not challenge wider structures of inequality but, rather, contribute to the normalisation of a hegemonic discourse that sees a certain section of society as the bar for normality.

Sahizer Samuk asks 'Can integration be temporary?'. Temporary migration policies are made for those who are not supposed to integrate. This may include seasonal agricultural workers, construction workers, domestic workers and many more. Those who do not have the 'high skills' depicted and decided by the immigration categorisations are forced to be temporary. They are needed but they are not wanted. They stay but no integration budget is spent on them. They are here to work, not to integrate. However, they are disintegrated via temporariness and a lack of access to the most basic social and economic rights. In some countries they do not have the right to strike or to become a member of a union, nor can they benefit from the pension or unemployment system. So, what if they stay? The chapter examines the cases of Canada and the UK comparatively, seeing that, despite their diverse immigration histories, they do follow similar logics in devising policies for temporariness. The life of continuous disintegration led by temporary migrant workers is not only of six months' duration but, in some cases, a whole life, unless they apply for permanent residence schemes if these possibilities of transition to permanent stay are within their avail. The chapter calls for the attention of the policy-makers. Apart from whether they stay or not, the migrant workers need the empowerment of their own agency, supported by changes to the institutional frameworks that surround them and that determine their living conditions.

In her chapter, **Nina Sahraoui** examines migrant and minority-ethnic workers' experiences in older-age care. From the specific perspective of racialised workers' experiences in this highly segmented section of the labour market, she sheds light on some of the mechanics of disintegration in three European capitals. Sahraoui's chapter illustrates how labour-market segmentation, while representing a form of inclusion, translates into everyday experiences of (dis)integration for migrant and minority-ethnic workers. Her empirical section, by focusing on cases of racist behaviour by colleagues and harassment/discrimination by managers, sets out to relate the level of individual interactions to the workings of institutions in order to inform our understanding of how policies produce (dis)integration. It offers insights into the workings of (dis)integration at the workplace level and the coping strategies that arise at the level of interpersonal relationships. Overall, this chapter demonstrates that anti-discrimination legislation often remains out of reach for racialised precarious workers and argues that anti-racism is too often reduced to the legal framework of anti-discrimination policies, falling short of analysing the structural dynamics that foster racism at multiple levels.

The chapter by **Mateusz Karolak** acknowledges the heterogeneity of contemporary migration patterns and expands the field of analysis on the oft-neglected experiences of labour migrants voluntarily returning to their countries of origin. Through the analysis of the life histories of Polish post-accession migrants returning from the United Kingdom, Karolak looks at the subjective and objective dimensions of the returnees' labour market (dis)integration. He argues that, in spite of the fact that the returnees do not lack the foundations for integration, they often fall into the 'experience trap' and transfer their vulnerable labour-market position from abroad. Moreover, due to the internalised feeling of 'permanent temporariness', returnees resign from collective attempts to change their situation and instead employ individualised strategies of re-emigration. In this way, despite the pricing discourse on the universal advantages of intra-EU mobility, it turns out that, for some Central and Eastern-European migrants, the current regime of EU mobility, alongside passive state policies and self-fashioned neoliberal subjectivities contributes to the further fragmentation of migrants' careers and precarisation of their work.

In the following chapter, **Reinhard Schweitzer** turns to the UK's experience of implementing the 'hostile environment'. Immigration control is gradually shifting from external borders to the interior of the state and society. As part of this broader trend, irregular migrants face policies that explicitly aim at preventing their settlement, integration and access to services. The UK government explicitly presents these as an effort to create 'a hostile environment' for this part of the population. In order to be effective, many of these policies have to be implemented *within* some of the core institutions of the liberal welfare state, which at the same time fulfil a crucial role for the integration of society as a whole. Based on original interview data from London, this chapter looks at various sites where the exclusionary logic of immigration law intersects with the different inclusionary logics underlying public service provision. Crucial insights from organisation theory help to show how (and why) different public institutions (hospitals, universities and social-service centres) have responded to this by establishing specialised subdivisions that deal specifically with migrant irregularity. Schweitzer argues that, while this allows them to shield their core staff from contradictory logics and demands, it further increases the dangerous overlap between these institutions and the immigration regime.

In her chapter, 'Disintegration within integration', **Amandine Desille** examines more recent transformations of Israel's Law of Return – the Israeli immigration policy which provides the (imagined) repatriation of Diaspora Jews to Israel – in a context of liberalisation of the Israeli economy and the devolution of power to local authorities. Today, new immigrants follow two paths of 'integration': 'direct absorption', where immigrants are granted benefits while being free to settle wherever they find fit; and 'community absorption', where immigrants are placed in 'absorption centres' and see their entitlements conditioned by residence, religious observance and more. Those two paths are 'ethnicised' in the sense that they depend on country of origin – Western immigrants, considered as economically useful, benefit from direct absorption and a more pluralist attitude of local governments, while immigrants from Africa and Asia are the objects of an assimilationist policy. This situation of '(dis)integration' within what is supposed to be an inclusive immigrant policy for all Jews, shows the extent to which new criteria of perceived economic performance limit the integration of specific segments of newcomers. The rescaling of immigration and immigrant policies to subnational governments, although it has introduced a more multicultural approach, antagonist to the assimilationist ideology at work in Israel, has not enabled an alternative policy framework which is more accommodating to all.

Céline Cantat examines the way in which a politics of spectacle is employed by Hungarian authorities in their government of migrants. She argues that this spectacle of the border participates in the delineation of a legitimate Hungarian public and in the representation of the Hungarian state as the protector of a 'desirable' national order. The chapter then looks at how this process of hyper-visibilisation is complemented by more discreet practices of negligence towards migrants and refugees. It argues that these less-visible acts of destitution directly contribute to the unweaving of the social, economic and political ties and spaces available to migrants and refugees in the country, thus contributing to a calculated process of social disintegration targeting migrants and refugees. Against this background, the chapter goes on to investigate instances of solidarity with and support for migrants and sets out to assess their potential in countering dynamics of disintegration.

Finally, the chapter by **Sarah Nimführ, Laura Otto** and **Gabriel Samateh** is concerned with the so-called 'integration paradox' in the Maltese manifestation of the European border regime. Despite a lack of public effort in support of integration – moreover, even the active pursuit of making integration more difficult – refugees are nevertheless required to integrate themselves into society, resulting in an ambivalent situation. The authors focus on refugees' coping strategies by looking at practices of (dis)integration acted out by governing and non-governing actors. Based on ethnographic data, they argue that (dis)integration is a continuum, created by both legal frameworks and individuals' action, producing different forms of differentiated in- and exclusion. By employing a textualisation strategy based on collaborative research with Gabriel, who is a classified refugee in Malta, their contribution offers an analysis and representation beyond the merely scholarly, White perspective. In so doing, the authors provide an example of how research is possible that enables understanding of the lived reality of refugees and, at the same time – through Gabriel's contribution – intervenes into hitherto normalised power relations in the scientific knowledge production on forced migration.

In the conclusion, **Violetta Zentai** reviews key messages from the volume as a whole, regarding the conceptual, political and policy formations on the management of migration and the relations that these interventions shape and re-shape in wider societal affairs amidst weakening mechanisms for protecting human dignity, rights and equal citizenship in Europe and beyond.

References

Andrijasevic, R. (2009). Sex on the move: Gender, subjectivity and differential inclusion. *Subjectivity, 29*(1), 389–406.

Ataç, I., & Rosenberger, S. (2013). Inklusion/Exklusion als relationales Konzept der Migrationsforschung. In I. Ataç & S. Rosenberger (Eds.), *Politik der Inklusion und Exklusion* (pp. 35–52). Göttingen: V&R Unipress.

Bommes, M. (2013). *Migration und nationaler Wohlfahrtsstaat: ein differenzierungstheoretischer Entwurf*. Wiesbaden: Springer.

Bojadžijev, M. (2008). *Die windige Internationale: Rassismus und Kämpfe der Migration*. Münster: Westfälisches Dampfboot.

Brubaker, R. (1992). *Citizenship and nationhood in France and Germany*. Cambridge, MA/ London: Harvard University Press.

Castles, S. (1995). How nation states respond to immigration and ethnic diversity. *Journal of Ethnic and Migration Studies, 21*(3), 293–308.

Chauvin, S., & Garcés-Mascareñas, B. (2012). Beyond informal citizenship: The new moral economy of migrant illegality. *International Political Sociology, 6*(3), 241–259.

Chauvin, S., & Garcés-Mascareñas, B. (2014). Becoming less illegal: Deservingness frames and undocumented migrant incorporation. *Sociology Compass, 8*(4), 422–432.

Dua, E. (2007). Exclusion through inclusion: Female Asian migration in the making of Canada as a white settler nation. *Gender, Place and Culture, 14*(4), 445–466.

Favell, A. (2019). Integration: Twelve propositions after Schinkel. *Comparative Migration Studies, 7*(1).

Garcés-Mascareñas, B., & Pennix, R. (2016). *Integration processes and policies in Europe. Contexts, levels and actors.* Heidelberg: Springer.

Heitmeyer, W. (1994). Entsicherungen. Desintegrationsprozesse und Gewalt. In U. Beck & E. Beck-Gernsheim (Eds.), *Riskante Freiheiten* (pp. 376–401). Frankfurt am Main: Suhrkamp.

Hess, S. (2012). De-naturalising transit migration. Theory and methods of an ethnographic regime analysis. *Population, Space and Place, 18*(4), 428–440.

Hess, S., Binder, J., & Moser, J. (2015). *No integration?!: kulturwissenschaftliche Beiträge zur Integrationsdebatte in Europa.* Bielefeld: Transcript Verlag.

Imbusch, P., & Heitmeyer, W. (2012). Dynamiken gesellschaftlicher Integration und Desintegration. In W. Heitmeyer & P. Imbusch (Eds.), *Desintegrationsdynamiken: Integrationsmechanismen auf dem Prüfstand* (pp. 9–25). Wiesbaden: Springer.

Isin, E., & Nielsen, G. (Eds.). (2008). *Acts of citizenship.* Chicago: Chicago University Press.

Mezzadra, S., & Neilson, B. (2013). *Border as method, or, the multiplication of labor.* Durham, NC: Duke University Press.

Morris, L. (2002). *Managing migration: Civic stratification and migrants' rights.* London/New York: Routledge.

Morris, L. (2003). Managing contradiction: Civic stratification and migrants' rights. *International Migration Review, 37*(1), 74–100.

Nassehi, A. (1999). Inklusion, Exklusion: Integration, Desintegration. Die Theorie funktionaler Differenzierung und die Desintegrationsthese. In A. Nassehi (Ed.), *Differenzierungsfolgen. Beiträge zur Soziologie der Moderne* (pp. 105–131). Wiesbaden: Springer.

Ngai, M. (2004). *Impossible subjects: Illegal aliens and the making of modern America.* Princeton/Oxford: Princeton University Press.

Oxford English Dictionary. (2016). *Disintegration.* Retrieved 07 September 2018 from https://en.oxforddictionaries.com/definition/disintegration.

Portes, A., & Zhou, M. (1993). The new second generation: Segmented assimilation and its variants. *Annals of the American Academy of Political and Social Science, 530*(1), 74–96.

Schweitzer, R. (2017). Integration against the state – The state against integration? *Politics Blog.* Retrieved 07 September 2018 from http://politicsblog.ac.uk/2017/02/05/integration-state-state-integration/.

Standing, G. (2014). The Precariat. *Contexts, 13*(4), 10–12.

Täubig, V. (2009). *Totale Institution Asyl. Empirische Befunde zu alltäglichen Lebensführungen in der organisierten Desintegration.* Munich: Juventa Verlag.

Travis, A. (2013). Immigration bill: Theresa may defends plans to create 'hostile environment'. *The Guardian, 10 October.* Retrieved 07 September 2018 from https://www.theguardian.com/politics/2013/oct/10/immigration-bill-theresa-may-hostile-environment.

Treibel, A. (2015). *Integriert Euch! Plädoyer für ein selbstbewusstes Einwanderungsland.* Frankfurt/New York: Campus Verlag.

Yuval-Davis, N., Wemyss, G., & Cassidy, K. (2018). Everyday bordering, belonging and the reorientation of British immigration legislation. *Sociology, 52*(2), 228–244.

Chapter 2
Integration Through Disintegration? The Distinction Between Deserving and Undeserving Refugees in National and Local Integration Policies in Germany

Sophie Hinger

2.1 Introduction

Until recently, refugees[1] with an insecure residence status were, just like undocumented migrants, not a target group for integration policies in Germany. What is more, they were explicitly excluded from national integration provisions, such as German language and integration courses. They were largely prohibited from taking up employment, from moving out of accommodation centres into private flats and from leaving their assigned locality of residence. These and other measures had been introduced by the German government in the 1980s to make the stay of (rejected) asylum-seekers in Germany as unattractive as possible and to deter other potential asylum-seeking persons. Even though municipal authorities generally adopted a much more pragmatic and inclusive approach knowing that many of the protection-seekers would end up staying for many years they often did not explicitly include them in integration plans and, in some cases, also explicitly excluded them (Aumüller 2009; Bommes 2012).

However, the perception of and take on the integration of refugees with an insecure residence status seems to have changed. In the 2000s, a few city municipalities started to make plans to decentralise the accommodation of refugees – that is, to move away from mass accommodation to providing access to private flats. Since 2013, it has also become increasingly common for local authorities to adopt encompassing strategies or concepts for the integration of refugees, including those

---

[1] I use 'refugee' not (only) in its limited legal sense but in the broad sense of a person who has sought or is seeking asylum, thus including persons with different legal statuses. When I refer to 'refugees without a secure residence status' I mostly mean persons who are in the process of claiming asylum or whose claims have been rejected, some of whom have a so-called *Duldung*. I reflect on my own use of categories in the second section of this chapter.

S. Hinger (✉)
Osnabrück University, Osnabrück, Germany
e-mail: sophie.hinger@uni-osnabrueck.de

© The Author(s) 2020
S. Hinger, R. Schweitzer (eds.), *Politics of (Dis)Integration*,
IMISCOE Research Series, https://doi.org/10.1007/978-3-030-25089-8_2

without a secure residence status. Some of the *Länder* (federal states), too, have adopted measures to improve the living situation of asylum-seekers – e.g. by financially or otherwise supporting the decentralisation of accommodation and introducing quality standards for collective accommodation centres (Aumüller 2018). The national government has relaxed some of the measures of discomfort and deterrence, like the residency obligation (in 2015) and the employment prohibition (since 2014). With the adoption of the Integration Bill in July 2016, refugees without a secure residence permit even became the main focus of national integration policies.

This chapter enquires into the functioning and underlying logics of recent integration policies in Germany. In line with the literature on integration policies that notes clashes between different levels of policy-making (Chauvin and Garcés-Mascareñas 2012; Mügge and van der Haar 2016), it especially explores the links and tensions between integration measures at municipal and the national levels. The integration policies and measures of the *Länder* are beyond the scope of this paper. The analysis of the local level is based on a case study of one German city. The in-depth analysis of one local case allows to go beyond an analysis of integration policies as they are described in official documents and to trace the implementation of policies over time (Penninx and Garcés-Mascareñas 2016). Looking at both levels, this chapter asks: How do the policies construct and distinguish between the different target groups? Who is (not) to be integrated? And in how far are the national framings of integration reproduced or contested at the local level?

In order to grasp the logics of integration policies at different levels, the chapter places special emphasis on their explicit and implicit category structures. The following section lays out some of the principles of category analysis and its relevance for understanding integration policies. The third section presents the methods employed in this study. The fourth section turns to the national Integration Bill, which will then be contrasted, fifth, with an analysis of local integration policies and practices in the city of Osnabrück.

2.2 Integration Policies, Disintegration and Category Analysis

Integration policies can be understood as attempts by State authorities to guide and control the integration processes of immigrants (Penninx and Garcés-Mascareñas 2016). They are

> part of a normative political process, in which the issue of integration is formulated as a problem, the problem is given a normative framing, and concrete policy measures are designed and implemented to achieve a desired outcome (ibid., p. 19).

While the lack of integration of immigrants is often the proposed problem, one can also consider *disintegration* measures as part of the policy repertoire of states to attempt to control immigration and (post-)migration social relations. Vicki Täubig

(2009) has used the concept of *organised disintegration* to describe the living situation of refugees with an insecure residence status in Germany. Building on Erving Goffmann's (1973) concept of a *total institution*, Täubig (2009 pp. 45–54) describes how the German state undermines asylum-seekers' right to a self-determined life and integrated social relations by obliging them to reside in collective accommodation centres, where their daily lives are subjected to strict bureaucratic regimentation. Sieglinde Rosenberger (2012) ties in with Täubig's work by distinguishing between *residential segregation* on the one hand and *material disintegration* on the other, the latter referring to the erecting of barriers to asylum-seekers' access to resources and institutions. In line with the conceptualisation of *(dis)integration* as spelled out by Collyer et al. (2020), this chapter looks for connections between integration and disintegration. It seeks to contribute to the argument that disintegration is not only an aim of policy-makers but is also, in fact, legitimised within a broader integration framework (*Ibid.*).

Categories are, in many ways, at the heart of migration and integration policies, as they define 'who is a wanted and who is an unwanted migrant and who requires integration and who does not' (Mügge and van der Haar 2016, p. 77). The desirability or *deservingness* of immigrants is framed in different and sometimes contradictory ways, as Sébastien Chauvin and Blanca Garcés-Mascareñas (2014) have highlighted. For refugees, vulnerability has been a major criterion for deservingness but, as I argue below, other framings such as economic performance or cultural deservingness also (increasingly) play a role. We can see in the shift of categories and the underlying framings of deservingness over time, as well as in diverging practices at the national and local levels, that the categorisations on which integration policies rest are always due to change. Even though, especially in policies, they appear as if they were fixed and natural, they are always social constructions. Multiple actors at multiple levels engage in the construction of categories, including those who are categorised.

From a critical perspective, it is especially important to reflect how we, as researchers, (co-)produce categorisations. For example, the use of a presumably neutral legal category such as 'asylum-seeker' is, in fact, highly problematic if we consider that it was introduced by Northern governments to mark the distinction between asylum claimants and those who are granted asylum, thus preventing access to the label 'refugee' and entailing the 'wholesale withdrawal or reduction of established rights' (Zetter 2007, p. 181). In a similar vein, the use of 'refugee' as an analytical term has been questioned, both because it is intimately tied to a specific legal status and because it seems to confirm the political differentiation between forced and voluntary migration (Fiedler et al. 2017). I have nevertheless opted to use the term because the constitution of the (non-)refugee subject in and through integration policies is the very focus of this chapter. In what follows, categories are mainly regarded as a construction of states and policy-makers. State actors and the policy documents they produce are of special relevance due to their power position and because their formal systems of categorisation are particularly apt for deconstruction (Martiniello and Simon 2005, p. 8).

Category analysis can help 'to identify the architecture of the argument that underlies a policy issue and that, while often not discussed explicitly in policy debates, nevertheless is part of policy-relevant publics' sense-making' (Yanow 2000, p. 55). In order to reveal the organising principle of category systems, it helps to question their supposedly exclusive, exhaustive and neutral nature (Yanow 2000; Mügge and van der Haar 2016). Category systems rest on the assumption that categories are mutually exclusive, an assumption which, however, can be questioned from an analytical point of view – people may move between and fit into several categories. The supposed exhaustiveness of category systems can be deconstructed if we look beyond those groups or individuals highlighted by the policy and ask who is obscured or only targeted implicitly by a policy and why. Integration policies, for example, rarely or never mention undocumented migrants, just as they remain silent on those groups deemed automatically integrated. Intended or not, category systems often (re-)produce stereotypes, prejudice and inequality (Mügge and van der Haar 2016). While some elements or groups are presented as problematic or deviant, others are constructed as normal (Yanow 2000, p. 52). Category analysis explores this as the *marking* of categories (Ibid.).

In the literature on integration policies, differential organising principles or markings have been noted between policy levels. For example, according to the institutional discourse of the European Union, EU citizens are integrated in all EU member-states and should therefore not be considered as specific targets of integration policies. However, the issue is handled quite differently by policy-makers at the national level, as the discrimination against some EU citizens – especially the Roma and citizens of Eastern European countries – in other EU member-states shows (Lind and Persdotter 2017; Magazzini 2020). Differences have also been observed between national and local levels, especially towards immigrants without a secure residence permit (Chauvin and Garcés-Mascareñas 2012; Mügge and van der Haar 2016; Schweitzer 2020).

2.3   Methodology

Given the interest in categorisations, the analysis of national and local policy documents will focus on their diagnostic parts as well as the solutions – i.e. the actual measures – they propose. For the (national) Integration Bill, this means that I also take into account the Draft Bill, the executive order and other statements connected to the bill. The local case study consists of an analysis of policy documents, ethnographic data and interviews generated during my PhD project on local asylum practices in Osnabrück between 2014 and 2016. I chose Osnabrück, a city of about 160,000 inhabitants in the German state of Lower Saxony, as the entry point for my fieldwork because the city has a long history of accommodating refugees and thus an established 'asylum landscape' (Hinger et al. 2016) with a diversity of relevant actors and sites, yet not as many as in bigger cities. I conducted interviews with key actors in the municipal administration and government, as well as local NGOs and initiatives, in order to understand how asylum is negotiated in a particular local setting and how this changes over time. Given the focus of this chapter on comparing the national and local levels, a differentiated analysis of conflicts and contradictory logics within and among local institutions has to be omitted. In line with category analysis, as laid out above, I look at the construction, demarcation and markings of the (non-) targets of recent integration policies, as well as the understanding of integration and (urban) society that these policies convey.

2.4 The National Integration Bill

The Integration Bill of 2016 concerns, despite its general framing, only a specific group: refugees. In fact, most of its regulations address asylum applicants and rejected asylum-seekers with a *Duldung* (certificate suspending their deportation). This presents a rupture with earlier national integration provisions,[2] from which refugees without a secure residence permit were, more or less explicitly, excluded. The introduction of the Integration Bill has to be read as part of a series of legal changes that were introduced in 2015 and 2016 in reaction to the heightened number of persons seeking asylum in Germany. As the draft Bill clearly states, the augmented number of refugees and their supposed lack of integration are defined as a problem:

> Only last year, 476,649 persons have applied for asylum in Germany […] A lack of integration does not only lead to social problems in the medium and long term, it also leads to high costs (Gesetzentwurf für das Integrationsgesetz 2016, p. 1).

To counter the influx of asylum-seekers and their lack of integration, the bill introduces a legal division between putative 'genuine' and 'bogus' refugees through the notion of strong or weak 'likelihood of staying' (*Bleibeperspektive*). For the asylum applicants considered as being likely to stay, it establishes fast-track integration and, for those who are not, accelerated asylum procedures and deportations. The following sections look at the explicit and implicit categories constructed in and through the Integration Bill.

2.4.1 'We' and the 'Others': An Ethno-National Framing of Integration

In addressing only refugees and the problem of their (non-)integration, the German government marks them as 'others' – that is, as persons who do not (yet) belong to German society. The distinction between 'us' and an asylum-seeking 'other' rests on the imagination of German society as a homogenous ethno-cultural entity. This

---

[2] The National Integration Plan (2007) and the National Action Plan Integration (2012).

container model of society and culture comes to the fore in the Integration Bill in several ways: First, it posits refugees as a potential threat to social cohesion and stability. While it points to the humanitarian obligation of the German state to protect asylum-seekers, it also underlines the national government's duty 'to maintain a peaceful, liberal and communal society' (Gesetzentwurf für das Integrationsgesetz 2016, p. 23). The arrival of asylum-seekers is thus constructed as a menace to a supposedly cohesive and conflict-free German society. Second, it frames integration as an obligation on behalf of the asylum-seeker and not as a two-way or even a three-way process (Penninx and Garcés-Mascareñas 2016). That is, it mainly focuses on the duties of refugees and foresees sanctioning mechanisms in cases of non-compliance but barely targets discrimination and other barriers to their equal participation in the institutions of the receiving society. The only exception is the removal of barriers to the labour market and education schemes for refugees considered as likely to stay. Third, it places special emphasis on 'cultural integration', which is understood as the learning of German and the acceptance of 'German values'. As the executive order to the Integration Bill explicates, 'The content of the orientation courses [for asylum-seekers] will be extended and will focus primarily on the conveying of values' (Verordnung zum Integrationsgesetz 2016, p. 9). The integration courses can be made compulsory and, in cases of non-compliance, the living allowance cut.

This approach to integration ties in with the idea of the German nation as a community of descent and culture as well as with debates about a German 'leading culture'. What exactly is to be understood as German culture and values is not spelled out by the government. It also remains unclear who is assumed to be part of German society and who is not. In Germany, as in other Western countries, Muslims in particular and other persons associated with non-Western countries have been defined as target groups of integration measures (Lanz 2016), whereas migrants from the 'global North' as well as so-called 'expatriates' and their families are usually exempt from integration requirements (Hess and Moser 2009, p. 18). While integration is considered unnecessary for most and an obligation for some, it is also constructed as an exclusive privilege. Not everyone is supposed to integrate. While the Integration Bill includes some asylum-seekers without a secure residence permit, it excludes others.

2.4.2 Differentiating Between 'Genuine' and 'Bogus' Refugees

To a certain extent the Integration Bill breaks with the differentiation between refugees with and without a secure residence status, as it grants some asylum applicants and persons with a *Duldung* easier access to the labour market and job training. Whether asylum applicants are included or excluded from integration provisions depends on their assumed 'likelihood of staying'. Asylum applicants assumed to be 'likely' to be granted a secure residence status can take part in language and integration courses before a decision in their asylum procedure is taken. This right was hitherto reserved for persons with a secure residence status. According to the Integration Bill, 'being likely to stay' (*gute Bleibeperspektive*) means that 'a regular and permanent stay is to be expected' (Integrationsgesetz 2016, Art. 1). The distinction between asylum applicants who are likely to stay and those who are not is based on their nationality. Only if a considerable number of persons of one nationality ask for asylum in Germany and if the unadjusted protection rate for persons of this nationality exceeds 50%, they are assumed as being likely to stay (Bundesamt für Migration und Flüchtlinge 2019). This label has been attributed to persons from Syria, Eritrea, Iraq, Iran and temporarily also to Somalian nationals. Every 6 months the attribution of this label is reconsidered (ibid., 2019).

Critics have pointed out that the distinction between asylum applicants on the basis of the notion 'likely or not to stay' is inconsistent because it does not include all those who have a high probability of being granted asylum in Germany, as it is based on the unadjusted protection rate, which encompasses all asylum decisions, including those rejected on formal grounds (Pro Asyl 2017; Voigt 2016). This way of arguing, while making the case for a much larger number of asylum-seekers, follows the same logic as the Integration Bill as it holds that the line between those to be integrated and those to be excluded can be drawn on the basis of their likelihood of staying. In a more substantiated way, it can be argued that the Integration Bill and the notion of being 'likely or not to stay' contradicts the very principle of asylum as a right that is accorded to individuals on the basis of a proper hearing.

Among the asylum applicants with a poor likelihood of staying are all those whose countries of origin have been white-listed.[3] Persons from these so-called 'safe countries of origin' are not only subjected to material disintegration but also to residential segregation. Unlike other asylum applicants, they are not transferred from the so-called 'reception facilities' run by the regional authorities to municipal accommodation but they have to stay until the end of their procedure (and thus their deportation) in these facilities. Some *Länder*, such as Bavaria, have even established special camps for persons considered unlikely to stay since 2015.[4]

The distinction between asylum applicants who are or not likely to stay is related but not equal to the discourse on *economic refugees*. The former notion seems more technical and less stigmatising than the latter. Economic refugees are marked as less deserving than other refugees and assumed to be moving voluntarily and in order to attain better working and living conditions, which is seen as 'asylum abuse' (Bade 2015, p. 6). 'Genuine' refugees are thought to be moving due to war, political persecution or a well-founded fear of persecution. The label thus serves to devalue the motives of persons seeking asylum and the persons themselves (Flüchtlingsrat

---

[3] Besides the EU member-states, the six Balkan states (Albania, Bosnia and Herzegovina, Kosovo, Macedonia and Serbia), Ghana and Senegal have been white-listed. That of Morocco, Tunisia and Algeria was rejected by the German Federal Council (*Bundesrat*) in March 2017.

[4] Whereas these special camps were at first reserved for persons from putatively safe countries of origin, soon persons from countries of origin with a protection quota of less than 50 per cent were also targeted (Bayerischer Flüchtlingsrat 2017). In 2018, the Bavarian government eventually transformed all reception facilities into so-called '*Ankerzentren*', which are geared towards an accelerated selection and deportation of persons whose asylum claims are rejected.

Niedersachsen 2017, p. 33). The notion of '(not) likely to stay' is more open to interpretation, as it does not entirely rule out the possibility of a person eventually and rightfully obtaining asylum. However, it strongly suggests that this will not happen and it is often used as a synonym for economic refugee. It also suggests that voluntary migration can be clearly distinguished from forced movement and comes with certain representations and ideas of what constitutes violence and who deserves protection and who does not. Both notions are therefore in opposition to the findings of empirical studies, which have shown that migration flows are usually mixed and that migration motives are complex and may change over time (e.g. King 2002, pp. 92–93; Zetter 2007, p. 175).

The *a priori* distinction among asylum applicants and their differential treatment through the notion of (not) likely to stay is legitimated by the argument that the country has a limited capacity for reception and integration. The government has claimed that 'We have to concentrate our efforts on those people who flee from war and political persecution and really need protection' (Bundesregierung 2016a). In other words, the disintegration of some is legitimated by the need to reserve integration capacity for others. This logic is in line with the model of society as a container, thus constituting a finite space with limited integration capacity (Nimführ et al. this volume). Along with the humanitarian legitimation of the preferential treatment of some refugees on the basis of their nationality, a relatively new logic can be noted that ranks asylum-seekers according to their assumed usefulness (for the German labour market) and thus links protection to economic performance.

2.4.3   *'Promoting and Demanding' the Integration of Entrepreneurial Subjects*

The expansion of the integration dispositive to include asylum applicants considered 'likely to stay' and those with a *Duldung* has to be read above all as the triumphant success of a *workfare approach to integration* (Lanz 2009). In line with the workfare principle, the Integration Bill asks asylum-seekers to actively look for a job and become independent of social benefits. To enable their fast integration into the German labour market, barriers such as the interdiction to work and the proof of precedence[5] have been relaxed. Moreover, asylum applicants and those with a *Duldung* can – after a certified period of stay in the country – claim educational and vocational grants. Besides the easing of access to the labour market, the integration law includes a number of activating measures. In addition to the mandatory language and integration courses, asylum-seekers may be obliged to take part in so-called 'refugee integration measures' – low-paid jobs (with a remuneration of 80 cents an hour) which are supposed to serve as a 'meaningful occupation' during the

---

[5] According to the proof of precedence regulation, employers had to give preference to German or EU job applicants over asylum-eekers.

asylum procedure and to make asylum-seekers fit for the German labour market (Bundesregierung 2016b).

In the workfare state, social benefits are only attributed under certain conditions. If a welfare recipient fails to (re-)enter the labour market or contribute to society by engaging in some form of work scheme, social benefits may be cut or other sanctioning mechanisms put into place. The slogan of 'promoting and demanding' labour market integration has been at the heart of such approaches and also takes a central place in the Integration Bill. As explained by the German government: 'They [asylum-seekers] are [however] obliged to also make an effort to integrate. If asylum-seekers refuse integration measures or the obligation to cooperate, benefits will be cut' (Bundesregierung 2016b). Not only social benefits but also residence permits are tied to participation in integration measures. Those who do not fulfil the requirements may have their settlement permit withheld, while those who can prove advanced German skills and secure their own livelihood may be rewarded with a permanent 'settlement' permit after 3 years. These regulations imply that (non-) participation in integration measures has to be controlled, which can be challenging for local institutions and individuals responsible for controlling and informing the national ministry (Schweitzer 2020).

While workfare regulations are not new – they have marked the treatment of unemployed persons in Germany since the 1980s (Lanz 2009, p. 111) – the extension of this logic to the area of asylum is relatively recent. By promoting and demanding asylum-seekers as *entrepreneurial subjects*, the government seeks to kill two birds with one stone. One aim is to prevent a lack of integration and long-term dependence on social benefits. The other is to have refugees contribute to meeting the challenge of demographic change and skills shortages in certain sectors (Gesetzentwurf 2016). As several authors have pointed out, the 'refugee problem' has partly been made up not to confront the challenge of how to deal with international migration in a globalised world (Zetter 2007). As Castles (2003) has put it, Northern governments 'tacitly use asylum and undocumented migration as a way of meeting labour needs without publicly admitting the need for unskilled migration' (p. 16).

In short, the national Integration Bill partly breaks with the distinction between persons recognised as refugees and asylum applicants, in the sense that (some) asylum applicants and persons with a *Duldung* now also have access to integration courses and the labour market. Yet the binary approach to deservingness is not in fact challenged and becomes even more strongly enmeshed within a frame of performance and utility. In line with a workfare approach to integration, some refugees may be obliged to take part in integration schemes. If they refuse, they can be punished with a reduction of their social benefits and the prolongation of their legal insecurity. While, for this group, integration becomes an obligation, other refugees – namely those considered as 'not likely to stay' – are deliberately disintegrated, in terms of both residential segregation and material disintegration.

2.5   A Different Narrative? Local Integration Policies and Practices

Having explored the way in which disintegration is entangled with integration policies at the national level, this section now turns to (dis)integration policies and practices at the local level. 'Integration takes place locally' has been a much-repeated phrase in both political and academic debates on integration (Bommes 2012). While Germany was not perceived as an 'immigration country' by the national government until the 2000s, many municipalities, especially cities,[6] have been developing integration plans for their immigrant populations at least since the 1980s (Gesemann and Roth 2009). While these integration concepts rarely mentioned persons with an insecure residence status, municipalities often provided some services to all residents no matter their legal status (Aumüller 2009). The first integration documents explicitly targeting refugees (with various legal statuses) were developed in the late 1990s and early 2000s and mostly focused on the area of housing. City authorities found that decentralised accommodation was better not only for those directly concerned but also for urban society as a whole as well as the public budget (Wendel 2014, p. 79). With their decentralisation plans, some city municipalities contradicted the national and *Länder* regulations, which stipulated (and in some cases still do) that refugees with an insecure resident status should be housed in accommodation centres. Fully fledged integration concepts explicitly targeting refugees were adopted by many German cities in 2015 and 2016 as a reaction to the heightened number of refugees arriving in the country.

In Osnabrück, such policies were first developed in 2013, thus preceding both the discourse of a 'refugee crisis' in 2015 and the official re-framing of integration by the 2016 Integration Bill. The 2013 'Plan for the Integration and Accommodation of Refugees in the City of Osnabrück' was a reaction to increasing allocations of refugees and the desire to organise their accommodation in a way that corresponded with their needs, following the example of other city municipalities (Stadt Osnabrück 2013). It officially established decentralised housing and introduced 'proactive' social work. The Osnabrück Integration Plan was the first of its kind in Lower Saxony and was soon copied by other municipalities. However, it was quickly outmoded by the dynamics of the *long summer of migration* (Kasparek and Speer 2015): Between 2013 and 2017, more than 4000 refugees were allocated to the city (Stadt Osnabrück 2017) and both a regional 'initial reception centre' and several new municipal accommodation centres were opened, some of which were closed again in 2017 when fewer refugees were allocated to the city due to the renewed success of European and German authorities in keeping refugees out. In 2018, the municipality published an updated Integration Plan for refugees. As I show below, the changing local integration policies differ (increasingly) from the national

[6]While town and rural administrative district municipalities have also adopted integration plans, cities are often the pioneers of local integration policies (Gesemann and Roth 2009).

policies in terms of how they understand integration and construct refugee subjects and their deservingness.

2.5.1 Refugees as Part of a Heterogeneous Urban Society

With the 2013 Plan, the Osnabrück municipality stated officially, for the first time, that the integration of refugees with insecure legal status was a policy aim and that the long-established differentiation between persons with a 'migration background' – hitherto the main target group of integration measures – and 'refugees' or 'asylum-seekers' who had been officially excluded from such measures, was to be discontinued 'as far as possible' (Stadt Osnabrück 2013, p. 3). As the Municipal Commissioner for Integration in Osnabrück underlined in an interview on 6 July 2015:

> That we decided to focus on this [the integration of refugees] and that we even used the word 'integration' was completely new, because the Asylum-Seekers Benefits Act actually forbids this; integration should not take place [for persons with an insecure residence status].

The 2013 Plan identified refugees as persons who have suffered and are in need of special guidance and care (Stadt Osnabrück 2013, p. 3). This served, on the one hand, to justify the expenditure on additional social workers; on the other hand, it legitimised the continued accommodation of refugees with an insecure residence status in centres, where social workers could more easily intervene. The city authorities established decentralised housing only for those refugees who had stayed for two or more years in the city, with the exception of persons – like families or the elderly – for whom a prolonged stay in an accommodation centre was considered inappropriate. The decision to link access to private housing to the length of stay in the city or the migrants' supposed vulnerability was harshly criticised by some civil society initiatives and the City's Migrant Advisory Board, which had been involved in developing the Integration Plan and demanded access to decentralised housing for all refugees (Migrationsbeirat der Stadt Osnabrück 2013; No Lager 2013).

Throughout the long summer of migration, the city authorities often reverted to the image of refugees as victims in order to mobilise support and sympathy for the newcomers in the local community. At the same time, refugees were increasingly framed as an integral part of urban society. In 2015, the city administration decided that all refugees, regardless of their legal status and length of stay in the city, could move into private flats. In the same year, the Municipal Integration Department presented an integrated activity report, which no longer differentiated between activities targeting refugees and those aimed at other migrants. The report simply highlighted that the urban community was growing and becoming more diverse:

> Migration is becoming more and more important in the city – today every fourth person has already a so-called migration background. Among children (younger than six) it is already 48 per cent (Stadt Osnabrück 2016, p. 4).

By underlining that the local population consists to a large extent of migrants and their children, local authorities portray migration as the norm and migrants as members of the local community. This also counts for refugees, who are addressed as '(new) Osnabrückers' in the latest Integration Plan (Stadt Osnabrück 2018). This perception of migrants as rightful residents or 'citizens' is also reflected in the local authorities' concern to facilitate the transition of migrants with different legal statuses as soon as possible from immigration reception and orientation services to regular municipal services (Stadt Osnabrück 2018).

In addition, and in line with a more general shift from a problem-oriented to a potentiality-focused perspective on migration-based diversity among German city municipalities (Pütz and Rodatz 2013), (refugee) migration to Osnabrück is increasingly referred to as a potential advantage. The authorities have underlined time and again that Osnabrück is growing and flourishing and that this is at least partly thanks to (refugee) immigration. A recent municipal demographic forecast for 2017–2030 states:

> Compared to the composition of the population in 2016, the population will become older and more diverse as a result of international immigration and the integration of refugees. This development fits in with the picture of the expected population in other German cities, which attracts (young) people with a good infrastructure and qualified education and job offers. A particular challenge is to bind this population group in the long-term, especially once they have completed their education and during the family phase (Stadt Osnabrück 2017, p. 55).

While the positive discourse on migration-based diversity is challenged by some (within both local institutions and the wider urban community), it still dominates local political debates and practices, as an incident in 2014 illustrates. As part of a publicity campaign to promote diversity in the city, the municipality had displayed a large poster which read 'Diversity is our strength' and showed images of several Osnabrück residents with a 'migration background'. When the poster was deliberately destroyed in 2014, the local authorities reinforced their statement by selling the remaining paper shreds to locals and replacing the poster. While certainly also driven by a desire to make a stance against xenophobic and racist violence, the positive take on migration and diversity by local governments can at least partly be explained by inter-locality competition. In their quest for financial and human resources, city governments seek to position themselves as *entrepreneurial cities* using migration-based diversity and the way in which they are managing it as a location factor (Desille 2020; Pütz and Rodatz 2013; Schmiz 2017). In Osnabrück, for example, refugee accommodation and integration in the city have been used to reinforce the city's image as the 'City of Peace' (a reference to the signing of the Treaty of Westphalia in 1648):

> The City of Osnabrück already paved the way, in 2013, […] for a culture of welcome so that we did not experience the arrival of refugees in 2014/15 as a 'refugee crisis'. Since then, more than 4,000 persons, who fled from war, persecution and paucity of prospects, have found a safe haven in the City of Peace of Osnabrück (Stadt Osnabrück 2018, p. 6).

The above-mentioned 'paradigm shift' to a potentiality-oriented perspective entails the risk of reducing migrants to 'human resources' and reformulating deservingness on the basis of economic concerns in a similar way to the workfare approach to integration at the national level. However, it also has the potential to break with ethno-centric models of citizenship, particularly if participation and integration are not only framed as a duty on behalf of the newcomers.

2.5.2 We All Need to Integrate: Integration as a Two-Way Process

While the Integration Bill frames integration above all as a duty on behalf of the individual refugee, the local integration policies analysed here frame integration as a two-way process which concerns the whole of urban society and its institutions. In quite explicit opposition to the national discourse on 'integration', the local Integration Department states:

> Any demands for 'integration' are based on the erroneous assumption that integration processes are shaped above all by the immigrants themselves, since they have to integrate into the 'host society'. However, if we understand integrationas a task for society as a whole, including the opening up of established social institutions, it becomes clear that the concept of integration must be based on a broader conceptual foundation (Stadt Osnabrück 2018, pp. 9–10).

For the municipal authorities, the problem is not a supposed unwillingness or incapacity to integrate on behalf of certain individuals but an inequality of access to and participation in social systems. The aim of local integration policies is, accordingly, to establish equality of access to and participation in different spheres of social life (like health, housing, employment, law, politics, religion and so on). One of the main barriers to equal participation in these spheres, from the perspective of the municipality, is the legal insecurity and differential access tied to the different legal statuses of their residents. Discrimination on the basis of legal status is not only an additional administrative burden and cost but also a factor that contributes to inequality and insecurity in the urban community, as a representative of the Integration Service in Osnabrück explained in an interview:

> [...] the municipality takes on the expenses, for example, for health and accommodation, and that is really *insane* compared to the normal system, isn't it? Why are they [refugees] not covered by statutory health insurance? Why do they not have access to integration courses? These are all federal funds. So this is the pecking order; in the pecking order we are at the very bottom as a municipality, we have to take responsibility for public order regulations like Dublin [...].

There is thus a clash of interests and logics between national and local government insofar as the latter 'are obliged to make available to their inhabitants and thus also to foreigners – that is, migrants – the required economic, social and cultural institutions and services' (Bommes 2012, p. 128), whereas the former seek to protect their borders and social systems from non-citizens. Another reason for the different approach of local authorities to migrant integration is the strong engagement of civil society initiatives, and the fact that local politicians often feel more pressure to react to demands of local initiatives and migrant organisations than politicians at other levels of government (Cantat 2020; Ellermann 2009).

In the US and Canada, opposed interests between city and national authorities concerning undocumented residents led to the development of 'sanctuary practices' (Bauder 2017) or even forms of 'local citizenship' (Varsanyi 2006) and also in many German cities, including Osnabrück, so-called 'solidarity-city' initiatives have formed. While the German initiatives, unlike the American and Canadian Sanctuary-City movement, are above all bottom-up initiatives, they seek dialogue with local authorities and often obtain political approval: The Osnabrück City Council, for example, endorsed the local initiative to resettle 50 refugees from camps in Greece to Osnabrück and, more recently, followed the demands of several civil society organisations to become part of an alliance of cities across Europe which declare themselves as 'safe havens' in order to protest against the (supra-)national politics of deterrence (Dörn 2018). In turn, the local government also relies on civil society initiatives to support newcomers. In Osnabrück, the Municipal Service for Refugee Integration is, in fact, a collaboration between the municipality and several NGOs. The municipality also relies on informal initiatives, particularly where integration support – like language courses for refugees who are considered 'unlikely to be able to stay' – is not funded by the *regional* or national government.

Yet the cooperation between local government and the administration with local activists also has its limits, as became apparent in Osnabrück in 2017, when activists asked the local council to take a stance against deportations. A broad alliance between different groups had prevented more than 36 Dublin deportations in the city in 2014/15, before changes regarding the deportation procedure by the *Land* rendered their prevention more difficult (Hinger et al. 2018). While part of the City Council supported the demand to 'avoid deportations whenever possible', the conservative parties emphasised their political backing of European and national legislation stipulating that rejected asylum-seekers should be deported (Kröger 2017). This shows the contested nature of the local asylum regime and highlights the fact that local governments also (re-)produce certain framings of belonging and deservingness based on legal status.

2.5.3   The Distinction Between 'Our' and Other Refugees

Although local integration measures thus tend to follow a different logic than national legislation, (city) municipalities sometimes also distinguish between those who (ought to) belong to the urban community and those who do not. Precisely because the discrimination of residents on the basis of their legal status is highly contested at the local level, municipalities demand selection of refugees *before* they become 'their' residents. As Bommes (2012, p. 128) noted, '[f]or municipalities, unless they are in a position to reject migrants, there has been no alternative but integration'. In other words, municipalities, like national governments, attempt to attract some immigrants and to reject others. In fact, German municipalities cannot reject refugees allocated to them by the *Land* government but can, at least to some degree, influence dispersal and accommodation policies and processes. First, municipal administrations can (try to) negotiate who is allocated to them in dialogue with the responsible service at the level of the *Land*. An employee of the Osnabrück Social Services, responsible for the reception and accommodation of refugees in the city, explained to me that he could express his preferences regarding the nationality of newcomers – namely, Syrians – and that, most of the time, persons were allocated in line with this preference, because it was 'in everyone's interest that there were no frictions in the allocation process'.

Second, municipalities negotiate with the *Länder* and the national government about the distribution of responsibilities and the cost of refugee accommodation. Even though individual municipalities or services might distance themselves from national asylum policies, as we have seen in the case of Osnabrück, city municipalities have, in fact, played a vital role in shaping migration and integration policies at the national level, including the Integration Bill. When the number of refugees arriving in German municipalities rose significantly in 2015/2016, it was also city representatives who pressed for accelerated asylum procedures and an early selection. The President of the Association of German Cities, for example, demanded that only 'genuine' refugees should be allocated to municipalities:

> Besides international efforts [to curb the number of asylum-seekers] the government and the *Länder* have to quickly implement the accelerated asylum procedures and then consistently return persons with no likelihood of being allowed to stay to their countries of origin. This is necessary, so that only those refugees who need our protection as civil war refugees and the politically persecuted are transferred into the municipalities (Lohse, cited in Deutscher Städtetag 2015).

This quote illustrates how city representatives contribute to the fractioning of the refugee label through the use of the notion of (not) being likely to stay and how this notion is equalised to the binaries genuine/bogus or civil war/economic refugee. This way of categorising refugees provides a deceptively simple moral compass and way of handling an intricate problem. Instead of waiting for the outcome of long and complex asylum procedures, the authorities simply assign refugees to one or the other category on the basis of their nationality (or, more precisely, the likelihood that persons of that nationality will be granted asylum). For the municipalities, such a preliminary selection is attractive, because the accommodation of persons who later have to be deported comes at a high cost – on the one hand, because the reception and orientation phase presents a financial burden, which is at least partly carried by the municipality, and on the other, because the enactment of deportations is a contentious issue. In Osnabrück, for example, the (planned) deportations of refugees to other EU member-states according to the Dublin regulation led to a series of protests and the actual prevention of deportations by a civil society initiative, as already mentioned above. While this engagement of the local community was welcomed by (part of) the local government, it also presented a problem, given that the local administration is expected to collaborate in the enactment of deportations. In order to forego such conflicts, the Mayor of Osnabrück asked the *Land* authorities in 2014 to discontinue the transfer of 'Dublin cases' to the municipality and instead keep them in the regional 'reception centre'. What is more, the mayor argued that such a measure of residential segregation was necessary in order to ensure successful integration at the local level:

> For meaningful and successful social work with refugees as well as for the engagement of volunteers, it is extremely difficult if, shortly after becoming acquainted with a refugee, they learn that this person is transferred to another [EU] member-state for their asylum procedure. Such very short encounters are a burden for everyone and have, as you probably know, already led to public outrage (Letter to the Minister of Interior by the Mayor of Osnabrück 2014).

The mayor's letter did not lead to a change in the allocation of refugees but shows how local authorities attempt to limit and select who comes to the city and how they, like their national counterparts, link the successful integration of some to the disintegration of others.

Finally, I want to highlight that the distinction between those who belong to the urban community and those who do not is not simply a question of *presence*, as suggested by Bommes (2012). The mere presence of refugees in the city does not actually suffice for them to be considered rightful members of the urban community. The example of refugees living in reception centres, run by the *Länder* authorities but located in cities, proves this point. Those accommodated in such centres are residents of the city but their stay is considered to be only temporary – since they are still awaiting their allocation to a municipality[7] – and their integration thus not expected. My interviewees in the local administration in Osnabrück, for example, did not consider the refugees accommodated in the reception centre that was opened in Osnabrück at the end of 2014 as 'their' refugees. Interestingly, they are not only excluded from municipal integration measures, but also civil society initiatives perceived those accommodated in the reception centre as somehow not belonging to the city, as a Solidarity-City activist in Osnabrück reflected:

> We only started to think about the [reception centre] sometime in the beginning of this year and that was partly because of Brenda, a Roma woman who appeared at one of our meetings one day. She told us a bit about what happened inside the camp. And this also spread among the *No Lager* group so that they also said we have to focus more on [the reception centre]. The whole time deportations were taking place there. Also when we celebrated our deportation preventions [elsewhere], the whole time people were being deported from the reception camp. So eventually we said we have to see the whole truth and this also includes [the reception centre].

The example of Brenda shows that 'acts of integration' (Collyer et al. 2020) are possible even for persons whose integration in (urban) society is put on hold. However, their (supposedly) only temporary stay, in addition to their accommodation in camps which are often located on the outskirts of cities, renders their participation in the life and institutions of the urban community very difficult.

---

[7] Which is normally not the one in which the reception centre is based, with the exception of city states.

2.6   Conclusions

This chapter has explored the functioning and logics of recent integration policies targeting refugees in Germany. While at both local and national levels the (dis)integration of refugees has become a policy issue, the perceived problem and proposed solutions differ. At the national level, an official integration policy targeting refugees was developed in response to their rising numbers in 2015/2016 – perceived and presented mostly as a threat to social cohesion and stability. The 2016 Integration Bill introduced a two-class asylum system with possibilities of fast-track integration for asylum claimants deemed 'likely to stay', and systematic disintegration – involving both residential segregation and material exclusion – for those considered 'unlikely to stay'. This categorisation, which is based on protection rates for different nationalities, conveys the message that decisions in asylum procedures are infallible and that a clear distinction between deserving and undeserving asylum claimants can be made. While economic performance also plays an increasing role in the determination of deservingness of refugees at the national level, the integration bill remains grounded in an ethno-national understanding of integration.

On the contrary, municipalities – especially city municipalities – developed integration measures for refugees with different legal statuses well before 2015, with the aim of reducing both financial and social costs. The distinction of residents on the basis of their legal status and the disintegration of some of them turned out to be impractical and against the very interests of municipalities in maintaining stable and flourishing local communities. The study of integration policies and practices in Osnabrück showed that migrants in general and refugees in particular, are still distinguished from other residents, however, not to mark them as non-members but to detect social inequalities. To overcome these and ensure equal participation in social systems is the main aim of local integration measures. Contrary to the national logic of integration as a duty and privilege, integration is here understood as a process also involving the opening of local institutions. Moreover, the integration of immigrants, including refugees, is seen not only as a challenge and burden but also as a chance and potential in the inter-locality competition for talent and resources.

At the same time, however, local governments also pursue *integration through disintegration* as they seek to select who comes to the city in the first place and to concentrate their efforts on those newcomers who are 'likely to stay'. While this notion is not used in the Osnabrück Integration Plans, the question whether or not a refugee will stay or be transferred/deported in a near future does play a role for local decisionmakers as illustrated by the letter of the Mayor cited above. While municipalities thus break with certain logics and framings of deservingness, they (re-) produce others, partly out of the (perceived) necessity to create cost and planning security and the desire to avoid local conflict. As my analysis shows, the way in which local authorities use their room for manœuvre ultimately also depends on the local actor constellations and dynamics, e.g. the influence of civil society initiatives. In my case study, the latter mostly lobbied for a more generous implementation of asylum provisions. It needs to be stressed, that this is not always the case – in many

German localities, civil society has also mobilised against the reception of asylum-seeking newcomers. The negotiations between local state and non-state actors here served as an example to illustrate that negotiations take part on the local level. While not highlighted in this chapter, this observation also regards negotiations and conflicts among local government institutions. For example, the municipal Integration Department follows quite different institutional logics than the local Foreigners' or the Welfare Office. More research is needed to further explore integration policies and practices at the local level, highlighting the competing logics and forces within and among municipal administrative and political bodies, as well as comparative analyses, also including rural municipalities.

This chapter sought to contribute to the debate on (dis)integration, by pointing out that disintegration is not only an aim of policy-makers but is also legitimised within a broader integration framework. Above all on the national level, but to some extent also on the local level, policymakers (as well as parts of civil society) stress that integration capacities are limited and that successful integration requires a selection among refugees, and a systematic disintegration of those considered undeserving.

References

Asyl, P. (2017). *Die Einstufung nach 'Bleibeperspektive' ist bewusste Integrationsverhinderung*. Retrieved March 06, 2019, from https://www.proasyl.de/news/die-einstufung-nach-bleibeperspektive-ist-bewusste-integrationsverhinderung/

Aumüller, J. (2009). Die kommunale Integration von Flüchtlingen. In F. Gesemann & R. Roth (Eds.), *Lokale Integrationspolitik in der Einwanderungsgesellschaft: Migration und Integration als Herausforderung von Kommunen* (pp. 111–130). Wiesbaden: VS Verlag für Sozialwissenschaften.

Aumüller, J. (2018). Die kommunale Integration von Flüchtlingen. In F. Gesemann & R. Roth (Eds.), *Handbuch Lokale Integrationspolitik* (pp. 173–198). Wiesbaden: Springer.

Bade, K. J. (2015). Zur Karriere und Funktion abschätziger Begriffe in der deutschen Asylpolitik. *Aus Politik und Zeitgeschichte, 65*(25), 3–8.

Bauder, H. (2017). Sanctuary cities: Policies and practices in international perspective. *International Migration, 55*(2), 174–187.

Bommes, M. (2012). 'Integration takes place locally'. On the restructuring of local integration policy. In C. Boswell & G. D'Amato (Eds.), *Immigration and social systems: Collected essays of Michael Bommes* (pp. 125–156). Amsterdam: Amsterdam University Press.

Bundesamt für Migration und Flüchtlinge. (2019). *Was heißt gute Bleibeperspektive?*. Retrieved March 06, 2019, from https://www.bamf.de/SharedDocs/FAQ/DE/IntegrationskurseAsylbewe rber/001-bleibeperspektive.html

Bundesregierung. (2016a). *Fluchtursachen bekämpfen, Flüchtlingszahlen reduzieren*. Retrieved March 06, 2019, from https://www.bundesregierung.de/Content/DE/Infodienst/2016/03/2016-03-09-fluechtlingszahlen-reduzieren/2016-03-09-fluchtursachen-bekaempfen.html

Bundesregierung. (2016b). *Meseberger Erklärung zur Integration*. Retrieved 11 July 2019 from https://www.bundesregierung.de/Content/DE/Pressemitteilungen/BPA/2016/05/2016-05-25-meseberger-erklaerung.html?nn=694676

Cantat, C. (2020). Governing migrants and refugees in Hungary: Politics of spectacle, negligence and solidarity in a Securitising state. In S. Hinger & R. Schweitzer (Eds.), *Politics of (Dis) Integration* (pp. 183–199). Cham: Springer VS.

Castles, S. (2003). Towards a sociology of forced migration and social transformation. *Sociology,* *37*(1), 13–34.

Chauvin, S., & Garcés-Mascareñas, B. (2012). Beyond informal citizenship: The new moral economy of migrant illegality. *International Political Sociology, 6*(3), 241–259.

Chauvin, S., & Garcés-Mascareñas, B. (2014). Becoming less illegal: Deservingness frames and undocumented migrant incorporation. *Sociology Compass, 8*(4), 422–432.

Collyer, M., Hinger, S., & Schweitzer, R. (2020). Politics of (Dis)Integration – An introduction. In S. Hinger & R. Schweitzer (Eds.), *Politics of (Dis)Integration* (pp. 1–18). Cham: Springer VS.

Desille, A. (2020). Jewish Immigrants in Israel: Disintegration within Integration? In S. Hinger & R. Schweitzer (Eds.), *Politics of (Dis)Integration* (pp. 141–159). Cham: Springer VS.

Deutscher Städtetag. (2015). *Deutscher Städtetag zu Asylverfahrensbeschleunigungsgesetz.* Retrieved March 06, 2019, from http://www.staedtetag.de/presse/mitteilungen/075486/index. html

Dörn, S. (2018). *Osnabrücker Unterstützung der Seebrücke ist mehr als Symbolpolitik. NOZ.* Retrieved March 06, 2019, from https://www.noz.de/lokales/osnabrueck/artikel/1510004/ osnabruecker-unterstuetzung-der-seebruecke-ist-mehr-als-symbolpolitik

Ellermann, A. (2009). *States against migrants: Deportation in Germany and the United States.* Cambridge: Cambridge University Press.

Fiedler, M., Georgi, F., Hielscher, L., Ratfisch, P., Riedner, L., Schwab, V., & Sontowski, S. (2017). Umkämpfte Bewegungen nach und durch EUropa. Zur Einleitung. movements. *Journal for Critical Migration and Border Regime Studies, 3*(1). Retrieved September 06, 2018, from https://movements-journal.org/issues/04.bewegungen/

Flüchtlingsrat, B. (2017). *Transitzentren & ARE: Die bayerischen Abschiebelager.* Retrieved March 06, 2019, from http://www.fluechtlingsrat-bayern.de/ankunfts-und-rueckfuehrungsein-richtungen.html

Gesemann, F., & Roth, R. (Eds.). (2009). *Lokale Integrationspolitik in der Einwanderungsgesellschaft: Migration und Integration als Herausforderung von Kommunen.* Wiesbaden: Springer.

Gesetzentwurf für das Integrationsgesetz. (2016). *Entwurf eines Integrationsgesetzes.* Retrieved March 06, 2019, from http://www.bmas.de/SharedDocs/Downloads/DE/PDF-Meldungen/2016/entwurf-integrationsgesetz.pdf%3F__blob%3DpublicationFile%26v%3D4

Hess, S., & Moser, J. (2009). Jenseits der Integration. Kulturwissenschaftliche Betrachtungen einer Debatte. In S. Hess, J. Binder, & J. Moser (Eds.), *No Integration. Kulturwissenschaftliche Beiträge zur Integrationsdebatte in Europa* (pp. 11–26). Bielefeld: Transcript Verlag.

Hinger, S., Schäfer, P., & Pott, A. (2016). The local production of asylum. *Journal of Refugee Studies, 29*(4), 440–463.

Hinger, S., Kirchhoff, M., & Wiese, R. (2018). 'We belong together!' collective anti-deportation protests in Osnabrück. In S. Rosenberger, V. Stern, & N. Merhaut (Eds.), *Protest movements in asylum and deportation* (pp. 163–184). Cham: Springer.

Integrationsgesetz. (2016). *Bundesgesetzblatt Jahrgang, I*(39), 1939–1949.

Kasparek, B., & Speer, M. (2015). *Of Hope: Hungary and the long summer of migration.* Bordermonitoring.eu, 09 September. Retrieved March 06, 2019, from http://bordermonitoring. eu/ungarn/2015/09/of-hope-en/

King, R. (2002). Towards a new map of European migration. *Population, Space and Place, 8*(2), 89–106.

Kröger, D. (2017). *Osnabrücker Rat streitet um Abschiebung NOZ.* Retrieved September 06, 2018, from https://www.noz.de/lokales/osnabrueck/artikel/847252/ osnabruecker-rat-streitet-um-abschiebung

Lager, N. (2013). *Stellungnahme der Initiative No Lager zum Konzeptentwurf zur Wohnraumversorgung und Integration von Flüchtlingen der Stadt Osnabrück, 24.07.2013.* Retrieved March 06, 2019, from https://www.nds-fluerat.org/wp-content/uploads/2013/07/ stellungnahme-no-lager-os.pdf

Lanz, S. (2009). In unternehmerische Subjekte investieren. Integrationskonzepte im Workfare-Staat. Das Beispiel Berlin. In S. Hess & J. Moser (Eds.), *No Integration. Kulturwissenschaftliche Beiträge zur Integrationsdebatte in Europa* (pp. 105–122). Bielefeld: Transcript Verlag.

Lanz, S. (2016). Politik zwischen Polizei und Post-Politik: Überlegungen zu 'urbanen Pionieren' einer politisierten Stadt am Beispiel von Berlin. In M. Behrens, W. D. Bukow, K. Cudak, & C. Strünck (Eds.), *Inclusive City* (pp. 43–61). Wiesbaden: Springer.

Letter to the Minister of Interior by the Mayor of Osnabrück, In No Lager (2014). *Wie willkommen sind Geflüchtete in Osnabrück, wirklich? Diesmal geben Geflüchtete und Unterstützer*innen eine Antwort. Pressemappe*, 18 December (pp. 21–22). Retrieved March 6, 2019, from http://nolageros.blogsport.eu/files/2014/12/pressemappe.pdf

Lind, J., & Persdotter, M. (2017). Differential deportability and contradictions of a territorialised right to education: A perspective from Sweden. *movements Journal for Critical Migration and Border Regime Studies, 3*(1). Retrieved March 06, 2019, from https://movements-journal.org/issues/04.bewegungen/04.persdotter,lind--differential-deportability-contradictions-territorialised-right-education.html

Magazzini, T. (2020). Integration as an essentially contested concept: Questioning the assumptions behind the National Roma Integration Strategies of Italy and Spain. In S. Hinger & R. Schweitzer (Eds.), *Politics of (Dis)Integration* (pp. 41–59). Cham: Springer VS.

Martiniello, M., & Simon, P. (2005). Les enjeux de la catégorisation: Rapport de domination et luttes autour de la représentation dans les sociétés post-migratoires. *Revue Européenne des Migrations Internationales, 21*(2), 7–19.

Meseberger Erklärung zur Integration. (2016). Retrieved September 06, 2018, from https://www.bundesregierung.de/Content/DE/Pressemitteilungen/BPA/2016/05/2016-05-25-meseberger-erklaerung.html?nn=694676

Migrationsbeirat der Stadt Osnabrück. (2013). *Stellungnahme zum 'Konzept zur Wohnraumversorgung und Integration von Flüchtlingen' des Osnabrücker Migrationsbeirates*, beschlossen am 19.11.2013. Retrieved March 06, 2019, from https://www.osnabrueck.de/fileadmin/eigene_Dateien/0611_Quartierstreff-Dodesheide/user_upload/Stellungnahme_Fluechtlingskonzept.pdf

Mügge, L., & van der Haar, M. (2016). Who is an immigrant and who requires integration? Categorizing in European policies. In B. Garcés-Mascareñas & R. Penninx (Eds.), *Integration processes and policies in Europe* (pp. 77–90). Cham: Springer.

Niedersachsen, F. (2017). *Mal ehrlich! Flucht und Asyl in Niedersachsen*. Flüchtlingsrat, 151(1). Retrieved March 06, 2019, from https://www.nds-fluerat.org/wp-content/uploads/2017/04/Brosch%C3%BCre-Asyl-A5-NDS-v10.pdf

Nimführ, S., Otto, L., & Samateh, G. (this volume). *Denying, while demanding integration:An analysis of the integration paradox in malta and refugees' coping strategies*. In S. Hinger & R. Schweitzer (Eds.), *Politics of (dis)integration*. Cham: Springer.

Stadt Osnabrück. (2013). *Konzept zur Wohnraumversorgung und Integration von Flüchtlingen der Stadt Osnabrück*. Retrieved September 06, 2018 from https://www.nds-fluerat.org/wp-content/uploads/2014/01/2014-12-17_Fluechtlingskonzept_aktuell.pdf

Stadt Osnabrück. (2016). *Tätigkeitsbericht 2015*. FB Integration, Soziales und Bürgerengagement, 14 April 2016. Retrieved March 06, 2019, from https://www.osnabrueck.de/fileadmin/eigene_Dateien/Ta-tigkeitsbericht-2015-FD-50-5.pdf

Stadt Osnabrück. (2017). Bevölkerungsprognose Osnabrück 2017–2030. Band 1 –Gesamtstadt. *Osnabrücker Beiträge zur Stadtforschung*. Retrieved March 06, 2019, from https://www.osnabrueck.de/fileadmin/eigene_Dateien/01_osnabrueck.de/011_Rathaus/Statistik/Bevolkerungsprognose-Band-I.PDF

Stadt Osnabrück. (2018). *Von der Erstaufnahme zur Überleitung in die Regelsysteme: Integration von Geflüchteten in der Stadt Osnabrück*. Retrieved March 06, 2019, from https://www.osnabrueck.de/fileadmin/eigene_Dateien/Integrationskonzept-der-Stadt-Osnabru-ck-2018.pdf

Penninx, R., & Garcés-Mascareñas, B. (2016). The concept of integration as an analytical tool and as a policy concept. In B. Garcés-Mascareñas & R. Penninx (Eds.), *Integration processes and policies in Europe* (pp. 11–29). Cham: Springer.

Pütz, R., & Rodatz, M. (2013). Kommunale Integrations-und Vielfaltskonzepte im Neoliberalismus: Zur strategischen Steuerung von Integration in deutschen Großstädten. *Geographische Zeitschrift, 101*(3–4), 166–183.

Rosenberger, S. (2012). Integration von AsylwerberInnen? Zur Paradoxie individueller Integrationsleistungen und staatlicher Desintegration. In J. Dahlvik, H. Fassmann, & W. Sievers (Eds.), *Migration und Integration. Wissenschaftliche Perspektiven aus Österreich: Jahrbuch 1/2011* (pp. 91–106). Göttingen: V & R Unipress.

Schmiz, A. (2017). Staging a 'Chinatown' in Berlin: The role of city branding in the urban governance of ethnic diversity. *European Urban and Regional Studies, 24*(3), 290–303.

Schweitzer, R. (2020). How Inclusive Institutions Enforce Exclusive Immigration Rules: Mainstream Public Service Provision and the Implementation of a Hostile Environment for Irregular Migrants Living in Britain. In S. Hinger & R. Schweitzer (Eds.), *Politics of (Dis)Integration* (pp. 121–140). Cham: Springer VS.

Täubig, V. (2009). *Totale Institution Asyl: Empirische Befunde zu alltäglichen Lebensführungen in der organisierten Desintegration.* Weinheim and München: Juventa.

Varsanyi, M. W. (2006). Interrogating 'urban citizenship' *vis-à-vis* undocumented migration. *Citizenship Studies, 10*(2), 229–249.

Verordnung zum Integrationsgesetz. (2016). *Verordnung der Bundesregierung.* Retrieved September 06, 2018, from http://www.bmas.de/SharedDocs/Downloads/DE/PDF- Meldungen/2016/ent-wurf-verordnung-zum integrationsgesetz.pdf?__blob=publicationFile&v=5

Voigt, C. (2016). *Die Bleibeperspektive.* Wie ein Begriff das Aufenthaltsrecht verändert. Asylmagazin, 8/2016, 248.

Wendel, K. (2014). *Unterbringung von Flüchtlingen in Deutschland. Regelungen und Praxis der Bundesländer im Vergleich.* Frankfurt am Main: Pro Asyl.

Yanow, D. (2000). *Conducting interpretive policy analysis.* London: Sage.

Zetter, R. (2007). More labels, fewer refugees: Remaking the refugee label in an era of globalization. *Journal of Refugee Studies, 20*(2), 172–192.

Chapter 3
Integration as an Essentially Contested Concept: Questioning the Assumptions behind the National Roma Integration Strategies of Italy and Spain

Tina Magazzini

3.1 Introduction

Integration is a term that can fittingly be included in what W. B. Gallie (1956, p. 169) labelled 'essentially contested concepts' – those notions 'the proper use of which inevitably involves endless disputes about their proper uses on the part of their users'. Gallie warned that the indetermination suffered by this kind of concept cannot be settled by appeal to linguistics or logic, since it is caused by a dispute, a substantive disagreement on the reasons for attributing any given meaning to the concept. As argued in the introduction to this volume, integration has become a key term in the social sciences and yet it can be used – as it is – for a variety of meanings.

The indetermination of the notion of integration is closely related to what the aims or the target of integration are considered to be: whether the underlying 'problem' that integration is to tackle is seen in terms of cultural distance from the majority or as socio-economic disadvantage and whether the belief is either that the minority should integrate into the majority or that society as a whole should undergo an integration process as a response to increased diversity.

This chapter is concerned with the underlying assumptions that underpin the concept of integration aimed at a specific minority, the Roma, in two Mediterranean Western European countries, Italy and Spain. In both countries Roma minorities have been present in the territory for over five centuries.[1] Yet, over the past two decades, Italy and Spain have also become destination countries for Roma individuals or families fleeing poverty and discrimination in their home countries.

---

[1] For an overview of the historical context in Italy see Sigona 2005; Armillei 2014; Picker and Roccheggiani 2014; for Spain see Charnon-Deutsch 2004; Sánchez 2017.

T. Magazzini (✉)
European University Institute, Fiesole, FI, Italy
e-mail: tina.magazzini@eui.eu

© The Author(s) 2020
S. Hinger, R. Schweitzer (eds.), *Politics of (Dis)Integration*,
IMISCOE Research Series, https://doi.org/10.1007/978-3-030-25089-8_3

While Italy and Spain have fairly similar political and administrative structures and migration histories, and have both been heavily affected by the 2008 economic crisis, they differ radically in their treatment of Roma. While Spain is usually presented as a model of successful integration,[2] Italy has been condemned repeatedly by the UN Committee on the Elimination of Racial Discrimination and other international bodies for its treatment of Roma.

In order to understand such different approaches, I here carry out a discourse and thematic analysis of the Roma-targeted integration legislation that exists in Italy and Spain. The National Roma Integration Strategies (henceforth NRIS), which both countries adopted in 2012 in compliance with the 'European Roma Integration Framework' promoted by Brussels, represent the cornerstones of the Roma integration policies in each country in terms of goal-setting and objectives to be achieved, and thus are critical to our understanding of how integration is interpreted. I combine the analysis of these policy documents with interviews with a range of actors involved, who are part of the politics of (dis)integration. This means attempting to uncover processes of negotiation and political dynamics around integration and disintegration. By giving policy-makers a voice on what Roma integration is about, according to them, and what they meant by it when drafting policies, we gain some insight into what the expectations of such measures and the politics behind them are.

This chapter is part of a broader study which builds on the hypothesis that the Spanish state historically focused mainly on the socio-economic dimension of the integration of the Roma, while Italy has adopted a more culturalist approach towards this specific minority. Analysis of the NRIS confirms the different levels of importance granted in each of the two countries to the cultural and economic aspects of integration. Yet, what emerges is also a picture in which the declared intent of promoting integration coexists with – and is part and parcel of – wider processes of disintegration. As explained in this volume's introduction, disintegration processes and measures are hereby understood as policies that actively 'do harm [...], although they are sometimes justified within a broader integration framework' (Collyer et al. 2020, p. 2), and experiences of disintegration are not a problem experienced by a few individuals but a phenomenon of mainstream society and its institutions.

In the case of Roma minorities and of racialised migrants more broadly, the discourses have shifted over the past decade from protection against discrimination to the issue of 'integration' (Ciulinaru 2018). More specifically, 'being integrated' in the case of Roma minorities in Italy and Spain seems to be associated with 'being a national' which, in turn, is perceived as belonging to the mainstream, understood as the white middle-class sector of society (Magazzini 2018). In this sense, it appears that normative assumptions of integration have not radically changed in contemporary Western Europe from that described as 'segmented assimilation' in the United States in the early 1990s (Portes and Zhou 2016). 'Segmented assimilation' chal-

---

[2] For a problematisation of Spain's 'successful Roma integration' see Magazzini and Piemontese 2016; Vrăbiescu 2016; Vrăbiescu and Kalir 2017.

lenged the idea that assimilation goes hand-in-hand with upward mobility, recognising that immigrants and their descendents might experience 'downward' assimilation and/or selective acculturation. While the vocabulary employed in policy discourses aimed at minorities in contemporary Europe celebrates diversity and rejects assimilation, the assumptions behind the new concept of 'integration' are still rooted in an assimilationist idea of what it means to belong to a given community. Disintegration practices are thus the result of an understanding of 'integration' that either requires assimilation – Spain compels Roma to be 'proper Spaniards' in order to be the recipients of inclusion policies – or pits the majority and minority as so inherently culturally different as to require physical separation or mediation – Italy compels Roma to be 'ethnic others' or 'cultural others' for them to benefit from integration policies.

3.2   (Roma) Integration as a Stratified Process

While, in European literature and policies, the concept of minority integration is usually understood to address the situation of migrants – and specifically of third-country nationals (Garcés-Mascareñas and Penninx 2016; Murphy 2010; Penninx et al. 2008) – it has also become an increasingly pivotal term in directives and policies explicitly targeting Roma groups and individuals, even though the vast majority of them are European citizens and only relatively few have left their country of origin (Matras and Leggio 2018).

Roma minorities are specifically addressed in Italy's and Spain's reports pursuant to Article 25, paragraph 2 of the Framework Convention for the Protection of National Minorities, a framework that, as a general rule, does not include 'new' minorities (even though it is not forbidden to do so).[3] This would lead them to be thought of as 'old' or national minorities; however, at the same time, a specific set of 'integration' policies aimed at the Roma has emerged, which is an atypical way of conducting diversity management of, or accommodating, traditional minorities.[4] The rationale for the distinction between migrants and national minorities is fairly straightforward: since historical, autochthonous minorities became numerical

---

[3] 'New' minorities refer to migrants. For a distinction between 'new' (migrant) and 'old' (national) minorities, see Tina Magazzini 2018; Medda-Windischer 2014.

[4] Long-established minorities in European countries, whether officially recognised or not as national minorities by the state in which they reside, have generally, albeit to different degrees, been granted some sort of autonomy from the state, and such autonomy (linguistic, fiscal, etc.) has typically not included interaction with mainstream society as a necessary feature of majority–minority relations. While important historical, political and legal differences exist between Western and Eastern European countries, the protection of national minorities is not generally framed in terms of 'integration'. The only exception I am aware of is the case of the 'integration programmes' developed by Estonia and Latvia for their Russian minorities but, even in these cases, an attempt was made to frame the policies as addressed to 'residents with immigrant background' or 'immigrant settlers' (Cianetti 2015, p. 201).

minorities in the territories they have traditionally inhabited as a result of conquest, colonisation, state-building and/or the redrawing of international borders, their incorporation into the state is seen as 'involuntary' which, in turn, makes it difficult for the state to ask for concessions in terms of cultural integration[5] (Medda-Windischer 2014, p. 3). The rights and protections afforded to refugees rest on similar assumptions of their migration being caused by external reasons of *force majeure* and thus being 'involuntary'.

Conversely, minority integration in the European academic literature is commonly conceived of as a process shaped by the interaction between so-called 'economic migrants' and the receiving society, even though it is 'an interaction between parties that are fundamentally unequal in power and resources' (Ponzo et al. 2013, p. 2), and, more recently, has been presented as a three-way process that also includes countries of origin (Garcés-Mascareñas and Penninx 2016). However, as is noted in the chapter by Nimführ et al. (2020), the burden of integration, in most cases, tends to fall on the migrants, refugees or minorities, rather than on the state – even if this latter might subscribe to the principles of integration as a desirable goal for society as a whole.

'Integration' as a category of analysis may well fit the definition contained in the Ljubljana Guidelines on Integration of Diverse Societies as a 'two-way process of mutual accommodation by minorities and residents of Member States' (OSCE High Commissioner on National Minorities 2012), yet the actual policies and practices related to it differ greatly. Indeed, to use the concept of 'integration' is to enter a minefield which can cause great political and theoretical concern, confusion and, in some cases, hostility, because of the diversity of meanings which the term can have. Lorenzo Cachón and Ben Gidley, amongst others, have pointed at how conceptualising integration means making choices regarding the kind of 'issue' to be addressed (Cachón 2008; Gidley 2014). This can take radically different turns depending on whether we interpret it as an individual or a collective 'integration', as an issue involving a study of the actors or rather an analysis of the structures, as a process, a 'measurable' result reflected upon general society or as a result/outcome measurable only with reference to the minority community, and whether 'integration' should study the behaviour (and/or processes) at an empirical level (including analysing policies) or instead delve into the normative regulatory field of how integration 'should be' and 'should take place' (Cachón 2008; Gidley 2013, 2014). These choices open up important questions related to the various dimensions of rights (civic and political, social, economic and cultural) as well as the interplay and relations between them, and issues such as whether there is a trade-off between different types of integration (i.e. cultural versus socio-economic).

Thus – given all these variables and potential for misunderstandings – the first temptation is to criticise the concept of 'integration' and jettison it, as a number of authors have proposed (Merry 2014; Schinkel 2017). It is, however, a term that is increasingly difficult to avoid as it has entered the jargon of international politics

---

[5]The idea that migrants should integrate into the host society because of their migration being 'voluntary' is debated, particularly in the case of refugees (see Lundberg 2016; Spencer 2004).

and of EU policy to such an extent that to do away with it would mean to give up on analysing altogether the causes and consequences of one of the most compelling current debates, both in terms of minority rights and of diversity management. In the case of Roma-targeted policies, 'integration' has turned into the officially declared goal of the EU as a whole as well as of individual countries, becoming an inescapable component of Roma politics itself. The departing point of this chapter is that integration, as stated in this volume's introduction, encompasses a set of normative assumptions, practices, policies and discourses that are always embedded in specific context.

3.3   Roma Integration Regimes: European Narratives and Fragmented Collectivities

Against this background, how can and should we situate the 'Roma integration' concept and policy framework? The emergence of the Roma minority as a category to be 'integrated' saw a significant hoist in the late 1990s and early 2000s, along with a more general preoccupation with minority protection in Europe, following the fall of the Berlin Wall and the breakup of Yugoslavia and the wars that accompanied it. The 1993 Copenhagen criteria required member-states to demonstrate 'respect for and protection of minorities'. Such a principle led to the Framework Convention for the Protection of National Minorities, which came into effect in 1998 and which, beyond fighting discrimination, is concerned with the preservation and development of the culture and identity of national minorities. This, in turn, translates into certain legal guarantees dealing with minorities' access to media, education and basic services accessible in their language. The Roma were included by some countries as a 'national minority' that falls within the scope of the convention and that is therefore in need of 'protection', but such a narrative has run counter to a parallel discourse on Roma 'integration'. This narrative has gained traction in recent years and tends to frame the Roma as a minority that is disadvantaged *vis-à-vis* the majority but that is more in need of 'getting up to speed' with the rest of society than of 'protection' as an indigenous cultural minority – or even of protection from discrimination. As Ciulinaru argues in reference to Eastern European Roma who migrated to France and have faced repatriation:

> [P]rejudice against the Roma took over the debate about their discrimination as migrants
> [...]. Of particular importance is *the shift in discourse from protection against discrimination to integration*, and the implications this shift had on diminishing the responsibility of national and EU authorities for protection of migrants from discrimination (2018, pp. 2–3).

A 2003 meeting of 12 European countries to promote the socio-economic inclusion of Roma minorities in the region resulted in the launch of the Decade for Roma Inclusion initiative (2005–2015), 'an unprecedented political commitment by European governments to eliminate discrimination against Roma and close the unacceptable gaps between Roma and the rest of society' (Brüggemann and Friedman 2017). While the elimination of discrimination is mentioned, the real focus of the Decade, as can be seen by its funding allocation and programmes, is rooted in the idea of 'uplifting' a vulnerable population from extreme poverty and marginalisation. The 'acknowledging' or 'constructing' of the Roma as a vulnerable category – a group considered to be especially susceptible to social exclusion (European Commission 2010) – and the representation of Roma exclusion as a public problem differed, however, from the accounts of other disadvantaged or marginalised groups. While the European Commission never singled out Roma exclusion in documents on welfare, economic growth and social inclusion, it developed a parallel set of reports, directives and recommendations addressing the Roma as a specifically disadvantaged group. Similarly, other international organisations, researchers and often also Roma activists have tended to reinforce the idea that the Roma face a set of obstacles that are completely different from the issues faced by other minority groups or by the majority population, which sets them in a category of their own. Thus, the growing debate around Roma marginalisation –and the need for Roma integration– has made for the hybridisation of a discourse that is highly ethnicised and yet, at the same time, centred on poverty and exclusion.

This has led to a Roma Integration Strategy Framework which sets the same markers and means as those typically used to assess the integration of migrants and refugees, but without addressing what Ager and Strang identified as the foundation of integration, namely the issue of rights and citizenship.

In their 2008 paper 'Understanding integration: a conceptual framework', Ager and Strang carried out a thorough review of the ways in which the term integration had been used in policy documents in an attempt to identify those elements that were consistently central to perceptions of what constituted integration (Ager and Strang 2008). In their article, the target population to be 'integrated' were refugees and, by analysing the 200 indicators of integration proposed by the 1997 Council of Europe's Report *Measurements and Indicators of Integration* and combining an additional literature review with fieldwork in refugee camps, they came up with the recurrent dimensions of integration, illustrated in Fig. 3.1.

In the following sections I take a similar approach, looking at how 'Roma integration' is defined in the Italian and Spanish NRIS, which lay the conceptual framework for the actions that governments are expected to pursue with regard to Roma minorities. While not focusing on all of Ager and Strang's domains, I look at the understanding of 'integration' of policy-makers and how they translated such understandings into a conceptual framework for the national strategies. This shows how integration is not a set 'package' of measurable characteristics but, rather, a stratified and, at times, contradictory narrative in which different voices overlap and coexist.

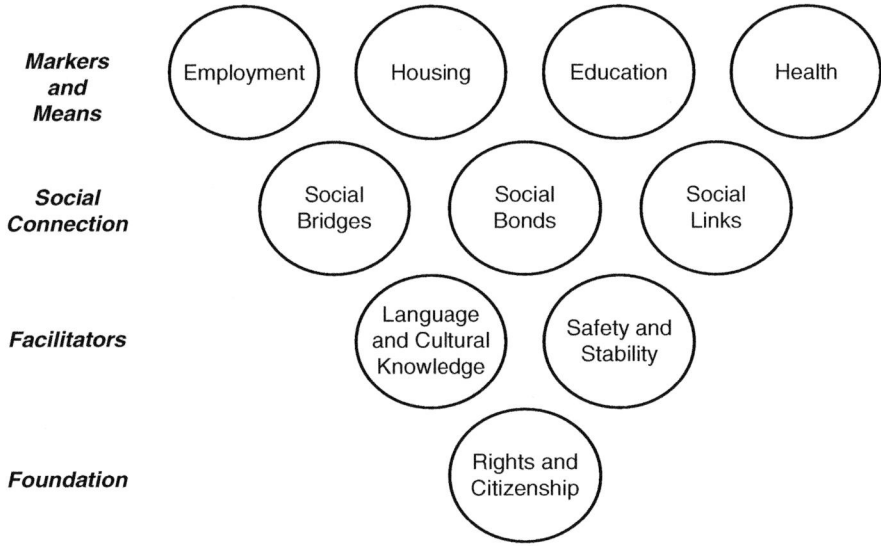

Fig. 3.1 A conceptual framework defining core domains of integration

3.4   The 'Subjectivisation' of Roma Integration: Political Contexts and Actors

This section provides the context and content of integration strategies aimed at the Roma in Italy and Spain. I firstly outline the political background of the NRIS, then look at the different definitions of the target population and analyse the use of 'integration' within the documents that is made in relation to this target population.

The rationale for introducing explicitly targeted measures to reduce inequality for the Roma was rooted in the conviction that Roma integration would both foster social cohesion and bring economic benefits to society as a whole (Vermeersch 2012). As explained in the introduction, this is also one of the core arguments that this book makes and which encompasses the (dis)integration processes faced by refugees, migrant and non-migrant minorities alike: the disintegration of some (including barriers to their access to resources and institutions) is inherently connected to the disintegration of society as a whole (Collyer et al. 2020; Hinger 2020; Lundberg et al. 2016).

The concern of Western European countries to deter large numbers of Eastern European Roma from migrating westward – what Liz Fekete (2014) defined as an attempt to curb a 'free movement of poverty' – also played an important role in promoting Roma-specific policies. Particularly following Italy's and France's repatriation of EU Roma citizens, the concern that freedom of movement from Romania and Bulgaria would translate into significant numbers of impoverished Roma migrating to Western Europe functioned as a catalyser for action.[6]

In 2012, both Italy and Spain submitted an NRIS to the European Commission, as requested by the EU. While there was no officially agreed-upon definition of integration, the European Commission (2011) communication *An EU Framework for National Roma Integration Strategies up to 2020* identified the issue in the following manner:

> Since non-discrimination alone is not sufficient to combat the social exclusion of Roma, the Commission asks the EU institutions to endorse this EU Framework for National Roma Integration Strategies. It is a means to complement and reinforce the EU's equality legislation and policies by addressing, at national, regional and local level, but also through dialogue with and participation of the Roma, *the specific needs of Roma regarding equal access to employment, education, housing and healthcare.*

The two countries therefore found themselves with two comparatively similar documents which were, however, the result of very different processes: Spain in 2011–2012 already had a fairly long trajectory of Roma inclusion plans and practices to draw upon for the drafting of its NRIS. In fact, the European Framework for Roma Integration put forward by the European Commission borrowed a number of features – i.e. the focus on four priority areas (education, health, housing and employment) – from the structure and goals set by the Decade for Roma Inclusion, of which Spain was a strong driver, and from Spain's 'explicit but not exclusive' approach. It is therefore not surprising that the 2011 EU Framework was well received by the Spanish government and that Spain did not encounter major difficulties in producing a national strategy in line with European guidelines. In terms of institutional responsibility for the development and implementation of Roma integration guidelines, the Ministry of Health, Social Services and Equality was charged with producing the strategy and it remains the National Contact Point to manage and implement it.[7]

Italy, instead, selected the Italian Office against Racial Discrimination (UNAR) as the National Contact Point for the strategy. The UNAR, established at the Presidency of the Council of Ministers within the Department for Equal Opportunities, was instituted by Decree no. 215 of 9 July 2003, which transposed into Italian law the European Directive 43/2000. It has, however, seen a series of setbacks, scandals and changes in its directorate and staff composition since its inception, mainly because of it being very much dependent upon the ruling government. When asked about the structure and responsibilities of UNAR, one senior Italian policy advisor stated:

---

[6] Between 2008 and 2010, under the justification of a 'nomad emergency' promoted by the Berlusconi government, five Italian provinces fingerprinted, evicted and relocated to encampments many Roma families who had been living in so-called 'unauthorised camps'. Around the same time, Sarkozy's government in France evicted hundreds of Romanian and Bulgarian Roma and provided economic incentives to those who agreed to leave the country (Kóczé 2017.).

[7] For a contextualization of the Gitano-Roma nuance in Spain see Magazzini and Piemontese 2016.

UNAR is not independent, it doesn't have its own budget nor political autonomy; it is completely dependent upon the Prime Minister, who can appoint and revoke the staff; and it is attached to the Department for Equal Opportunities, which isn't even a Ministry...in short, it is not worth a hill of beans (Interview 12).

Another interviewee commented that '[t]he UNAR staff basically lives off the National Roma Integration Strategy. Without it they would have no purpose, even though they couldn't care less about the integration of the Roma' (email follow up to an interview with a senior consultant, Ufficio Rom, Sinti e Caminanti).

The way in which the term 'integration' is used in both national strategies is noteworthy, and appears to be more of an adaptation of EU vocabulary than a term of choice for the two governments. In Spain, the '*Estrategia Nacional para la Inclusión Social de la Población Gitana en España 2012–2020*' uses the term 'social inclusion' rather than 'integration' in its Spanish version (Ministerio de Sanidad Servicios Sociales e Igualdad de España 2012, emphasis added). This is also reflected in the body of the text: the word 'inclusion' is used over 50 times, while 'integration' features fewer than 15. Both terms are employed not as a 'two-way process', but rather as a *de facto* synonym for a poor section of society that needs to overcome socio-economic marginalisation. When describing the challenges that the strategy aims to tackle, the document reads:

In general terms, Roma people in Spain have seen significant social progress in the last 40 years; such progress is the result of the arrival of democracy in Spanish society, economic growth on a national scale, the establishment of a Social state, generalized access to social welfare systems (particularly housing, education, healthcare and social services and benefits) and specific measures and programmes aimed at correcting disadvantages. However, there is still a long way to go for there to be equality in the four fundamental areas for social inclusion, and on which the targets of this National Roma Integration Strategy for Spain are based (*Ibid.*, 2012, p. 5).

A NRIS section entitled *The 2020 National Roma Integration Strategy: Definition and Targets* provides a detailed description of the targets aimed at improving the living conditions of Roma in Spain and includes mid-term quantifiable targets to be reached by 2015 and 2020 for each of the key areas of social inclusion: education, health, employment and housing. However, it does not offer an explicit definition of what 'integration' or 'inclusion' mean.

An adviser to the Ministry of Health, Social Services and Equality (MSSSI) who contributed to the Spanish strategy's conceptual framework, offered the following explanation when asked to define the term 'integration' for the purposes of the NRIS:

Well, the semantics of a term always carry nuances and are important. It's not the same to say 'handicapped' or 'disabled' or 'person with a disability'. The terminology has been changing and evolving with Roma as well ... but basically the NRIS uses the term [integration] that was established by the European Framework. *The term was really just adopted because of that.* However, when [later in the document] the meaning that is given to [integration] is explained, you can see that the principles for Roma integration are defined, and *basically what is meant by integration is the improvement of the living conditions of the Roma population, their normalisation into society,* while respecting their differences and their particularities. And for this reason, the Spanish strategy should not be reduced to the four axes established by the European framework (education, housing, etc.) but we also included aspects related to culture, discrimination, etc – aspects that we have always worked on and that we considered important (Interview 7).

It is true that the concept of Roma identity and culture is neither dismissed nor totally excluded from the Spanish strategy,[8] but it is certainly not the main pillar of what Roma integration is understood to require or entail. In talking about the trade-offs between an identity-based approach and a socio-economic one, the same interviewee summarised his position, and the way he framed the NRIS, in this way:

For years there has been, in Spain and also in Europe, something that I would call 'a negative empowerment' or a 'misunderstood empowerment'[9] of Roma with a focus in some cases towards defending and using more 'ethnic arguments' for Roma integration. I don't share this view: I don't think that it's the right approach. I am more in favour of an intercultural approach, for many reasons, which doesn't mean that I am against Roma identity … on the contrary, I am completely in favour of the empowerment of Roma – that is to say, I believe that we must seek the leadership and participation of Roma. But when you have an ethnic approach – and I have seen this quite a bit in the countries of Central and Eastern Europe – the fundamental risk is that the Roma issue becomes a problem *of the Roma*, not a problem *of society*, and therefore specialised agencies are created, and the integration of Roma is of course delegated to these organisations. And that does not work, and nowhere has it been shown that this works because, in the end, *the key to the integration of Roma lays fundamentally in the access to standardised, normalised services, in policies by the ministry, which then have to be balanced with targeted measures* (Interview 7).

Similar considerations about this understanding of integration, consistent with the idea of it being a matter of improving Roma's socio-economic conditions – often referred to in terms of 'normalising' or 'bringing to the same level' the rate of unemployment, education outcome etc. of Roma persons as that of the non-Roma population – were made by a number of other Spanish interviewees in charge of policy-making and/or implementation (Interviews 2, 3, 4, 5, 6, 8 and 9). While none of the policy-makers interviewed denied nor wanted to antagonise Roma identity and culture, these aspects are seen as residing outside the integration paradigm which is, instead, understood to be a matter of access to services.

Italy presents some common features from a superficial terminological outset but a very different – and almost specular – focus with respect to the content and meaning of integration. In Italy's NRIS, which is approximately twice the Spanish one in length, the word 'integration' is also not featured in the title, which is *'National Strategy for the Inclusion of Roma, Sinti and Caminanti Communities'*.[10] Footnote 1 of the text specifies that

In view of the differing legal status of the members of relevant groups (please see below para.1.5), it would better respond to the current heterogeneous Italian situation, the following title: 'Strategy for the *Inclusion/Integration* of Roma, Sinti and Caminanti communities' (National Office on Anti-Racial Discriminations National Focus Point 2012, p. 3).

---

[8] The document mentions the creation, in 2007, of the Institute for Roma Culture, and contains the creation of educational materials on Roma culture and history to be included in schools.

[9] *'Un mal empoderamiento o un empoderamiento mal entendido'*.

[10] *'Strategia Nazionale per l'Inclusione dei Rom, Sinti e Caminanti'* in Italian.

The terms 'inclusion' and 'integration', in the Italian National Strategy, are linked to the principles of anti-discrimination and equality, but the usage of rights and equality is in turn very much tied to the differentiation between citizens and non-citizens. As Nina Sahraoui's chapter in this volume illustrates, if integration is a tool for establishing 'equality of both access and outcome for migrants and racialised minorities' (Sahraoui, 2020), the legal dimension of anti-discrimination policies alone clearly falls short of addressing the structural power dynamics that allow and reproduce racist behaviours. Not only does it fall short of ensuring equality, but it also can be used as window-dressing for state naturalisation of inequalities within society. Disintegration, for Roma residing in Italy is, therefore, at least in part, the result of the government having successfully constructed the illusion of neutrality by merely granting individuals the same rights and opportunities, without concerning itself with the outcome: '[t]he assumption that we live in post-racial societies de facto obscures the continuity of 'race' as an organising dynamic in European societies' (Sahraoui, 2020, p. 84). In the Italian NRIS, there is a general preoccupation with defining the excluded groups as either 'regular' or 'irregular'. Such legalistic differentiations are, however, difficult to implement in terms of concrete policy actions. As the UNAR senior legal adviser who drafted the NRIS' conceptual framework argued, when explaining the way in which 'integration' is employed in the Italian strategy:

> From a juridical point of view, we should keep the concept of integration and inclusion separated, because integration applies to those who, for instance, are not European citizens, while inclusion is for those who are European citizens but are not Italian. This is a distinction that I made in the strategy. Honestly it is, however, a bit useless to make these distinctions between integration and inclusion. I prefer to speak of outright inclusion because if, let's say, you are a European citizen, it is now useless to make these distinctions between European and Italian citizens, we are all Europeans now ... so I think we should enter the order of ideas that the concept of integration must be overcome, even if it is true that part of the Roma who are in Italy are from places such as Bosnia, Albania, Montenegro, so they are not yet in the European Union. I did specify in the first footnote of the strategy that the concept of integration is different from that of inclusion.... But I tell you, really, it's quite useless to make that distinction, because we should really just speak of inclusion and that's it (Interview 10).

Despite the interviewee's choice of terminology, there is no objective legal basis to claim that 'integration' should refer to Third Country Nationals while 'inclusion' has to do with European citizens. Yet, making such a differentiation in the NRIS contributes to frame differently the targets of the strategy based on their citizenship status.

As shown in Sophie Hinger's chapter in this volume, '[s]tate actors and the policy documents they produce are of special relevance, because of their power position and because their formal systems of categorisation are particularly apt for deconstruction' (Martiniello & Simon 2005 cit. in Hinger 2020, p. 21). If Germany places special emphasis, in the case of asylum-seekers, on the legal status of those eligible as recipients of integration strategies, Italy operates similarly with regard to Roma individuals. As has been observed with respect to refugees and migrants, integration policies are mainly marked by a national framing of integration

(Hinger, 2020). It is noteworthy that, while it is more evident in the case of Italy, the 'national' dimension of integration is just as strong in Spain's approach.

In fact, an interesting element that emerges from both strategies is that the (dis) integration processes are deeply linked to what constitutes the *idea* of being a 'national'. Those who are perceived as 'in need of integration' are either portraid as foreigners (Italy) or as second-class citizens (Spain) (Magazzini 2018).

3.5   Whose Integration?

While in Spain the Ministry of Health, Social Services and Equality seems to have incorporated in the NRIS some cultural elements advanced by the *Segretariado Gitano*, the *Unión Romaní*, the *Fundación Instituto de Cultura Gitana* and other entities, the focus and benchmarking remain strongly centred around the economic aspect of integration and, particularly, the employment and schooling dimensions. The Director of the Roma Social Programme Unit at MSSSI described the 'Spanish model' of Roma integration and its line of action thus:

> The key to the Spanish model has been a programmatic approach that has prioritised measures to redress inequalities and improve living conditions over other approaches more focused on issues of identity, advocacy for minorities or political participation which, in fact, have also started to emerge but later. … *we privileged a socio-economic approach over the ethnic approach* (Interview 1).

This does not mean that there is unanimity amongst the different stakeholders on the success of such an approach or that its implementation has been consistent or uniform in different autonomous communities (Bereményi and Mirga 2012). However, there was general agreement among Spanish policy-makers in understanding the concept of integration as 'raising the living standards of the Roma population', *as members* of the Spanish population. The rejection of a cultural lens can be seen in the conflation of the 'cultural' with the 'ethnic', two terms that most interviewees used interchangeably. If the stress is on bettering the living conditions of part of a population, it is only natural that policies will omit any reference to the 'ethnic or cultural other', even though this has often meant, in practice, that Roma immigrants end up being excluded from such integration policies (Magazzini and Piemontese 2016).

Conversely, while, in Spain, it was considered necessary to not single out the Roma as recipients of specific policies in order to prevent the promotion of 'difference' over 'equality' (Kostka 2015, p. 82), the Italian strategy focuses, instead, precisely on differential treatment for different categories:

> When considering the human rights-based approach, *it should be always very clear who are the recipients of relevant measures, the rights-holders and the duty-bearers.* […] With this strategy Italy intends to achieve the effective integration/social inclusion of Roma, Sinti and Caminanti communities, besides effectively enabling them to fully exercise fundamental rights, as enshrined in Art. 2 of the Italian Constitution. […] It has been stressed, under Part One of the present strategy, the differing legal statuses of members of the minority under

reference, to whom to apply the fundamental principles of the Italian Constitution, primarily Art. 3, being dedicated to the principle of equality and non-discrimination. […] On a practical note, such principle [the equality principle] envisages that: it shall be treated on a equal basis what is equal; and on a different basis, what is different (National Office on Anti-Racial Discriminations National Focus Point 2012, pp. 19–20).

This passage is interesting because it makes explicit that one of the main concerns of the Italian strategy is to identify and categorise the various Roma groups based on their legal status, and that those categories should function as a criterion for which rights and duties belong to each category. This is also reflected in Paragraph 1.5 of Italy's NRIS, which does not explicitly define either inclusion or integration but does provide an extensive overview of demographic estimates broken down by citizenship status. The data provided, however, are inconsistent: on Page 12, the estimate given for the totality of the Roma residing in Italy is about 140,000 (around 0.23 per cent of the total population – the approximate calculation provided by the Council of Europe), 'most of whom are children and youngsters based in Italy, with Italian nationality'. This is, however, immediately contradicted by a paragraph in which the estimates add up to over 160,000 persons, most of whom do not hold Italian citizenship:

They can be divided into three main groups in relation to the citizenship and period of immigration: The first group consists of approximately 70,000 people (Italian citizens) whose first records date back to the fourteenth century and are distributed throughout the country.; The second group consists of about 90,000 Roma people from the Balkan region (non-EU citizens) who arrived in Italy, in the 90s, especially after the disintegration of the former Yugoslavia. This group is mainly settled in Northern Italy. The third – more recent – group … is made up of Roma people with Romanian and Bulgarian nationality (EU citizens), who mainly live in large cities (Milan, Turin, Rome, Naples, Bologna, Bari, Genoa) (National Office on Anti-Racial Discriminations National Focus Point 2012, p. 12).

It is noteworthy that, even for the first group – Italian citizens – the 'foreign' ancestry dating back to the fourteenth century is stressed. Mention is also made a page later in the strategy to

[t]hose irregular Roma people, whose exact number has not been set yet, officially. For example, the Prefecture of Rome detected the presence, on the local territory, of 12,000/13,000 *irregular* Roma people, compared with 7,000 *regular* Roma people living in around 20 unauthorized camps (National Office on Anti-Racial Discriminations National Focus Point 2012, p. 13, emphasis added).

The last sentence is particularly telling of how, despite the claim that the NRIS represented a radical rupture with the previous paradigm in Italy, Roma are still very much tied, in the government's view, to either the so-called 'authorised camps'[11] or the 'unauthorised camps'.[12] As articulated in Hinger's chapter in this volume and by Mihai Surdu in his 2016 book *Those Who Count: Expert Practices of Roma Classification* (Surdu 2016), the power and danger of categories and categorisations

---

[11] In practice, segregated ghettos run by local administrations that sub-contract their 'management' – mainly surveillance – to private agencies or NGOs.

[12] Slums/shantytowns, generally built on publicly owned land on the outskirts of cities.

to integration policies lies in the fact that, even though they are social constructions, they are framed as natural and mutually exclusive, while people may move between and fit into several categories. 'The supposed exhaustiveness of category systems can be deconstructed if we look beyond those groups or individuals highlighted by the policy and ask who is obscured or only targeted implicitly by a policy and why' (Hinger 2020).

On the whole, it seems that the approach adopted by the Italian government in its 2012 strategy is indeed an attempt to comply with European demands, but that the Roma minority is still seen (not only sociologically but also institutionally) as cultural and ethnic 'others'. While the Spanish approach conceives Roma exclusion as a product of wider socio-economic changes, the Italian one points directly at Roma groups with alleged particular problems and regards the issue as cultural and behavioural, thus focusing on group identity and characteristics rather than on discriminatory patterns or institutional incapacity to address a systemic lack of affordable housing.[13]

The strategies are, by and large, a reflection of how the majority of policy-makers understand the Roma's role in society and the role they can 'fill' in either economic or political terms. Based on policy-makers' way of speaking about the beneficiaries of Roma policies, we notice that Spain focuses on the socio-economic dimension of integration while Italy highlights cultural integration. Beyond this difference, an equally important distinction between the two approaches is that, while the Spanish narrative is about improving living conditions for part of its population (who might well be overly represented among the poor and less-educated, as well as culturally different and/or subject to ethnic discrimination), Italy's discourse is about incorporating, integrating or accommodating an 'external' group (or rather multiple external groups) who are not part of the Italian nation and its society, even though they might hold Italian citizenship. In Italy, the problem is framed as being about integrating foreigners or citizens of foreign origin who, in any case, hold a culture and values that are seen as distant, and often opposed, to 'Italianity'. Therefore, the indicators and framework adopted are those usually employed in the 'migrant integration' literature, including the need to respect 'migrant' identity and 'diversity' while making sure that they [the migrants/Roma] accept (unspecified) 'Italian' values. In Spain, it is instead about bringing 'up to level' an impoverished and 'deficient' section of the population, therefore the indicators and categories used are those linked to social exclusion, employment and economic growth.[14]

---

[13] For a more detailed account of Roma classifiers as targets of specific policies in Italy and Spain, see Magazzini (2018).

[14] A sentence that is repeated more than once in the Spanish strategy, and in the numerous plans and actions, and that represents the main pillar of Spain's approach towards Roma integration is 'Roma are full and equal citizens in Spain' ('*Los gitanos son ciudadanos de pleno derecho en España*'). See, for instance, the position of the Spanish Ombudsman on the Roma: https://www.defensor-delpueblo.es/grupo-social/gitanos/

3.6 Concluding Remarks: (Dis)Integration Dynamics within Integration Policy Frameworks

This chapter has built upon an analysis of the Roma integration strategies adopted by Italy and Spain, and on interviews with the policy-makers in charge of these strategies, to explore how 'integration' is understood and acted upon by policy-makers in these two settings. By looking at the NRIS and their formulation in Italy and Spain, what emerges in terms of general trends is that the Spanish framework revolves mainly around socio-economic elements, while the Italian one prioritises the differentiation between different legal statuses and the alleged need for cultural mediation. There are, however, some commonalities in the ways in which Roma are seen as 'deficient', lagging behind the majority population (in either cultural or economic terms). The fact that national identity dominates both strategies –even more than the concept of integration itself– is highly consequential for their outcome, and for the ways in which the recipients of integration policies are categorised.[15] On the whole, the fundamental difference – beyond the economic or cultural approach – seems to be whether or not Roma are framed as belonging to the national polity. It could actually be said that it is precisely whether Roma individuals are perceived as citizens of the respective country (regardless of their actual legal status) that determines a socio-economic or a cultural approach.

Because group solidarity relies heavily on the contingency of perceptions of commonality and otherness, the dichotomy 'in group' vs 'out group' is crucial, particularly in times of economic crisis, in constructing categories of deservingness (Kymlicka 2015). Who belongs to 'us' and is therefore rightfully entitled to welfare benefits, social housing, health services and so on? Each case responds to distinct political necessities and societal contexts, and neither is accidental. While Spain decided to 'use' Roma policies as an effective tool to attract European funds and develop what has been called 'a strategy of competitiveness with a human face' (Kostka 2015, p. 82), Italy wrapped its plan in an eloquent human rights discourse which, however, has proven quite shallow (thus flexible) in terms of concrete measures. This can be problematised and declined in various ways, but the baseline narrative is that Roma 'have problems' (or are themselves a problem) and are thus in need of 'integration'.

This distinction points at the necessity to delve, beyond integration's markers and means, into its foundation, as defined by Ager and Strang: rights and full citizenship. In their definition Ager and Strang (2008) acknowledge that such a foundation is by no means consistent across different countries, nor does citizenship necessarily respond to fulfilling the same criteria everywhere:

---

[15] While the words 'integration' and 'inclusion' are used cumulatively about 60 times in the Spanish strategy and 130 times in the Italian, the Spanish document used the terms 'national', 'Spain' or 'Spanish' 188 times, and the Italian one the words 'national', 'Italy' or 'Italian' 483 times, inciting us to question who the Roma targeted by these integration policies are for policy-makers.

Definitions of integration adopted by a nation inevitably depend on that nation's sense of identity, its 'cultural understandings of nation and nationhood' (Saggar 1995, p. 106). This sense of identity as a nation incorporates certain values; and these are values that significantly shape the way that a concept such as integration is approached' (Ager and Strang 2008, pp. 173–174).

They suggest that a discussion about citizenship and rights should be made explicit whenever applying the notion of integration in any given setting. How to do so is, however, less clear, precisely because 'notions of nationhood, citizenship and rights will vary across settings' (*Ibid.*, p. 176). Of course, the political dimension of the exclusion and marginalisation is hardly, if ever, really separated from either cultural or economic inequalities or both. To the non-citizen who enjoys a sense of cultural belonging and recognition in the host country and who does not suffer from economic hardship and the personal insecurity that comes with it, the idea of being a citizen is largely superfluous. It is when a group has access to neither cultural nor economic rights that the lack of civic and political rights comes at a high cost.

One way to overcome the exclusion and disintegration processes that racialised minorities are subjected to might be, as suggested by some of the chapters in this book (Desille 2020; Hinger 2020) to focus more on the local dimension of integration, which is where the practicality of integration measures holds the potential to override ethno-nationalist rhetoric. Yet the wider issue that this raises is that state institutions are themselves engaged in producing and reproducing not only integration but also disintegration, by selectively organising and categorising 'deserving' and 'underserving' individuals. What Chauvin and Garcés-Mascareñas have called 'probationary citizenship' with respect to irregular migrants (2012, p. 243), applies similarly to racialized minorities such as the Roma. Integration measures are granted to (or forced upon) Roma groups based on their perceived 'deservingness' and/or ability to participate in the majoritarian society. To be 'integrated' becomes therefore to become 'closer' to an imaginary ideal national citizen.

Against this backdrop, an analysis of the Roma integration strategies in Spain and Italy shows us that, while widely different in scope and trajectories, they share two problematic assumptions with other European integration strategies aimed at migrants and refugees. One is an ethno-national framing of integration, which is rarely made explicit but permeates most integration policies, fostering the illusion of a homogenous ethno-national identity that 'others' should ntegrate into. The other assumption is the understanding of integration as a 'privilege' to be either 'earned' by the outsiders through hard work or that might be 'granted' to them by the institutions upon proof of good conduct (Hinger 2020). As argued in the introduction to this volume, the perceived desirability of the integration of specific individuals ultimately depends on how they are categorised by the state in which they live, with those who are seen as too 'foreign' or 'deviant' increasingly becoming the target of disintegration policies or practices which, in turn, harm society as a whole. As long as even explicit integration policies rest on these assumptions, however, they will continue to produce and reproduce disintegration dynamics at both the individual and collective levels.

3.7 List of Interviews

Interview 1: Director of the Roma special programme unit, Ministry of Health, Social Services and Equality (MSSSI), Spain, 14 October 2014.

Interview 2: Local councillor (social services), City Council of Aviles, Spain, 16 October 2014.

Interview 3: Member of the Board of Trustees, Fundacion Secretariado Gitano (FSG), Spain, 16 October 2014.

Interview 4: Member of the Welfare Committee, Parliament of Catalunya, 17 October 2014.

Interview 5: Member of the Social Service Department, City Council of Zaragoza, 17 October 2014.

Interview 6: Member of the Governing Board, Instituto de Realojamiento e Integracion Social (IRIS), Spain, 18 October 2014.

Interview 7: Legal adviser, Ministry of Health, Social Services and Equality (MSSSI), Spain, 17 April 2015.

Interview 8: Head of the Promotion of Social Action Programme, City Council of Bilbao, 9 June 2016.

Interview 9: Member of the Governing Board, City Council of San Sebastian, 8 July 2016.

Interview 10: Senior legal adviser, National Office Against Racial Discrimination (UNAR), Italy, 6 August 2015.

Interview 11: Senior consultant, Ufficio Rom, Sinti e Caminanti, Italy, 14 November 2015.

Interview 12: Senior policy adviser, Roma Capitale, Italy, 19 December 2015.

References

Ager, A., & Strang, A. (2008). Understanding integration: A conceptual framework. *Journal of Refugee Studies, 21*(2), 166–191.

Armillei, R. (2014). Neither included, nor excluded: The paradox of government approaches towards the Romanies in Italy. *Citizenship and Globalisation Research Paper Series, 5*(3), 1–22.

Bereményi, B.-Á., & Mirga, A. (2012). *Lost in action? Evaluating the 6 years of the comprehensive plan for the Gitano population in Catalonia.* Barcelona: FAGiC and EMIGRA/CER-M.

Brüggemann, C., & Friedman, E. (2017). The decade of Roma inclusion: Origins, actors, and legacies. *European Education, 49*(1), 1–9.

Charnon-Deutsch, L. (2004). *The Spanish gypsy: The history of a European obsession.* University Park: The Pennsylvania State University Press.

Cianetti, L. (2015). Integrating minorities in times of crisis: Issues of displacement in the Estonian and Latvian integration programs. *Nationalism and Ethnic Politics, 21*(2), 191–212.

Ciulinaru, D. (2018). When 'inclusion' means 'exclusion': Discourses on the eviction and repatriations of Roma migrants, at national and European Union level. *International Migration & Integration, 19*(4), 1059–1073.

Collyer, M., et al. (2020). Politics of (dis)integration – An introduction. In S. Hinger & R. Schweitzer (Eds.), *Politics of (dis)integration* (pp. 1–18). Cham: Springer VS.

Desille, A. (2020). Jewish immigrants in Israel: Disintegration within integration? In S. Hinger & R. Schweitzer (Eds.), *Politics of (dis)integration* (pp. 141–159). Cham: Springer VS.

European Commission. (2010). *Investing in Europe's future – Fifth report on economic, social and territorial cohesion.* Brussels. Retrieved at https://ec.europa.eu/regional_policy/sources/docoffic/official/reports/cohesion5/pdf/5cr_part1_en.pdf

Fekete, L. (2014). Europe against the Roma. *Race & Class, 55*(3), 60–70.

Gallie, W. B. (1956). IX.—Essentially contested concepts. *Proceedings of the Aristotelian Society, 56*(1), 167–198.

Garcés-Mascareñas, B., & Penninx, R. (2016). Introduction: Integration as a three-way process approach? In B. Garcés-Mascareñas & R. Penninx (Eds.), *Integration processes and policies in Europe.* Cham: IMISCOE Research Series. Springer.

Gidley, B. (2013). Landscapes of belonging, portraits of life: Researching everyday multiculture in an inner city estate. *Identities, 20*(4), 361–376.

Gidley, B. (2014). Integration. In B. Anderson & M. Keith (Eds.), *Migration: A COMPAS anthology.* Oxford: ESRC Centre on Migration, Policy and Society.

Hinger, S. (2020). Integration through disintegration? The distinction between deserving and undeserving refugees in national and local integration policies in Germany. In S. Hinger & R. Schweitzer (Eds.), *Politics of (dis)integration* (pp. 19–39). Cham: VS Springer.

Kóczé, A. (2017). Race, migration and neoliberalism: Distorted notions of Romani migration in European public discourses. *Social Identities, 24*(4), 459–473.

Kostka, J. (2015). Implementation of Roma inclusion policies: Why defining the problem matters. *Social Inclusion, 3*(5), 78.

Kymlicka, W. (2015). Solidarity in diverse societies: Beyond neoliberal multiculturalism and welfare chauvinism. *Comparative Migration Studies, 3*(1).

Lundberg, A. Squire, V. Strange, M. Schweitzer, R. (2016) Integration against the state: Irregular migrants' agency between deportation and regularisation in the United Kingdom. *Politics, 37*(3), 317–331.

Magazzini, T. (2018). What's in a name? Causes and consequences of labelling minorities as "national" or "migrant": Roma in Italy and Spain. *International Migration, 56*(3), 203–220.

Magazzini, T., & Piemontese, S. (2016). Roma' migration in the EU: The case of Spain between 'new' and 'old' minorities. *Migration Letters, 13*(2), 228–241.

Matras, Y., & Leggio, D. V. (Eds.). (2018). *Open borders, unlocked cultures. Romanian Roma migrants in Western Europe.* London: Routledge.

Medda-Windischer, R. (2014). Integration of new and old minorities in Europe: Different or similar policies and indicators? INTEGRIM Working Papers Series No. 10. Retrieved from www.integrim.eu

Merry, M. (2014). Is there a positive case for segregation in a liberal society? In D. Goodhart (Ed.), *Mapping integration* (pp. 83–89). London: Demos.

Ministerio de Sanidad Servicios Sociales e Igualdad de España, (2012) Estrategia Nacional para la Inclusión Social de la Población Gitana en España 2012–2020. Retrieved from https://www.mscbs.gob.es/ssi/familiasInfancia/PoblacionGitana/docs/WEB_POBLACION_GITANA_2012.pdf

Murphy, C. (2010). The concept of integration in the jurisprudence of the European court of human rights. *European Journal of Migration and Law, 12*(1), 23–43.

National Office on Anti-Racial Discriminations National Focus Point. (2012). National strategy for the inclusion of Roma, Sinti and Caminanti communities. *European Commission Communication, 173*, 1–90. Retrieved from http://ec.europa.eu/justice/discrimination/files/roma_italy_strategy_en.pdf.

Nimführ, S., Otto, L., & Samateh, G. (2020). Denying while demanding integration: An analysis of the integration paradox in Malta and refugees' coping strategies. In S. Hinger & R. Schweitzer (Eds.), *Politics of (dis)integration* (pp. 161–181). Cham: Springer VS.

OSCE High Commissioner on National Minorities. (2012). *The Ljubljana guidelines on integration of diverse societies*. The Hague: OSCE HCNM. Retrieved from http://www.osce.org/hcnm/96883.

Penninx, R., Spencer, D., & Van Hear, N. (2008). Migration and integration in Europe: The state of research. In *Report commissioned by the Economic and Social Research Council (ESRC) for NORFACE (new opportunities for research funding cooperation in Europe)*. Retrieved from http://www.mighealth.net/nl/images/4/40/Compas.pdf.

Picker, G., & Roccheggiani, G. (2014). Abnormalising minorities. The state and expert knowledge addressing the Roma in Italy. *Identities, 21*(2), 185–201.

Ponzo, I., Gidley, B., Roman, E., Tarantino, F., Pastore, F., Jensen, O. (2013). Researching functioning policy practices in local integration in Europe: A conceptual and methodological discussion paper. Retrieved from http://www.eu-mia.eu/Eumia%20meth%20paper3.pdf.

Portes, A., & Zhou, M. (2016). The new second generation: Segmented assimilation and its variants. *The Annals of the American Academy of Political and Social Science, 530*(1), 74–96.

Rodríguez, L. C. (2008). Polítiques d'integració en el camp de la immigració redistribució, reconeixement i representació. *Nous Horitzons, 90*, 6–12.

Saggar, S. (1995). Integration and adjustment: Britain's Liberal settlement revisited. In D. Lowe (Ed.), *Immigration and integration: Australia and Britain*. London: Bureau of Immigration, Multicultural and Population Research and Sir Robert Menzies Centre for Australian Studies.

Sahraoui, N. (2020). From everyday racist incidents at work to institutional racism: Migrant and minority-ethnic workers' experiences in older-age care. In S. Hinger & R. Schweitzer (Eds.), *Politics of (dis)integration* (pp. 81–99). Cham: Springer VS.

Sánchez, D. M. (2017). *El pueblo gitano en Euskal Herria*. Txalaparta.

Schinkel, W. (2017). *Imagined societies: A critique of immigrant integration in Western Europe*. Cambridge: Cambridge University Press.

Sigona, N. (2005). Locating 'the gypsy problem'. The Roma in Italy: Stereotyping, labelling and 'nomad camps'. *Journal of Ethnic and Migration Studies, 31*(4), 741–756.

Spencer, S., Johnson, M. R. D., Phillips, D., Rudiger, A., Somerville, W., & Wintour, P. (2004). *Refugees and other new migrants: A review of the evidence on successful approaches to integration*. Oxford: Centre of Migration: Policy and Society. Retrieved from https://www.compas.ox.ac.uk/wp-content/uploads/ER-2006-Integration_Refugees_UK_HO.pdf.

Vrăbiescu, I., & Kalir, B. (2017). Care-full failure: How auxiliary assistance to poor Roma migrant women in Spain compounds marginalization. *Social Identities, 24*(4), 520–532.

Vrăbiescu, I. (2016). Roma migrant children in Catalonia: Between the politics of benevolence and the normalization of violence. *Ethnic and Racial Studies, 40*(10), 1663–1680.

Vermeersch, P. (2012). Reframing the Roma: EU initiatives and the politics of reinterpretation. *Journal of Ethnic and Migration Studies, 38*(8), 1195–1212.

Chapter 4
Can Integration Be Temporary? The (Dis)Integration of Temporary Migrant Workers in Canada and the UK

Şahizer Samuk

4.1 Introduction

Temporariness and integration are usually seen and treated as being in contradiction to each other and temporary migration policies more or less explicitly try to avoid or undermine the integration of temporary migrant workers (Hennebry 2012; Lenard and Straehle 2012). Also within the mainstream migration studies literature, integration is generally regarded as an arduous process that takes many years to achieve. Temporariness, therefore, does not fit with the nature of the integration process as understood by most scholars as well as policy-makers. At the same time, however, it is a necessary component of temporary migration policies (TMPs), which primarily serve the interests of businesses and sending and receiving states' economies at large. In the two countries which serve as case studies in this chapter – Canada and the UK – such employer-driven migration policies and programmes have been a common feature for decades. However, there are important differences in terms of their continuity, implementation, and the accompanying rhetoric, which I particularly focus on here.

The aim of this chapter is to understand what policy-makers and other relevant actors mean by 'integration' in relation to temporary migrant workers (TMWs). It treats this policy field as part of broader migration regimes, within which 'migration is not regulated, it is negotiated' (Rass and Wolff 2018, p. 21). How diverse actors negotiate and contribute to the understanding of temporary migration is one of the central questions that this chapter tries to answer. The question is important because first, the number of temporary migrants is increasing (Castles 2006; Hennebry 2012; Ruhs 2006), as has been the case in Canada since 2006 (Open Government Canada 2015). Also in the UK, the management of migration via temporary routes and categories has gained precedence since a points-based system that categorises

Ş. Samuk (✉)
Independent Scholar, Lucca, Italy
e-mail: sahizer.samuk@alumni.imtlucca.it

S. Hinger, R. Schweitzer (eds.), *Politics of (Dis)Integration*,
IMISCOE Research Series, https://doi.org/10.1007/978-3-030-25089-8_4

migrants into five 'tiers' – high-skilled, medium-skilled, low-skilled, students and temporary migrants – has been introduced. Between 2000 and 2009 the annual quota for temporary immigration was greatly increased (Consterdine and Samuk 2015). Second, despite the fact that international conventions exist, the rights of temporary migrant workers are extremely limited during their stay. Existing international conventions are either not ratified by the countries in which they work or simply not implemented (Basok 2004; Fudge 2012). For instance, Canada and the UK have not yet signed the International Convention on the Protection of the Rights of all Migrant Workers, which, like other conventions[1] contains basic rules regarding the employment and rights of migrant workers. Third, temporary migrant workers are deliberately excluded from the scope of integration policies precisely because they are expected to stay only for a limited amount of time. During this time, work dominates their lives, which keeps them from becoming part of the community in which they work as well as the one they come from (Foster and Taylor 2013). Yet, we also need to consider the fact that migrant workers can gain, even if only temporarily, at least partial access to certain rights and entitlements.

Examining the situation of temporary migrant workers with the notion of (dis) integration as set out in the introduction of this volume (Collyer et al. 2020) will highlight how their integration into particular segments of the host country's labour market is linked to their disintegration from wider social relations. As I will show, both result from the temporariness of their stay and the precariousness of their employment, which are reproduced in law, policy and discourse.

Many scholars have argued that the term 'integration' is problematic and needs to be reconsidered when used as an analytical concept (see Cantat 2020; Magazzini 2020). Integration has generally been considered a long-term process and its meaning is often considered interchangeable with that of 'assimilation' (Diehl and Schnell 2006). Berry (1997) states that 'integration' is a term which falls somewhere between 'acculturation' and 'assimilation', being not as lightweight as the first yet not as strong as the second. From a more critical perspective, Li (2003) indicates that integration policies have been promoting conformism rather than diversity, while Abu-Laban (1998) points out that the term 'integration' has started to become disconnected from multiculturalism and less tolerant of diversity.

Even if all these views can be challenged, two points are certain. First, policymakers believe that temporary migrant workers do not need to be integrated as they are only temporarily present on the territory and, that there is no need to create extra integration policies for them. In this chapter, however, integration is not only seen as a policy aim, but a process that is equally affected by what will be described as individual 'acts of integration' (see also Collyer et al. 2020). Even though these acts of migrant workers can lead to partial self-integration, the policies that regulate their

---

[1] Besides the ICMW, there are many other conventions such as the International Labour Organisation Declaration on Fundamental Principles and Rights at Work (1998), the Private Employment Agencies Convention (1997), the Domestic Workers Convention (2011), the Covenant on Civil and Political Rights, the Covenant on Economic, Social and Cultural Rights, and the UN Convention on the Elimination of All Forms of Discrimination against Women.

stay prevent them from furthering their long-term goals of gaining more rights and becoming a part of the host community. By asking why there is no genuine effort by receiving states to integrate temporary migrant workers, this chapter highlights the role of temporariness as a means of (dis)integration.

I specifically focus here on low-skilled migrant workers rather than highly skilled ones, because the latter can more easily access their right to stay (longer), to benefit from family reunification and to unionize, compared to the former (Rajkumar et al. 2012), despite the fact that they might be both entering into a country under a temporary immigration and work permit (Ruhs and Martin 2008). The highly skilled are usually perceived as more deserving (Chauvin and Garcés-Mascareñas 2014) than low-skilled migrant workers. However, this does not mean that all those who come to work in temporary sectors are low-skilled. They might be high-skilled but 'lose' or not be able to use their skills in the host country's labour market, a situation that seems to confirm what De Genova (2010) described as the universal disposability of labour.

Temporary migration policies divide the global labour force into categories. Deepening this view, De Genova (2018, 14) draws attention to the intersectionality of race, class, and migrant labour which is an important aspect to underline: 'The sociopolitical and legal branding of migrant labor as 'foreign' and especially as 'illegal' supplies a crucial disciplinary mechanism for managing all labor through a multiplication of the categories of difference that serve to decompose and fragment labor into competing rival factions riven by racialized antagonisms.'

The aim of this chapter is to better understand how policy-makers and other relevant actors – including bureaucrats, academics, migration lawyers and representatives of migrant-organisations – account for the integration of migrants whose stay is expected to be temporary. To this end, I firstly describe the research design and provide a brief rationale for comparing Canada and the UK. Secondly, I situate my argument within existing debates and literature on TMPs. Thirdly, I look in more detail at how my interviewees in Canada and the UK perceive the role of, and interplay between, (1) temporariness, (2) precariousness, (3) rights. In the final section, I summarise my findings and propose agendas for further research. My main argument is that TMPs actively hinder the integration of migrant workers, despite the fact that temporary integration is not only a theoretical possibility but is also being achieved in everyday practice, through the acts of migrant workers (Foster and Taylor 2013; Hennebry 2012; Lenard and Straehle 2012).

4.2   Research Design and Case Selection

Comparing Canada and the UK in regard to their temporary migration policies, allows an 'intensive examination of cases with limited resources' (Collier 1993, p. 107). Both countries initiated more open immigration policies in the 1960s – the UK because of decolonisation and emigration from previously colonised countries; Canada for demographic and economic reasons and the changing international context during the Cold War. In both countries priority was thereby given to 'high-skilled' over 'low-skilled' migrant workers. Most importantly, both countries have benefited greatly from temporary migration programmes.

My examination of how temporary migration policies cause (dis)integration of temporary migrant workers within these different historical contexts is based on qualitative data I collected between 2013 and 2015 as part of my PhD research. I conducted 53 semi-structured interviews with policy-makers, politicians, migrant lawyers, migrant associations and trade unions in Canada (Ottawa and Toronto) and the UK (Brighton, London, Sheffield and York).

The two countries share multiple similarities but also very different histories of immigration, which allows for a deep and multifaceted comparison. Both countries have similar socio-economic background features and diversity in their demographical composition. They both chose liberal economic policies and free markets, whilst also possessing certain welfare measures that make the health sector one of the priorities of the state (Esping-Andersen 2013) as a part of 'welfare capitalism'. On the other hand, Canada is defined as a settlement country and the UK as a post-colonial immigration country (Freeman 1995) and this difference has implications for the conception of foreign workers' rights and their prospects to make a transition to a (more) permanent stay, as I will show.

As a settlement country, Canada has traditionally enabled immigrants to be part of the nation-building process (*ibid.*), thus providing them with the idea that their immigration would be permanent rather than temporary (Hennebry 2010). In comparison to the UK, Canada has more nuanced policies on temporary (labour) migration, which assign different sets of obligations and opportunities to foreigners according to their level of skills; and allow at least some of them a transition to permanent status.[2] This chapter compares the Canadian Seasonal Agricultural Workers Programme (SAWP) and Low Skilled Temporary Foreign Worker Programme (LSTFWP) with the Seasonal Agricultural Worker Scheme (SAWS) and the Sector-Based Scheme (SBS) in the UK, as these programmes are similar in nature.

In a first step, I analysed legislation regarding temporary migration through a review of policy briefs, documents and scholarly articles. This chapter mostly draws on my interviews with policy-makers, politicians, migrant lawyers, migrant-organisation leaders and research centres working on migration policies. Secondly, I used semi-structured interviews, which enabled participants to speak freely about temporariness, rights and how integration policies consider or neglect TMWs. Analysing my data, I used thematic and discourse analysis – which was inductive in some ways and deductive in others. The analysis has been constructed regarding social, economic and political rights of temporary migrant workers. In my analysis,

---

[2] In Canada, Temporary Foreign Worker Programmes (TFWPs) include the Canadian Experience Class (CEC), Provincial Nominee Program (PNP) and Live-in Caregiver Programme (LCP), which all give great weight to the transition to permanent status in comparison with the Low-Skilled Temporary Foreign Worker Programme (LSTFWP) and the Seasonal Agricultural Workers Programme (SAWP), although not all can be compared to those in the UK.

I was particularly careful about which aspects of political economy and historical context the interviewees referred to when they provided justifications for the temporary migration policies whilst not having temporary integration policies.

4.3 Temporary Migration Policies and Integration: Rights and Numbers Within Temporality

Having a temporary workforce for many years without any attempt to integrate them has been criticised by many scholars (Hennebry and Mclaughlin 2012; Karolak 2020; Lenard and Straehle 2012; Sharma 2012). In the UK context, Rogaly (2008, 2009) and Scott (2013) wrote on the lives of TMWs, underlining the employer-imposed working conditions. Other research found that an active neglect of, and intentional undermining of the rights of TMWs leads to precariousness and exploitation (Preibisch 2010). As Sarkar (2017, p. 16) writes with regard to guestworker regimes:

> What is lost, however, in this policy and academic verbiage is a simple fact: at the heart of all guest worker programmes lies a set of legally-constructed constraints that makes them profitable. Without these fundamental denials – of the right to choose one's employer, the right to organise and protest, and most importantly, the right not to be deported at the whim of employers and receiving countries – guest worker regimes would lose their *raison d'être*. 'Effective management' may succeed in reducing the excessive abuses of this system, but it cannot begin to address the issue of the guest worker system itself as abuse in the service of inordinate surplus extraction through the work of non-citizen labour.

Wickramasekara (2011) has defined temporary migration in the eyes of the receiving states as 'labour without people'. In a similar way, De Genova (2010) draws attention to the universal disposability of labour, explaining the structure that shapes labour migration and that of the undocumented within restrictive migration policies. Similarly, Pessar and Mahler (2003, p. 816) indicate that 'People – irrespective of their own efforts – are situated within power hierarchies that they have not constructed'. Part of these power hierarchies for immigrants emanates from the status they have when they enter a host country – not all categories of immigration help migrants start on an equal footing (Mügge and van der Haar 2016) but they define to what extent integration and disintegration take place in the daily lives of the migrants. The status a person has on entering a country defines her or his path within the intertwined processes of integration and disintegration (Hinger 2020; Mügge and van der Haar 2016).

Ruhs and Martin (2008) famously proposed that there is a trade-off between rights and numbers when states need to make decisions about the intake of migrants: states who employ more migrants, tend to grant them less rights. This knowledge, however, does not challenge the status quo or state-guided and employer-driven system of TMPs but provides a general evaluation on these programmes. Within this discussion, regimes of inequality or concerns about global justice (Lenard and Straehle 2012) occupy an important position. Criticising the rights vs numbers discussion, Dauvergne and Marsden (2014, p. 529) note that the debate behind this trade-off ignores the fact that not everyone's temporariness is the same. Moreover, they posit that there is a need for a 'globally contextualised approach' (*ibid.*, p. 540) given the marked hierarchy of nation-states.

Within such contextualised approach, the differentiation of 'foreign' labour is rendered necessary and useful by TMPs (De Genova 2018). That these policies neglect migrant workers social, economic and political rights is partly justified by their only 'temporary' presence in the country and participation in the labour market. Within this picture, migrant workers are not permitted to have a future goal of completing their integration process, but are subjected to (dis)integration processes. And if the migrants overstay their residence and work permit, they become 'illegal' and deportable despite having sold their labour (De Genova 2018).

Inspite of these structural constraints, there is still some room for migrant agency. Rogaly (2009, p. 7) draws attention to migrant workers who are unorganised but still manage to gain more rights and better conditions for themselves:

> Temporary migration as an intentional move to counter entrenched inequalities with more powerful people at home; negotiation and contestation of employment arrangements; and the deliberate seeking of non-wage based livelihoods so as to avoid being subject to an employer's control.

The logic of employers in choosing migrant workers can be quite strict and deliberate. Having the choice between workers who possess 'soft skills' (McCollum and Findlay 2011, p. 3) and those with a 'strong work ethic', who are 'great workers', employers will usually choose the latter (MacKenzie and Forde 2009, p. 150). Findlay et al. (2013) draw attention to how these migrant workers self-describe by sketching themselves on paper as figures, exhausted but obedient and still cheerful.

Also from a normative perspective, the issue of temporary migration and the limitation of rights and possibilities for integration is mostly seen as a problem. Walzer (1983) argues that guestworkers cannot be retained for long periods of time without being granted further social and political rights, as this would imply a democratic dilemma for the constituency of the nation-state. Similarly, Attas (2000) suggests that they should have a route to citizenship and the right to be able to change employer(s). Lenard and Straehle (2012) approach the issue from a global justice perspective and claim that the current application of TMPs does not promise TMWs a dignified life and that they should have more guaranteed rights, together with an open path to citizenship. Sager (2012) defends TMWs' right to vote so that they can prevent exploitation by their employers. Ruhs (2013) mostly defends migrant workers' economic rights and, to a certain extent (after a period, such as four to 5 years), their right to vote. Carens (2013) claims that despite the rights and numbers trade-off, migrants' rights cannot be restricted during their stay. This is also true for migrant workers who engage in circular migration (Hennebry 2012) – livening up the economy in the towns and cities where they work. On the contrary, assuming that temporary plans *are* just temporary, Ottonelli and Torresi (2014) challenge these points of view, saying that people have personal projects and might not want to gain further rights nor stay for longer periods.

In this chapter, I argue that an additional problem is that no matter how many times migrant workers take up temporary labour in a host country, their rights will not accumulate. Instead, with every repeated temporary assignment, a migrant worker restarts to manoeuvre between integration and disintegration. (Dis)integration as a dialectic process thus has a strong presence in migrants' lives both in Canada and the UK. This dialectic of (dis)integration in decision-making is seen also in the discourse of the policy-makers. Ambiguity about granting a permanent stay to TMWs is under discussion, but when it comes to political and social rights, there is hesitancy.

4.4 Migrant Rights and Temporary Integration: Conceptions of Integration for TMWs in Canada and the UK

In this section, interview based data from the two case studies are presented and discussed in order to show how the situation of TMWs is perceived and presented by various key actors involved in the politics of (dis)integration that specifically affects migrant workers.

A major difference between the two countries is that the UK chose to discontinue these programmes while Canada has demonstrated an ambivalent attitude (Samuk 2015), although the government in 2016 and 2017 talked of reforming its TMPs. The Conservative administration decided to decrease the numbers who arrive via temporary channels and better inform the migrant workers of their rights (Open Government Canada 2015). Nevertheless, those who stayed for 4 or 5 years suddenly faced the risk of deportation because they were forced to leave (*CBC News* 2015). In the UK, programmes were discontinued not because they resulted in unjust consequences and the deterioration of the lives of migrant workers but because the labour force was thought to be available from the countries that joined the EU in 2004 and 2007, and thus not needed from outside the EU.

Both Canada and the UK have been keen on increasing their highly skilled labour force and to ensure the labour-market integration of TMWs but do not consider other aspects of their integration. For instance, in an interview I conducted on 11 October 2013 in Ottawa, a migrant lawyer particularly stressed how important the highly skilled are for the labour market and that they integrate more easily compared to low-skilled migrant workers. Still labour-market integration is given priority over cultural, social and residential integration. Mirroring official policy discourses, demographic reasons for immigration, while highly considered in Canada, seem to be avoided in the UK as a discourse for encouraging immigration. Demographic growth is not a consideration in the UK: security and keeping the numbers down were more often used by interviewees to explain the logic of immigration policies.

4.4.1   The Case of Canada

While integration is not planned for in Canada's TMP, some efforts to integrate TMWs at the local level are visible. Two Liberal Party MPs I interviewed in Ottawa seemed ambiguous when it comes to people migrating under temporary schemes, while the so-called 'Ottawa Immigration Strategy' prepared by the Ottawa Local Immigration Partnership (OLIP) and other local parties is explicitly open to providing settlement opportunities for TMWs, as confirmed by an OLIP and by a United Food and Commercial Workers (UFCW) representative. Despite the fact that temporariness goes against the historical way of drawing up immigration policies, it has become institutionalised in Canada (Goldring et al. 2009; Rajkumar et al. 2012). Hence, temporary schemes which allow migrant workers to stay for up to 5 years with limited rights are set to remain.

Due to the understanding of Canada being a 'settlement country' or 'immigration country' (Freeman 1995) Canadian authorities demonstrate more flexibility in terms of understanding the shortcomings of temporary migration and its limitations for the rights of migrant workers. It is true that policy-makers incline more towards a policy[3] that would grant TMWs permanent residence in the country and support their transition to permanent migration status. Nevertheless, the numbers of those transiting to permanent residence status are below 3% (Lu and Hou 2017, p. 13). Being temporary and low skilled, family reunification and voting are out of question as social and political rights. Moreover, TMPs are known to cause the exploitation of migrant workers. Policy-makers from diverse parties accepted the exploitative aspect and were aware of the deterioration of the situation of TMWs' living conditions. For instance, a Liberal Party MP told me in an interview:

> We are talking about people working in Tim Horton's [Canadian coffee chain store]. Canadians do not want to go to work in Tim Horton's. I don't buy that either. I think that they bring people in some cases and exploit them. And pay them less. I think that it is a programme that I know too well that is easily exploited [by employers].

TMPs demand sacrifices not only in the social but also in the private lives of the migrant workers (Hughes 2012). A representative of the UFCW emphasised that these policies have many negative outcomes: 'We don't want to separate families for four years. Those who have jobs, we want to bring the families too and let them work then they can get to stay here'. He clearly stated that family reunification as a social right is under threat for the migrant workers' families. When I asked him about the argument in the media (Hari 2018) about the replacement of Canadian workers by migrant workers, he said:

> Employers should pay decent wages, and then more Canadian people would be employed. I am saying if TFWP was not there, the employers would have been forced to pay the Canadian workers better. As TFWs [Temporary foreign workers] they take anyone and treat

---

[3] Such as CEC (Canadian Experience Class), PNP (Provincial Nominee Programme) and FSWP (Federal Skilled Worker Programme)

them as badly as they want, they think that that way… We have a Human Rights department at UFCW…

This interview reveals that economic rights are not guaranteed fully for temporary migrant workers in regard to wages. As a result, employers can undercut minimum wage levels, which in return lowers the general wages in the labour market. Furthermore, TMWs who work in agriculture have limited rights to become a member of a rights-based labour union or organisation, a right that depends on the province they are in, as provincial regulations might limit their political opportunities to defend their rights (Makin 2011).

The possibility of a transition to permanence helps guarantee better social and political rights (and even economic rights) for migrant workers. Interestingly, when the transition-to-permanence programmes are considered, the most knowledgeable policy organisation was the Chamber of Commerce; it was impressive to see to what extent the Chamber of Commerce in Ottawa was well-informed about the amended immigration laws, and 'transition to permanence' Schemes. A representative of the Chamber said:

> The provincial nominee programme has been very successful as a complement, right, as an addition to, well, the other programmes but certainly in some of the provinces there were very high skill shortages, like Alberta, Saskatchewan and Manitoba. Manitoba has always been considered the best with respect to its provincial nominee programme because of how it brought together the players so that employers and the provincial representatives were together at the table…. I think the same is happening in Saskatchewan, too, you know the premier of Saskatchewan has gone to Ireland on a recruiting mission, that is how vested he is on the part of his province recognising 'We need these workers' you know, so we need to show some real interest in attracting the right workers [with high skills or matching skills] to our province and to our projects. … So the Canadian Experience Class, very pleased to see that they have increased the numbers for that, so that is … a great addition, because it allows that 'segue from temporary to permanent residency' that is very encouraging.

This observation proves that the Chamber of Commerce is closely following the developments regarding temporary migration policies. Within this context, employer-based and pro-employer institutions have higher leverage in design and criticism of immigration policies. The expansiveness (letting higher numbers of immigrants enter the country and giving them permanent status) aspect – within so-called liberal democracies – is fulfilled (Freeman 1995) via the involvement of private interests, whilst the integration aspect (further social and political rights) is not planned in detail by pro-immigration private institutions.

Regardless of who contemplates inclusiveness within public and private bodies, temporary integration has become a social reality for migrant workers who stay and work in a place for often more than 3 years. A government official from Citizenship and Immigration in Canada (CIC) admitted that some of the TMWs are definitely integrated and do not want to return to their country of origin: 'Some of them are very integrated already so they won't go back. […] So it is a big challenge for us to force people to go back [even if they are temporary] if they are eligible to stay here'. In line with Schweitzer's analysis of 'integration against the state' (2017) this interview confirms that there is 'integration despite temporariness'. Hence, in Canada, sending people back after their temporary work permit has expired, is still taboo, although it does happen in some cases.

Interviewees in Canada used phrases such as 'bridge building' and 'multi-sector cooperation' which meant that integration necessitates collaboration of many institutions and that there should be bridge building between these institutions, which is precisely the intention behind the OLIP. Multidimensionality of integration also includes 'cultural and language interpretation' as a representative of the Immigrant Women Services Ottawa (IWSO) suggested: years of experience of immigration and settlement bring forward the fact that the interpretation of culture is not the job of the interpreter but it depends on the migrant who interprets her/his own culture. This is a historically valuable experience Canadian institutions possess. Regarding migrant workers, however, not speaking English or French is still a disadvantage as they need to learn/read more about their economic, political and social rights.

Overall, the ambiguity regarding the role of immigrants as a 'demographic contribution' and about possible limitations to immigration come to the fore in more technical terms such as 'absorptive capacity' and 'skills set', which pay attention to bringing highly skilled couples rather than low skilled, as observed in the discourse of one of the Liberal Party members.

Integration starts at the local level, whilst decisions on TMPs (which cause disintegration) are made at the national level. Immigrants are categorised *before* they arrive in Canada, since they are entering via diverse schemes which determine their potential status and the extent to which they can benefit from integration policies. While for highly skilled foreign workers there are explicit integration policies (Rajkumar et al. 2012) – such as benefiting from language courses and easier rules for family reunification – for low-skilled TMWs social rights are not easy to implement due to the time limitations; political rights are almost non-present and economic rights can be violated due to lower hourly wages.

4.4.2   The Case of the UK

My interviews in the UK reveal that there was less ambiguity about temporariness: the rules of the game were clearer – in other words, once one is temporary, one is temporary. On the other hand, ways of preventing exploitation were more institutionalised compared to Canada. The Gangmasters' and Labour Abuse Authority (GLAA)[4] – was established in 2004 to protect the rights of migrant workers and to check for violations of their working conditions. However, the GLAA has its limitations, since it can only check officially registered legal agencies, employers and documented migrant workers but is unable to make inquiries on the situation of undocumented migrant workers.

The categorisation of immigrants into different 'tiers' reinforces the underlying hierarchy of skills, which highlights what the introduction of this book describes as

---

[4] The previous name was Gangmasters' Licensing Agency (GLA)

the stratification of (dis)integration processes (Collyer et al. 2020). Tier 3 – designed as a work-permit route for the low skilled – was discarded. Tier 5, which is for temporary workers with medium to high skill levels, still exists. Other routes for migrant workers are via Tier 2 – for skilled workers with a job offer from outside the EU – and Tier 4 for students. The tiered admission system in the UK ensures that migrants have certain limitations regarding the timeframe of their residence, work permits and social rights. Within each tier 'there are further differentiations to parameters of presence depending on what types of conditions applicants meet' (Meissner 2018, p. 292). Finally, temporary programmes such as the Sector-Based Scheme and the Seasonal Agricultural Workers Programme were discontinued in 2013.

Following the end of these two of the TMW programmes in the UK in 2013, integration is now considered through a different lens and generally not in relation to temporary workers. This constitutes a major difference with Canada, where there are some attempts to integrate TMWs, as in Ottawa for instance. In the UK, the main focus of integration policies is on preventing radicalisation, promoting social cohesion, supporting liberal values and relying on local integration (Communities and Local Government 2012). However, if the government does not provide sufficient funding/support for local authorities, the latter are not able to support migrants in accessing their social, political and economic rights effectively.

The policy-makers I interviewed did not perceive any need to provide integration support to migrant workers who come via tiered immigration routes. Referring specifically to Tier 2 and Tier 5 visa-holders, a Home Office official told me that 'from a policy point of view [there is] not much there to support integration. Also, it could be argued, they are coming from Australia, New Zealand… so integration issues will not be a problem'. Hence, policy-makers differentiate between English-speaking and non-English-speaking countries. However, Tier 5, which was not mentioned by the interviewee, is the channel also used by migrants from non-English-speaking countries such as Turkey, for instance.

In contrast with the policy-makers' perspective, temporariness is a very fluid state which can unexpectedly change, as representatives of NGOs like the Haringey Migrant Centre in North London emphasised. For instance, temporariness *can* turn into permanence, as a caseworker for the Migrant Forum explained:

> Temporary migrants… I just don't really know if we can define them in the category of temporary migrants. There are people who say they just want to come to the UK to make enough money to build a house in their home [country], but then they end up staying for ten years. So, I don't really know if we can define them as accepted … or [as] temporary migrants, because if you don't give me a temporary time-frame I don't really know.

The real picture is thus much more intricate than the categorisations established by the tiered visa system and other TMPs indicate. Migration regimes render the integration of third country nationals impossible via temporariness: in this sense, the high-skilled and the low-skilled face similar difficulties regarding temporary status. Moreover, those who came to the UK from one of the countries that joined the EU in 2004[5] are not considered as migrants under EU law but despite their relatively privileged status (full political and economic rights) they face significant levels of discrimination and everyday as well as institutionalised racism (Parachivescu 2016; Sahraoui 2020). Also the lack of language skills is a major factor hindering integration that affects EU citizens to the same extent as third country nationals, as confirmed by an interviewee working for the Haringey Migrant Centre:

> …the migrants that we help can be coming from the EU and outside of the EU, I think [those from] outside of the EU would have more limited resources but of course those from the EU can benefit from more rights… I don't know. I think that the people we help here [who come from] within the EU, their problem is mainly language it seems; and increasingly benefits and housing because those are being limited for EU [citizens].

In addition, there is a major problem about providing language training and support to foreigners whose integration is not explicitly desired by the host state. An interviewee who worked at the South East Strategic Partnership for Migration (SESPM) responded in the following way to my suggestion of creating a temporary integration policy that would guarantee access to such support: 'They will be inclined to stay if we give them integration possibilities like teaching them the language'. So not wanting to encourage them to stay was an excuse for not supporting them to develop their language skills, which would ultimately also enable them to defend their rights. Nonetheless, the interviewee added, in Scotland migrant workers also receive English lessons during their stay, suggesting that regional practices regarding integration policies can differ greatly. An interviewee from UNITE indicated that they are directly involved in the provision of language support for migrant workers but struggling due to insufficient funding coming from central and local government since the budget for language courses was cut in 2010.

The policy-makers whom I interviewed suggested that integration policies require investment; some underlined that it is not worth having integration for those who will leave relatively soon. When I asked a case-worker at Migration Yorkshire about the concept of temporariness and how the policy conceives it she replied:

> Yeah, I think, that's… we know it is difficult to create policy that is actually for the people who are here temporarily. Then, kind of, you can spend a lot of resources on integration and they might not be here. So I think there are some interesting parallels with asylum here…

In accordance with the dilemma of temporariness and rights, a representative from CentreForum indicated that 'Even if the state devised a temporary integration programme, the state would spend the minimum budget that it could spend' – in other words, not enough money would be available for this cause.

A researcher from the Institute for Public Policy Research (IPPR) pointed to the hostile environment, which creates a kind of active strategy of disintegration:

> …certainly with lower-skilled migrants it would appear that the more who come, the less you do to integrate them. And with the fewer rights they are able to enjoy and with policy and rhetoric suggesting that migrants are unwelcome, it creates a very hostile environment… Some of the changes [Immigration Acts 2014 and 2016] that have been made to the

---

[5] Czech Republic, Estonia, Hungary, Latvia, Lithuania, Poland, Slovakia, Slovenia

benefit system recently in response to concerns about EU migration, have made it more difficult for certain groups of migrant workers who might be on temporary contracts and who don't have regular work, which might mean that their access to the benefits system is taken away and that tends to hurt the most vulnerable migrants, particularly the women migrants. I think that the changes that have been made recently have implications for the rights of migrant workers.

Likewise, my interviewee at the Haringey Migrant Centre in London underlined the gap between rights and their implementation: 'They have rights [political, social and economic] but they cannot access them' for reasons related to discriminative practices; she also said that there are 'no integration policies but disintegration policies'. She used disintegration practices and policies to mean those that create a hostile environment by depriving people of their basic social, economic and political rights so that, in the long term, they give up and decide to leave the country.

On the other hand, there is the question of what TMWs deserve – as long as their opportunities to find other employment are limited because of legal restrictions to their permits (Chauvin et al. 2013). In relation to this notion of deservedness over time and of achievement, a representative of the Home Office told me:

It is not that Britain is unwilling to protect the rights of the migrant workers. As I have said, we treat, we expect the migrants to be treated equally with domestic workers [domestic and seasonal agricultural workers] in the same way, but obviously as migrants there are certain things that we expect from those who come to work – not to go directly onto benefits, for example, so there is a delay before they can apply for benefits. You know, we might expect migrants to come and find work before bringing their families. There are things in that declaration [ICMW] concerning the rights of migrant workers, which go further than British policy would like to go. For a lot of countries [it is like this] as well.

This interview explains how integration cannot go beyond where 'British policy would like to go' and how the expectations of migrant workers are shaped by the logic of deservingness. This can be seen even in the case of family reunification, for instance, whereby the human right to family life (Art. 8 ECHR) is severely limited through unrealistic wage thresholds or the temporariness. Despite the fact that these basic rights are indicated in international conventions like the ICMW, states can easily escape from their responsibility simply by not signing them.

In this sense, historical institutions and path dependency (Consterdine & Hampshire 2014) explain a great deal about how integration, and migration in general, are understood. For instance, the UK Home Office has mostly focused on national security and keeping the number of immigrants low than about economic competitiveness, as my interviewee from CentreForum emphasised:

Temporary migration is quite short in the government's mind [meaning from six months to one year by law] and there is not so much integration you can do when you stay here for three months. Whereas if you are here for two years, that is plenty of time to integrate even if you are not going to stay longer. You have to define what you mean by integration.

In the UK, eliminating temporary migration policies is assumed to result in lower numbers of immigrants. Likewise, not providing any integration support is thought to further discourage potential migrants. Access to healthcare for instance, although it is a universal right, is rendered tricky and time-consuming via identity document checks, making sure that migrants are legally present and that their visa and work permit allow them to benefit from the health system. As Schweitzer discusses in this volume, those who enter the UK as 'visitors' (i.e. for 6–12 months) have no 'recourse to public funds', implying exclusion from the health system. The question of deservingness is hereby combined with the idea that the temporary visitor has not done anything to deserve access to public benefits, such as health.

Although, according to the Home Office, integration is primarily a matter of local policy in the UK, financial and administrative support to local governments is generally insufficient as my interview at Migration Yorkshire explained. Therefore, if integration is considered local, then there should be more funds for the integration of TMWs who stay in the same locality for the period over which they work. After all, TMWs have very similar needs to other newcomers, including housing, language learning and social protection, my Migration Yorkshire interviewee continued. Hence, both national and local integration policies could accommodate their needs.

On the other hand, the UK discontinued its TMPs as labour-market assessments suggested that there would be sufficient supply of foreign labour from within the EU. The government promised to check the numbers of labour migrants to ensure that there would be no shortages (NFU 2017). Currently, 75% of migrant workers are from Bulgaria and Romania whilst the rest are mostly from A8 countries (*ibid.*). If Brexit comes into force, however, there is a risk that the UK will re-establish and rely on 'foreign' labour even more than they did before 2013 (Consterdine & Samuk 2018). At least in the current situation, EU citizens have more political and social rights compared to third country nationals who migrate on a temporary basis. Therefore, violation of political, social and economic rights, are likely to be greater if also EU citizens become 'foreign' labour following Brexit.

4.5   The Disruption of Integration Via Temporariness and Processes of (Dis)Integration in Canada and the UK

The aim of this chapter has been, firstly, to describe two national approaches to temporary migration policies and to critically assess how these policies prevent – although never fully – a natural process of integration in both Canada and the UK, thereby neglecting the inherent changeability and fluidity of migrant workers' lives (Hennebry 2012; Lenard and Straehle 2012). This chapter elucidates four crucial aspects of comparison between Canada and the UK:

First, despite their diverse histories of immigration and despite the fact that they both greatly benefited from TMPs, their approaches to these programmes diverge. The UK ended their temporary migration programmes such as SAWS and SBS in 2013 but without closing temporary routes (based on tiers) for medium- to high-skilled migrants. However, in the UK, ending TMPs was not justified in terms of these policies being unjust to migrant workers; it was because, sufficient labour would be provided from within the EU. Moreover, the dominant discourse in the UK has been more concerned with national interest, security and keeping numbers down. In Canada, TMPs have been criticised for the fact that TMWs cannot stay permanently and donot have access to full social, economic and political rights. Yet, in Canada the programmes continue to be implemented.

A second crucial aspect is that, in Canada, the rhetoric is more pro-immigration and pro-rights when it comes to TMWs, whereas in the UK, temporary migration is still largely perceived as 'labour without people' (Wickramasekara 2011). In both countries, however, the policy rhetoric reflects a general preference for highly skilled workers. Canadian policy-makers make references to the history of Canada as an immigration country and acknowledge the fact that these policies can have exploitative consequences for migrant workers, particularly the low-skilled. In the UK, questioning of temporariness and its consequences by policy-makers is not so obvious, also because the country relies more on the labour of EU citizens, whose rights are much better protected.

Thirdly, the integration of TMWs is regarded as an anomaly in the two countries (though arguably less so in Canada) and the corresponding integration programmes and policies therefore often exclude especially low-skilled migrant workers. Rather than meeting the actual needs of the TMWs, especially in the UK, the discourse around who contributes enough is still predominating in policy decisions (Chauvin and Garcés-Mascareñas 2014). It seems that TMWs never contribute enough to escape from permanent temporariness and processes of (dis)integration. In Canada, the discourse is not about deservingness but about the instrumentalisation of the 'right workers'. Differently from the UK, Canada has two well-functioning programmes that include a transition to permanence, and the overall rhetoric in Canada is more inclusive and open-ended as the country continues to implement TMPs.

Fourthly, in Canada, the highly skilled are seen to be contributing much more than the low-skilled, in terms of both social and labour-market integration, whilst low-skilled migrants' contributions are considered as secondary. Therefore, there are more integration policies for the high-skilled to benefit from (Rajkumar et al. 2012). In the UK, the gap between the perceived contributions of high- and low-skilled migrant workers has narrowed in the last eight to ten years as the channel for the highly skilled within tier 1 has also been restricted (Samuk 2015). Also access to family reunification has become dependent on the salary level, not skill level: rights are a part of the discussion but the integration of TMWs is not, and the discourses of policy-makers are restrictive regarding how far the policy can proceed, while un/deservingness is still a dominant element of the rhetoric.

My interviews reveal that there is a certain level of ambiguity when possible integration policies for migrant workers are pronounced. However, ambiguity about the current treatment of TMWs is more visible in Canada, while integration of TMWs was clearly rejected by my interviewees in the UK. There is the presumption in the UK that migrant workers have access to rights, either because they are EU citizens, or because they come through tiers that allow certain access to rights (while upholding divergences between different tiers). And since the UK eliminated the

TMPs and tier/route for the low-skilled, the policy-makers assume that there is no need to spend on integration policies for 'the temporary'.

Finally, I would like to suggest ideas for further research. First, there is a need to examine TMPs in relation to the gendered dimensions of (dis)integration. Holliday et al. (2018) have recently written on this topic but gendered processes of temporariness requires more attention. Secondly, how Brexit might potentially affect TMPs could be a relevant theme – it might mean more restrictive immigration policies and more disintegration measures. In this paper, I aimed at drawing attention to this temporary integration and (dis)integration process – caused by states and employer-driven economic policies. However, I also wanted to underline that migrants *can* integrate, although this self-integration is ignored by the state and other economic actors. In line with this idea, thirdly, temporary integration and migrant agency require further research in diverse contexts of temporary migration. Finally, yet importantly, who can and cannot benefit from Canadian Experience Class and Provincial Nominee Programme have been researched less, and this would be a good area for further research and comparison. In addition to these topics, the role of temporary migrants' agency –what the editors of this volume have called 'acts of integration' (Collyer et al. 2020) – influencing the differential implementation of TMPs in dissimilar local contexts and how their agency becomes a part of resistance within (dis)integration, are crucial research themes.

References

Abu-Laban, Y. (1998). Welcome/stay out: The contradiction of Canadian integration and immigration policies at the millennium. *Canadian Ethnic Studies, 30*(3), 190–211.
Attas, D. (2000). The case of guest workers: Exploitation, citizenship and economic rights. *Res Publica, 6*(1), 73–92.
Basok, T. (2004). Post-national citizenship, social exclusion and migrants' rights: Mexican seasonal workers in Canada. *Citizenship Studies, 8*(1), 47–64.
Berry, J. W. (1997). Immigration, acculturation and adaptation. *Applied Psychology, 46*(1), 5–34.
Cantat, C. (2020). Governing migrants and refugees in Hungary: Politics of spectacle, negligence and solidarity in a securitising state. In S. Hinger & R. Schweitzer (Eds.), *Politics of (Dis) Integration* (pp. 183–199). Cham: Springer VS.
Carens, J. H. (2013). *The ethics of immigration.* New York: Oxford University Press.
Castles, S. (2006). Guestworkers in Europe: A resurrection? *International Migration Review, 40*(4), 741–766.
CBC News. (2015). Temporary foreign workers prepare to leave the country. *CBC News,* 31 March. Retrieved August 31, 2018, from http://www.cbc.ca/news/canada/edmonton/temporary-foreign-workers-prepare-to-leave-the-country-1.3017194
Chauvin, S., & Garcés-Mascareñas, B. (2014). Becoming less illegal: Deservingness frames and undocumented migrant incorporation. *Sociology Compass, 8*(4), 422–432.
Chauvin, S., Garcés-Mascareñas, B., & Kraler, A. (2013). Working for legality: Employment and migrant regularization in Europe. *International Migration, 51*(6), 118–131.
Collier, D. (1993). The comparative method. In A. W. Finifter (Ed.), *Political science: The state of discipline II.* Washington, DC: American Political Science Association.
Collyer, M., Hinger, S., & Schweitzer, R. (2020). Politics of (Dis)Integration – An introduction. In S. Hinger, & R. Schweitzer (Eds.), *Politics of (Dis)Integration* (pp. 1–18). Cham: Springer VS.

Communities and Local Government. (2012). *Creating the conditions for integration.* London: Department for Communities and Local Government.

Consterdine, E., & Hampshire, J. (2014). Immigration policy under new labour: Exploring a critical juncture. *British Politics, 9*(3), 275–296.

Consterdine, E., & Samuk, S. (2015). *Closing the seasonal agricultural workers scheme: A triple loss.* Working Paper No. 83. University of Sussex.

Consterdine, E., & Samuk, S. (2018). Temporary migration Programmes: The cause or antidote of migrant worker exploitation in UK agriculture. *Journal of International Migration and Integration, 19*(4), 1–16. https://doi.org/10.1007/s12134-018-0577-x.

Dauvergne, C., & Marsden, S. (2014). Beyond numbers versus rights: Shifting the parameters of debate on temporary labour migration. *Journal of International Migration and Integration, 15*(3), 525–545.

De Genova, N. (2010). The queer politics of migration: Reflections on 'illegality' and incorrigibility. *Studies in Social Justice, 4*(2), 101–126.

De Genova, N. (2018). Migration and the mobility of labor. In M. Vidal, T. Smith, T. Rotta, & P. Prew (Eds.), *The Oxford Handbook of Karl Marx.* New York: Oxford University Press. https://doi.org/10.1093/oxfordhb/9780190695545.013.25.

Diehl, C., & Schnell, R. (2006). 'Reactive ethnicity' or 'assimilation'? Statements, arguments, and first empirical evidence for labor migrants in Germany. *International Migration Review, 40*(4), 786–816.

Esping-Andersen, G. (2013). *The three worlds of welfare capitalism.* Princeton: Princeton University Press.

Findlay, A., McCollum, D., Shubin, S., Apsite, E., & Krisjane, Z. (2013). The role of recruitment agencies in imagining and producing the 'good' migrant. *Social & Cultural Geography, 14*(2), 145–167.

Foster, J., & Taylor, A. (2013). In the shadows: Exploring the notion of 'community' for temporary foreign workers in a boomtown. *Canadian Journal of Sociology, 38*(2), 167–190.

Freeman, G. P. (1995). Modes of immigration politics in liberal democratic states. *International Migration Review, 29*(4), 881–902.

Fudge, J. (2012). Precarious migrant status and precarious employment: The paradox of international rights for migrant workers. *Comparative Labour Law and Policy Journal, 34*, 95–132.

Goldring, L., Berinstein, C., & Bernhard, J. K. (2009). Institutionalizing precarious migratory status in Canada. *Citizenship Studies, 13*(3), 239–265.

Hari, A. (2018). Putting 'Canadians first': Problematizing the crisis of 'foreign' workers in Canadian media and policy responses. *International Migration, Early View.* https://doi.org/10.1111/imig.12453.

Hennebry, J. (2010). Who has their eye on the ball? 'Jurisdictional fútbol' and Canada's temporary foreign worker program. *Policy Options, 63*, 62–67.

Hennebry, J. (2012). Permanently temporary? Agricultural migrant workers and their integration in Canada. *IRPP Study, 26*(1), 1–41.

Hennebry, J., & Maclaughlin, J. (2012). The exception that proves the rule: Structural vulnerability, health risks and consequences for temporary migrant farm works in Canada. In P. T. Lenard & C. Straehle (Eds.), *Legislated inequality: Temporary labor migration in Canada* (pp. 117–138). Quebec: McGill-Queen's University Press.

Hinger, S. (2020). Integration through disintegration? The distinction between deserving and undeserving refugees in national and local integration policies in Germany. In S. Hinger, & R. Schweitzer (Eds.), *Politics of (Dis)Integration* (pp. 19–39). Cham: Springer VS.

Holliday, J., Hennebry, J., & Gammage, S. (2018). Achieving the sustainable development goals: Surfacing the role for a gender analytic of migration. *Journal of Ethnic and Migration Studies, Early View*, 1–15. https://doi.org/10.1080/1369183X.2018.1456720.

Hughes, C. (2012). Costly benefits and gendered costs: Guatemalans' experiences of Canada's 'low-skill pilot project'. In P. T. Lenard & C. Straehle (Eds.), *Legislated inequality: Temporary labor migration in Canada* (pp. 139–158). Quebec: McGill-Queen's University Press.

International Convention on the Protection of the Rights of All Migrant Workers and Members of Families. (1990) *A/RES/45/158*. Retrieved September 04, 2018, from http://www.refworld.org/docid/3ae6b3980.html

Karolak, M. (2020). R*eturning for (Dis)Integration in the labour market?*. The careers of labour migrants returning to Poland from the United Kingdom. In S. Hinger, & R. Schweitzer (eds.), Politics of (Dis)Integration. Springer.

Lenard, P. T., & Straehle, C. (2012). Temporary labour migration, global redistribution, and democratic justice. *Politics, Philosophy & Economics, 11*(2), 206–230.

Li, P. S. (2003). Deconstructing Canada's discourse of immigrant integration. *Journal of International Migration and Integration/Revue de l'integration et de la migration internationale, 4*(3), 315–333.

Lu, Y., & Hou, F. (2017). *Transition from Temporary Foreign Workers to Permanent Residents, 1990 to 2014*. Ottawa: Statistics Canada, social analysis and modelling division, catalogue no. 11F0019M, no. 389, ISSN:1205–9153.

MacKenzie, R., & Forde, C. (2009). The rhetoric of the good worker versus the realities of employers' use and the experiences of migrant workers. *Work, Employment & Society, 23*(1), 142–159.

Magazzini, T. (2020). Integration as an essentially contested concept: Questioning the assumptions behind the National Roma Integration Strategies of Italy and Spain. In S. Hinger, & R. Schweitzer (Eds.), *Politics of (Dis)Integration* (pp. 41–59). Cham: Springer VS.

Makin, K. (2011). *Farm workers have no right to unionize, top court rules*. In The Globe and Mail. Retrieved March 24, 2019, from https://www.theglobeandmail.com/news/national/farm-workers-have-no-right-to-unionize-top-court-rules/article578141/

McCollum, D., & Findlay, A. M. (2011). *Employer and labour provider perspectives on eastern European migration to the UK*. ESRC Centre for Population Change Working Paper, Number 14, 1–50.

Meissner, F. (2018). Legal status diversity: Regulating to control and everyday contingencies. *Journal of Ethnic and Migration Studies, 44*(2), 287–306.

Mügge, L., & van der Haar, M. (2016). Who is an immigrant and who requires integration? Categorizing in European policies. In B. Garcés-Mascareñas & R. Penninx (Eds.), *Integration processes and policies in Europe* (pp. 77–90). Cham: Springer.

NFU. (2017). *Supply for seasonal labour to British horticulture farms*. NFU labour provider survey results. Stoneleigh: National Farmers Union. Retrieved August 07, 2018, from https://assets.publishing.service.gov.uk/government/uploads/system/uploads/attachment_data/file/692743/Supply_of_Seasonal_Labour_to_British_Horticulture_Farms_2017.pdf

Open Government Canada. (2015). *Facts and figures 2015: Immigration overview*. Temporary Residents Annual IRCC Updates. Ottawa: Government of Canada. Retrieved August 31, 2018, from https://open.canada.ca/data/dataset/052642bb-3fd9-4828-b608-c81dff7e539c

Ottonelli, V., & Torresi, T. (2014). Temporary migration projects and voting rights. *Critical Review of International Social and Political Philosophy, 17*(5), 580–599.

Paraschivescu, C. (2016). Political belonging and fantasies of inclusion: Romanians in London and Paris. *The Age of Human Rights Journal, 7*, 120–140.

Pessar, P. R., & Mahler, S. J. (2003). Transnational migration: Bringing gender in. *International Migration Review, 37*(3), 812–846.

Preibisch, K. (2010). Pick-your-own labor: Migrant workers and flexibility in Canadian agriculture. *International Migration Review, 44*(2), 404–441.

Rajkumar, D., Berkowitz, L., Vosko, L. F., Preston, V., & Latham, R. (2012). At the temporary–permanent divide: How Canada produces temporariness and makes citizens through its security, work, and settlement policies. *Citizenship Studies, 16*(3–4), 483–510.

Rass, C., & Wolff, F. (2018). What is in a migration regime? Genealogical approach and methodological proposal. In A. Pott, C. Rass, & F. Wolff (Eds.), *Was ist ein Migrationsregime? What is a migration regime?* (pp. 19–64). Wiesbaden: Springer.

Rogaly, B. (2008). Intensification of workplace regimes in British horticulture: The role of migrant workers. *Population, Space and Place, 14*(6), 497–510.

Rogaly, B. (2009). Spaces of work and everyday life: Labour geographies and the agency of unorganised temporary migrant workers. *Geography Compass, 3*(6), 1975–1987.

Ruhs, M. (2006). The potential of temporary migration programmes in future international migration policy. *International Labour Review, 145*(1–2), 7–36.

Ruhs, M. (2013). *The Price of rights: Regulating international labor migration*. Princeton: Princeton University Press.

Ruhs, M., & Martin, P. (2008). Numbers vs rights: Trade-offs and guestworker programs. *International Migration Review, 42*(1), 249–265.

Sager, A. (2012). Political rights, republican freedom, and temporary workers. *Critical Review of International Social and Political Philosophy, 17*(2), 189–211.

Sahraoui, N. (2020). From everyday racist incidents at work to institutional racism: Migrant and minority-ethnic workers' experiences in older-age care. In S. Hinger, & R. Schweitzer (Eds.), *Politics of (Dis)Integration* (pp. 81–99). Cham: Springer VS.

Samuk, Ş. (2015). *Temporary migration and temporary integration: Canada and the UK from a comparative perspective*. PhD thesis Lucca: IMT Institute for Advanced Studies, unpublished.

Sarkar, M. (2017). The flipside of the integration question: Guestworker regimes and temporary circular/managed migration in history. *Refugee Watch, 49*, 1–25.

Scott, S. (2013). Migration and the employer perspective: Pitfalls and potentials for a future research agenda. *Population, Space and Place, 19*(6), 703–713.

Schweitzer, R. (2017). Integration against the state: Irregular migrants' agency between deportation and regularisation in the United Kingdom. *Politics, 37*(3), 317–331.

Sharma, N. (2012). The 'difference' that borders make: 'Temporary foreign workers' and the social organization of unfreedom in Canada. In P. T. Lenard & C. Straehle (Eds.), *Legislated inequality: Temporary labor migration in Canada* (pp. 26–47). Quebec: McGill-Queen's University Press.

Walzer, M. (1983). *Spheres of justice: A defense of pluralism and equality*. New York: Basic Books.

Wickramasekara, P. (2011). *Circular Migration: A Triple Win or a Dead End*. Global union research network discussion paper no. 15. Retrieved August 31, 2018, from https://doi.org/10.2139/ssrn.1834762

Chapter 5
From Everyday Racist Incidents at Work to Institutional Racism: Migrant and Minority-Ethnic Workers' Experiences in Older-Age Care

Nina Sahraoui

5.1 Introduction

> If you see somebody oppressing someone, you have to speak up or if you can't do anything, in your mind you have to be against it. But if you just sit down and watch, this makes you also a sinner, you understand? If you bear oppression, and if you don't fight it, you also make a big sin, that's why we have always to fight, we have to. Wherever you are, life is not easy, it's always a challenge, always. This will make you stronger. What about you, are you a fighter? (Sameera, 32, Mauritius, London).

Sameera had lived in the UK for 12 years when we met. She came from Mauritius, where she had been working in a pharmacy. On arrival in London she again found employment in a pharmacy, though in a lower position. For 4 years she did not have a single day of annual leave; she felt exhausted, left the job and looked for something else. She found a job as a care assistant in older-age residential care. In her new employment she again went through tough times; she was harassed by colleagues and felt discriminated against by her managers. Immersed in these unpleasant memories during the interview, Sameera made the statement quoted above. Seen as an individual experience, Sameera's narrative appears to be specific and personal. Analysed as part of an institutional context shaped by employment rights, migration policies and anti-discrimination legislation and practice, such narratives reveal how these experiences reflect differentiated forms of institutional racism.

Through the analysis of non-EU migrant' and minority-ethnic care workers' narratives around their experiences and perceptions of racism and discrimination within older-age care in London, Paris and Madrid, this chapter attempts to shed light on some of the mechanisms fostering disintegration. It addresses in this regard what is at the heart of integration – equality of both access and outcome for migrants and racialised minorities – named by the editors of this volume 'equal participation in social systems' (Collyer et al. 2020). The chapter does not focus on the concept of

N. Sahraoui (✉)
GTM-CRESPPA, Paris, France

S. Hinger, R. Schweitzer (eds.), *Politics of (Dis)Integration*,
IMISCOE Research Series, https://doi.org/10.1007/978-3-030-25089-8_5

integration *per se* (see also Nimführ et al. 2020; Chap. 9) but, rather, on racism and racist discrimination (the distinction between racism and discrimination is clarified below). Engaging the material implications of racism contributes, this chapter argues, to our understanding of some of the exclusionary processes leading to disintegration. Exploring the dynamics of labour-market segmentation outlines a form of systematic discrimination – and thus of institutional racism – against racialised workers through migration and employment policies that produce deskilling and entrapment. The literature on migrant domestic workers foregrounded in this regard the racist structures upon which this segmentation relies (Ehrenreich and Hochschild 2002; Parrenas 2000). As noted by Collyer et al. (2020, p. 5) 'The disproportionate inclusion of migrant workers in particular sections of the labour market [...] may make their exclusion from various other domains of social and everyday life more likely'. More precisely, this chapter illustrates how labour-market segmentation translates into everyday experiences of disintegration for migrant and minority-ethnic workers. It seeks to bring out how these experiences, on the one hand, and respondents' ways of coping with them on the other, inform the 'ruling relations' (Smith 2005) that characterise respondents' work environments. This method of inquiry 'works from the actualities of people's everyday lives and experience to discover the social as it extends beyond experience' (Smith 2005, p. 10). In this regard, respondents' daily experiences and collective responses are central to the analysis.

In this chapter I demonstrate that anti-discrimination legislation often remains out of reach for racialised precarious workers and thus argue that anti-racism is too often reduced to the legal framework of anti-discrimination policies, falling short of analysing the structural dynamics that foster racism at multiple levels. The focus on cases of racism by colleagues and managers informs our understanding of how policies and institutions can produce disintegration, a process nonetheless enacted by individuals. Like Schweitzer (2020), who traces how immigration control mechanisms increasingly run through education- and health-related institutions, I equally highlight neglected dimensions of how practices that foster exclusion manifest themselves within specific workplaces. Following a brief description of the methodology, the first section situates the concepts of racism, racialisation and racist discrimination as understood here and briefly presents how anti-discrimination policies are implemented in each of the three countries relevant to this chapter. This overview contextualises the specific environments within which experiences of racism and discrimination take place. The second section empirically explores cases of racist behaviour by colleagues and of harassment/discrimination by managers. It highlights that, against the background of contemporary manifestations of racism in interpersonal interactions being less overt, victims of racism often feel insecure about their ability to challenge such forms of racism. In addition, in the cases under study, managers tolerated the described manifestations of racism or sided with the dominant group. The section equally examines how managerial practices were at times directly discriminatory, ranging from unfair workloads to bullying and stigmatisation. The last section explores how workers coped with racism and racist discrimination and why these situations were particularly difficult to challenge legally.

5.2   Methodology

This chapter is based on fieldwork conducted in London, Paris and Madrid between December 2013 and January 2015. The three European capitals chosen for this research represent three urban centres of significant size that are, in many ways, at the forefront of modern societies' 'crisis of care' (Fraser 2016). At the same time, these three locations are embedded in significantly different migration, employment and care regimes (Williams 2012). The findings presented here build upon 83 interviews conducted with non-EU migrant and minority-ethnic care workers in these three European capital cities. Rather than adopting a systematically comparative approach, the chapter focuses on drawing links between respondents' experiences across contexts so as to provide insights into the shared patterns of racism in the workplace that underpin the chapter's overall argument.

In the UK and Spain, interviewees were working as (health-) care assistants (in some cases live-in). In France, three different statuses corresponded to this position in terms of daily tasks performed: life assistant (*auxiliaire de vie*), medical/psychological assistant (*aide médico-psychologique*) and healthcare assistant (*aide-soignant*). The interviews took place in coffee shops as well as in care homes, mostly behind closed doors. I usually spent several hours in a home on one visit and was immersed into the workplace atmosphere, observing daily working routines in the lounges and corridors. The interviews lasted from 35 min to more than 2 h and were about 1 h on average. All interviews were recorded and transcribed. Qualitative data analysis software was used for coding and analysing the collected data following thematic analysis (Boyatzis 1998).

5.3   Racialisation, Institutional Racism and Anti-discrimination Policies

While this chapter makes a strategic use of the concept of 'minority ethnic' (Aspinall 2002) in the spirit of the 'intercategorical complexity' (McCall 2005) within intersectional studies, the concepts of 'process of racialisation' and 'racialised groups' are here preferred in an attempt to capture the social process at work without granting 'ethnicity' or 'race' a material existence but acknowledging the sociological implications of the existence of both concepts as well as the role 'ethnicity' plays in struggles for recognition. This focus on racialisation as process is crucial given that the definition of what constitutes racism cannot be static either. Stuart Hall wrote: 'Racism [is] not a permanent human or social deposit which is simply waiting there to be triggered off when the circumstances are right' (Hall 1978, p. 26). Gilroy warns in an analogous way against interpretations which do not recognise that racism 'exists in plural form, and I have suggested that it can change assuming different shapes and articulating different political relations' (Gilroy 1987/2002, p. 42). The notion of 'total social phenomenon' forged by Balibar furthermore highlights that racism is to be found in everyday practices, discourses and imaginaries (Balibar and Wallerstein 1988). From this perspective, racist discrimination implies a practice and thus differs from the concept of racism, which entails a broad range of possible manifestations – racist discrimination constituting one of these.

The relationship between ideology and practice – or the question of intentionality – also needs to be clarified. The 'race relations' model of British sociology tended, for instance, to focus on personal prejudice up to the mid-1970s. Similarly, philosophical accounts of racism tend to put the issue of intentionality at the heart of the definition of racism, referring for instance to 'motivational racism' (Headley 2000). This is not, however, the assumption on which this chapter relies. Following Anthias and Yuval-Davis (1992, p. 13), it is accepted here that 'racist practices do not require the racist intentionality of structures (…). Practices may be racist in terms of their effects'. In a nutshell, racist discrimination can result from policies and practices, which might or might not be imbued with explicit racist ideology. In that sense, the concept of 'institutional racism' – developed to a much greater extent in the Anglo-Saxon literature than in French and Spanish studies of racism – proves to be particularly useful for conceptualising racist outcomes without systematic racist intentionality. Early conceptualisations of institutional racism are to be found in the Black Power movement and notably in Carmichael's writings (Carmichael and Hamilton 1967/1992). Later, Sivanandan (1985) distinguished between what he named 'racialism' – defined as prejudice displayed by individuals – and racism – understood as structural racism. At the heart of this oppression are power relationships, as stated by Ikuenobe (2010, p. 162): 'Not all forms of racial discrimination or prejudice may be characterized as racism. In order for racial discrimination or prejudice to be characterized as racism, it must involve social-political power'. Experiences lived by racialised workers are here analysed as racist in the sense that 'Xenophobia, or the dislike of the stranger or outsider, (…) becomes racism when there are power relations involved. These can then put into practice the sentiments of antipathy and produce racist effects' (Anthias and Yuval-Davis 1992, p. 12).

The assumption that we live in post-racial societies *de facto* obscures the continuity of 'race' as an organising dynamic in European societies. The political economy of the Western world is increasingly shaped by neoliberal values and, under neoliberal governmentality, 'everyone is expected to have full personal responsibility'; as a consequence, everyone risks a 'loss of right for a life mismanaged' (Lentin and Titley 2011, p. 163). While capitalist structures of production rely intrinsically on socially constructed divisions among people – including processes of racialisation – these stratifications are effectively covered up by a governmentality (Foucault 2004) that constructs the illusion of neutrality. Neoliberalism is perceived not as a 'particular set of interests and political interventions, but as a kind of nonpolitics' (Duggan 2003, p. 10). This obscures power relationships at work and forms of oppression on which neoliberalism relies and which shape the everyday life experiences of women, racialised groups and other minorities.

From this perspective, the paradox of anti-discrimination policies implemented alongside institutionally ingrained racist discrimination is only superficial. The system of values upon which neoliberalism relies effectively organises the ignorance of those in privileged positions. When the British government states for instance 'You're legally protected from discrimination by the Equality Act 2010'[1] it certainly aims at emphasing equal rights and opportunities. Yet, by assuming the existence of equal opportunities, meritocracy constrains our understanding of racism. While anti-discrimination regulations might be useful for challenging certain manifestations of racism, it also allows for a naturalisation of inequalities within society. If anti-discrimination legislation ensures that *anyone* can denounce discrimination, then *everyone* is held responsible for his/her individual position in the labour market and in society at large. Anti-discrimination policies pertain to the politics of diversity under neoliberal governance and are central to contemporary understandings of integration. The inclusive aspiration of anti-discrimination legal measures obscures the very unequal conditions of access to these rights. Unpacking the paradox of states' commitment to anti-discrimination alongside the reproduction of institutionalised forms of racism thus sheds light on (dis)integration processes. This chapter critically assesses the shortcomings of the anti-discrimination legislation and its associated discourse of equal opportunities. The situated perspective of racialised workers in older-age care reveals how anti-discrimination can thrive at the policy level while the political economy of society reproduces major inequalities along gendered and racialised lines of division. The following paragraphs provide insights into the practice of anti-discrimination legislation for the three national contexts relevant here.

In the UK, 3064 racial discrimination claims were lodged with employment tribunals in 2013–2014 (Thelwell 2015). The number of claims decreased after the government introduced claim and hearing fees in 2013; 5700 claims were lodged in 2009–2010 (Ministry of Justice 2012). Discrimination cases are the most expensive, claim and hearing fees reaching £1200 compared, for instance, with £410 for cases of unpaid wages (Department for Business Innovation and Skills 2014). To add to this, only a minority of employment tribunal cases progress to full hearings; most cases are either settled by the Advisory, Conciliation and Arbitration Service (33% in 2010–2011), withdrawn (27%) or struck out (13%) (Ministry of Justice 2012). Once at the hearing stage, cases of racial discrimination have the poorest chances, with a success rate of only 16% in 2010–2011 (Renton 2013). In his online article, published by the Institute of Race Relations, Renton (2013) questions why racial discrimination cases are so unlikely to be successful, compared not only to unfair dismissal or wage deduction cases but also to other discrimination cases – such as sex discrimination (37%) or sexual orientation discrimination (26%). On the basis of several case studies, he points out that the understanding of racial discrimination is often conflated with racist intentions by judges. It is therefore not enough for the concept of institutional racism to be discussed within the field of anti-discrimination policies – as is the case in the UK – for the judiciary to take into account its implications for individual cases. Racial discrimination often remains equated with the

[1] https://www.gov.uk/discrimination-your-rights

racist intentions of the perpetrator and cases tend to revolve around proving or dis-
missing racist intentions instead of establishing the existence or non-existence of
discrimination.

In France, insights into the figures published by the High Authority for the Fight
against Discrimination and for Equality (HALDE),[2] an institution created in 2005 to
comply with EU requirements, show that the number of complaints increased from
1410 in 2005 to 12,467 by 2010. The purpose of this state-funded body was to assist
victims of discrimination by supporting their legal fights after the HALDE had
reviewed the case and established that discrimination had, indeed, taken place.
Around half of these complaints concerned employment and, overall, between 2005
and 2009, 28.5% of them mentioned 'discrimination based upon ethnic origin'
(HALDE 2010). Rattansi (2011) notes, however, that far fewer resources were provided to this new agency than to the former British Commission for Racial Equality.
Moreover, the HALDE existed for only a few years, having been integrated in 2011
into an institution with a broader mandate, 'Défenseur des Droits', chaired by an
'Ombudsman', also in charge of children's rights, public service users' rights and
security ethics. The merger of the HALDE has been vigorously criticised by grassroots organisations; it appears that information accessible by victims of discrimination is limited and legal cases are no longer published online, nor are the success
rates of discrimination cases publicly available, contrary to the practice formerly
put in place by the HALDE.

In Spain, as in the UK and France, there exists an immense gap between the
extent of discrimination – as subsequent studies have demonstrated (Colectivo Ioé
2003) – and actual legal cases. Anti-discrimination legislation was introduced only
in the last decade and the economic crisis affected the state's capacity to implement
related programmes. For instance, the Council for the Promotion of Equal
Opportunities and Non-Discrimination on the Ground of Ethnic and Racial Origin,
created in 2007, only registered 167 individual cases of discrimination in 2010
(Ministerio de Sanidad, Política Social e Igualdad 2011) and soon started to lack
funding, according to a 2013 report by the European Network Against Racism
(Spitálszky 2013). This NGO also highlighted that Spain failed to publish a trans-
parent database of all discrimination cases, so that an assessment of the efficiency
of the legislation is hardly possible (Spitálszky 2013).

It seems overall that anti-discrimination legislation is mobilised in a limited
number of cases. Focusing on individual rights arguably only offers a very partial
way of addressing deeply rooted inequalities which require social change. Anti-
discrimination legislation has, furthermore, a differentiated impact along class and
gender divisions and the most privileged amongst racialised workers are in a better
position to make use of it; thus potentially contributing to the integration of a few
while entrenching the marginalisation of many others. The denial of the continued
relevance of racialisation processes in contemporary societies and of their social
implications for racialised individuals makes it more difficult to identify, understand

---

[2] Haute Autorité de lutte contre les discriminations et pour l'égalité, HALDE.

and challenge institutional racism. The following section provides insights into selected aspects of migrant and minority-ethnic care workers' experiences of racism at work and points out why some elements amount to institutional racism.

5.4 Everyday Racism at Work Embedded in Power Relationships

In the three capital cities studied here, about half of respondents recounted experiences of racism and discrimination in relation either to residents, colleagues or management in older-age care. Respondents had to deal with both overt and covert forms of racism. Systematically exposed to racist comments by residents (Sahraoui forthcoming), some of them were also discriminated against or harassed by colleagues and managers (the focus of this chapter). Individual stories equally revealed how different manifestations of racism often take place simultaneously. The empirical section of this chapter focuses on cases of racist behaviour by colleagues and harassment/discrimination by managers and relates the level of individual interactions to the workings of institutions. It provides, on the one hand, insights into the workings of disintegration as it takes place at and beyond the workplace level in the forms of racist discrimination and exclusion, and explores, on the other, the coping strategies that arise at the level of interpersonal relationships.

5.4.1 Racist Attitudes Amongst Colleagues: Abusive Work Environments

Respondents in Madrid and London shared negative experiences of colleagues' racist attitudes in the workplace. In Paris, none of the respondents complained about the racist attitudes of work colleagues, which could be partly related to the fact that, in the care homes visited for my fieldwork, racialised workers made up the great majority of the workforce (around 70–90% as indicated by the nurses in supervisory positions who were interviewed). Facing similar racism on behalf of certain residents might have fostered solidarity amongst workers by creating a shared condition.[3] An obvious form of negative experience with colleagues, implying racist hierarchies, were remarks – directly addressed to migrant workers – which offended them. Isabel, who had started a Master's degree in the Philippines, felt deeply insulted by her colleagues' comments:

---

[3] Importantly, these contingent data should not suggest that racist attitudes do not arise amongst racialised workers. Racialisation processes are multifold, creating divisions that might equally manifest themselves amongst racialised care workers.

I have experience in the previous job you know there are some people you know… Racists…
When I started there they said, one of the carers asked me, because I'm reading a newspaper
in front of a resident, then she just asked me, 'Oh can you read English?' I said 'Yes, I can't
come here if I don't know how to read English'. 'Oh, I see' … and then I was using the
remote control because one of the residents asked me to turn on the TV and set it on a programme. 'Oh, do you know how to use that?' As if they are thinking I am ignorant or I'm
illiterate because I'm foreigner, I don't know…They are just degrading you (Isabel, 37, the
Philippines, London).

In this case Isabel perceived her colleagues' remarks as demeaning and as an attempt
to belittle her. Often the same feelings were described in relation to more covert
attitudes that did not necessarily involve any voiced interaction but had no less far-
reaching implications. Pedro, who was born in Spain to Guinean parents, described
Spanish society as intrinsically racist and explained how he had to learn to navigate
a space of social relations systematically imbued with racist prejudice:

Even if you hate me I will know how to get along. That's something that I learned as a little
boy – ignore, carry on and keep on living. You can't do anything else, it's not worth it
because it's not viable. You can't fight your whole life against something that vast. So at
work I've observed it, you see it a lot, a lot. What happens is that then it depends on each
person how you deal with it. If you're a person who doesn't put up with this and you can't
channel it and ignore it so that you focus on what's really important, then yes you can have
problems. Because unfortunately they'll never tell you, very rarely they'll say it openly so
that you can justify it, the key is to prove it. So they'll say 'I didn't say anything'. So the
best thing is to take it in, deflect it and transform it into something good (Pedro, 25, born in
Spain to Guinean parents, Madrid).

In Pedro's account, racist prejudice is diffuse, permanently present but rarely prov-
able. It affects so many of his daily social relations that, even if he is highly aware
of the racist overtones of certain attitudes towards him, he feels he can do very little
about them, given that this prejudice is not expressed through insults or aggression
but through less obvious behaviour, which nevertheless leaves no doubt about its
meaning. The following account by Sameera, quoted in the introduction to this
chapter, also describes the difficulty of coping with covert forms of racist bullying:

And when I was working I could feel, they wouldn't even look at you while you're sitting,
they just move when you come to the staff room, you sit next to them, they move. I was
thinking ….what happened? I was thinking maybe I'm smelly…You know? Maybe something is wrong with me, maybe my clothes are dirty…Me I shower every day …slowly
slowly I feel the attitude. Now I start feeling what this is, you know. And then there was a
girl over there I will never forget, the way she treats you….how can I say. It's like you're
nothing (Sameera, 32, Mauritius, London).

These discriminatory attitudes at work deeply affected Sameera's well-being as her
marginalisation became more and more apparent. Her colleagues' behaviour was
not, as it might appear, a passive attitude but constituted an active form of bullying.
This form of interpersonal interaction illustrates racist prejudice at the individual
level. The attitude of Sameera's colleagues can be described as a form of 'aversive
racism' (Byrd 2011; Gawronski et al. 2008). Negative feelings towards a racialised
person are expressed by such behaviour but no opinion is voiced against egalitarian
values *per se*. The examples given here by Isabel, Pedro and Sameera all reflect the
fact that contemporary manifestations of racism in interpersonal interactions tend to

be less overt because of the stigmatisation of racism in mainstream political and societal discourse and the likelihood of it being sanctioned. Victims of racism often feel insecure about their ability to challenge a form of racism that is not accompanied by racist claims. From this perspective, anti-discrimination legislation risks falling short of addressing the social phenomenon it concerns itself with – this in spite of having reversed the burden of proof in corresponding judicial procedures.

In the Spanish context, Claudia, who had been working in the same care home for 10 years, lamented the discrimination against 'Latino' workers by Spanish colleagues:

> At work there's sometimes discrimination, a lot of discrimination. Those who go first for breaks are the Spaniards and, if the Latinos are there, 'What are you doing there?' So what happens? They always have their breaks first, the Spaniards, best things for them and the Latinos are as always left behind (Claudia, 53, Peru, Madrid).

Another form of harmful interaction amongst colleagues is favouritism between minority groups. Mary, for instance, worked in a care home where she was one of the few Black workers (she identified as 'Black British') and where migrant workers from the Philippines represented the numerical majority, including Filipino staff in most managerial positions (except for the manager of the home, who was White British):

> In a workplace where we have a lot of different minorities, Black, White, Asians, when there becomes a majority of a certain minority then it starts a little bit of unfairness going on and favouritism ... and which does happen here in (name of the care home) and I'm not gonna lie to you, there is a lot of favouritism here (Mary, 20, Black British, London).

Racist behaviour amongst colleagues should invoke employers' responsibility for ensuring a fair workplace, in that managers' harmful negligence creates abusive environments. However, in none of the cases described above did managers provide support to respondents recounting such experiences. When discriminatory attitudes by colleagues were pervasive, in all the cases in which respondents in this research reported it to their managers, the latter were complicit in that they tolerated it or sided with the dominant group. Workers discriminated against because of favouritism towards other groups of workers did not envisage challenging it formally, often out of fear of retaliation. This factor constituted a very common deterrent to the use of anti-discrimination legislation.

5.4.2 Discrimination and Harassment by Managers and Employers

This section examines respondents' narrated experiences of racist practices by supervisors, managers and/or employers. Precarious employment and work intersect here with discrimination and create specific sets of experiences. Analysis of the empirical material demonstrates how racialisation bears material consequences for workers against the background of intersecting regimes. Following Fiona Williams, the articulations of various regimes are here emphasised: 'A country's *care regime* intersects with its *migration regime* and its *employment regime* which provides the institutional context that shapes the experiences of both migrant women employed in domestic/care work and their employers, as well as the patterns of migrant care work to be found in different countries' (Williams 2014, p. 17, emphasis in original). The notion of migration regime encompasses both 'regulative and mobile practices of migration' (Rass and Wolff 2018, p. 22). Drawing further on Williams' definition, it is here understood as including migration policies, national norms and practices governing relationships between majority and minority groups, migrants' mobilisations and relevant national and transnational histories (Williams 2012, p. 371).

In all three national contexts, the vulnerabilities created by migration, employment and older-age care regimes generate specific implications for migrant and minority-ethnic workers along differentiated patterns. First, some of the ways in which managers dealt (or did not deal) with discrimination might amount, under certain circumstances, to racist discrimination. As foregrounded by MacQuarie's (2018) ethnography on night workers at a London grocery market, employers remain accountable for their turning a blind eye to certain practices, in this case exacerbating workers' precariousness. Several respondents recounted, for instance, being moved by the manager to another unit or floor in the case of racist attitudes by service users or colleagues. This, however, sent out the wrong message as to who was to blame and therefore weakened the position of the affected worker, who was further marginalised. In these cases, institutional practices effectively transformed the experience of individual prejudice into a form of institutional racism because of how the managers' position of power was used to entrench discriminatory outcomes. Such examples illustrate empirically that addressing racism in the workplace crucially requires managers' awareness and engagement for legal rights to be enforced. 'The transformation of racists themselves' that Balibar called for (Balibar and Wallerstein 1988, p. 29) requires the transformation of the majority group – here that of employers' and managers' practices. For this purpose, it is crucial to analyse how these interactions are imbued in power relationships. The following paragraphs look into how intersecting elements such as the commercial context, migration statuses or live-in employment conditions play a role in shaping the power relationships within which racism manifests itself in interpersonal relations.

The commercial context of the private care homes in which most respondents in this study were employed, by transforming residents into customers, exacerbated the tensions engendered by the juxtaposition of vulnerable service users and precarious workers. The vulnerabilities created by migration policies and labour-market segmentation, which weakened the position of workers, were deepened by the commercial context in which these relationships were embedded. Bacar clearly blamed this framework for the exacerbation of workers' vulnerability:

> In for-profit care homes that make profits, so residents are clients; 'The client is the king', so they prefer clients to carers. Because the client makes the money go in, for the carer the employer pays out, he pays at the end of the month but clients pay in, so he prefers clients, the person who makes the money go in, that's logical. So if a carer has a problem with a patient or a resident or with the family, automatically it's the carer who's sanctioned, the client is always right (Bacar, 35, Senegal, Paris).

In addition, managerial practices were at times directly discriminatory and ranged from unfair workloads to bullying and stigmatisation. In several cases a combination of these practices was present. The unfair division of tasks, as identified in the UK by Cangiano and his colleagues (2009, p. 137), constitutes a common form of discrimination in the care sector. This research also points out that unfair shift and annual-leave distributions are equally common discriminatory practices. Jade, who worked in Paris, complained that shifts and days off were assigned arbitrarily:

> I would say that it is not fair. For instance, I can ask for a day off, one time it can be accepted, the other it's not. It's not fair, it's all I know; it's not fair. Annual leave, absences, no, it's not fair (Jade, 46, Ivory Coast, Paris).

Such management practices created resentment and impacted to varying degrees on workers' well-being. An unfair workload distribution could have serious health implications for the workers given the physical labour involved in care. Furthermore, migrant workers were undoubtedly exposed to specific forms of discrimination and exploitation due to the 'institutional insecurity' created by migration policies (Anderson 2010) within the group of racialised workers as a whole. The more dependent migrant workers were on their employer – e.g. to support the formers' work permits and provide their accommodation – the more they were exposed to abuse. A limited knowledge of their rights or a lack of language skills further worsened migrant workers' experiences. Isabel's first employer in the UK attempted to forcibly retain her in a job in which she faced abusive practices; she was required to work any shifts that the employer saw fit, as he had provided her with accommodation in a room adjacent to the care home and she had her wages withheld.

> The environment is not really good. They are bullying, they are abusing us because they know that we are new and that we are foreigners. So we filed a resignation but they didn't accept it, they wanted us to stay though it is our right. If you're not happy you can go, yeah? We asked permission, we asked properly that we don't stay here any longer but they didn't allow us so we just leave (Isabel, 37, the Philippines, London).

Equally exposed to abuse, Sameera described how she felt oppressed in her workplace, where she experienced bullying but felt powerless and unable to challenge these behaviours; the stigma of being a migrant went beyond legal status. As Guillaumin (1972, p. 247, my translation) wrote several decades ago: 'Each individual who used to be a foreigner, alienated, condemned, always bears the scars of it, and his/her status of integration and conformism always remains ambiguous and submitted to the form of good will that constitutes tolerance or the silence of the majority'. Here, Sameera did not expect the planned acquisition of British citizenship to have any impact on how she would be perceived by managers and colleagues in the workplace and thus on their abusive attitudes towards her.

> And me as migrant I can't even open my mouth, you understand? How can I? Because these people are more powerful than me. (…) Even though I've got ten years now, I'm married, my status changed, tomorrow I apply for British [citizenship], I will get it because my husband is British it's still … I will be considered like different level, you understand? Because of my background, where I come from, because maybe of my skin colour, (…). This is always something which is always … how can I say? … Always inside you but you can't

open your mouth and talk about it. Sometimes you feel you just want to shout, you want to explode. But what can you do? You're scared, you do your job (Sameera, 32, Mauritius, London).

The vulnerable position of migrant workers left a space for employers' arbitrariness given the very low probability that their practices would be sanctioned in any way. In London, Jenifer, who was born in the UK to Asian parents, highlighted a case of harassment of foreigners at her workplace:

And she [the manager] has been reported by several witnesses on one day, she went upstairs and was telling, because it's mostly Filipinos and a few Asian people on the first floor, she was going around and saying 'You're lucky, you're in your jobs otherwise you could be back home, if you're not happy where you're working you should go back home to your own country' (Jenifer, 24, the Philippines, London).

This harassment of the staff by a manager was more than xenophobia. The space for arbitrariness created by migration policies facilitated abuse in employer–employee relationships. Grace, employed in the same care home, made the point that bullying happens as a result of a power relationship:

She [the manager] doesn't do that [bullying] to the White ones who are there, like you know who can just drop everything and go. She doesn't do that to them. That's the difference; she doesn't insult them like that. She does it to the foreigners (Grace, 61, the Philippines, London).

Harassment by employers, including racist insults, was the most common in the narratives of migrant workers in Madrid employed in live-in caring arrangements. This employment situation constitutes an extreme form of imbalance between the employer and the employee, whereby the rights of the employee are extremely limited – on the one hand by employment legislation and migration rules and, on the other, by the material conditions of the employment relationship. A quite typical quote in this regard is that of Lucia, whose employer (a member of the family of the person she cared for) got angry and attacked her after she announced that she could not travel with the family to a Spanish island as planned because of a health issue:

She insulted me. She told me that we were only coming to steal, that I was a thief because she had bought me a uniform, she had bought me supplies. Because workers who worked in the house didn't eat in the house. They had a small separate house where domestic workers ate. Until they [employers] had finished eating, everything needed to be done and then you were going to the small house to have something to eat. It was a very difficult situation there (Lucia, 56, Nicaragua, Madrid).

The imbalance of power between the employer and the employee tends to be exacerbated in specific contexts: notably, when privatisation increases pressures to reduce labour costs, or when the employment relationship is situated in the domestic sphere for migrant workers employed as live-in carers. The articulation of care regimes and migration regulations thus created important differences as to care workers' exposure to employers' abuse. In Madrid, the domestic setting was particularly precarious due to workers' frequent dependence on their employers sustaining their legal statuses. With a focus on residential care provision most respondents in this research had been living in Spain for over 10 years, consequently the vast majority was able to obtain Spanish citizenship owing to post-colonial regulations for Latin American migrants. In London, those on student visas were at risk of loosing their legal status even in the case of continuous employment within the care sector as their employment did not provide sufficient earnings. In Paris, most had either a long-term residency permit (10 years) or had become French citizens. And yet, respondents' accounts in relation to managers' and employers' direct discrimination epitomise the reasons why anti-discrimination policies are *de facto* of very limited relevance when a large proportion of the workforce is trapped in segmented sections of the labour market on precarious employment terms. Even when working legally or after having obtained the citizenship of their country of residence, few migrant workers can afford to invest time and money individually in lengthy judicial procedures.

In addition, the statistics cited above demonstrated that such procedures are unlikely to bring about positive results in the UK and the absence of figures in the case of Spain and France revealed a lack of political will and transparency. While the discourses and practices around anti-discrimination legislation present notable differences in each of these countries, as outlined above, the structural vulnerabilities created by the intersection of migration/racialisation, employment and care regimes produced similar challenges for the everyday experiences of racialised workers in the three cities under study here. These negative work experiences were nevertheless resisted and fought against individually and collectively in creative ways. The following section looks at collective forms of coping with and resisting harassment and discrimination by managers.

5.5 Challenging Racist Practices Collectively

Seeking support outside the workplace is all the more difficult when targeted workers are denizens – i.e. have limited rights compared to citizens according to one's legal and economic status (De Genova 2013; Standing 2011). Faced with harassment by employers, it appears that respondents in Madrid mostly resorted to informal support groups and associations, while unions struggled to be present in this feminised sector of the labour market where a large share of migrant workers is present. In the masculinised sector of the night workers of a food market studied by MacQuarie (2018), unions were equally absent and workers knew little about their rights. Here, unions' weak presence was partly due to the inadequacy of the union's organising tools (e.g. meetings at times when workers could not attend, priorities that did not correspond to care workers' demands) as well as to care workers' isolation in the case of domestic workers. Often, the creation of such associations was the outgrowth of a previously existing informal group who aimed to alleviate domestic workers' isolation. Such organisations played a significant role in Madrid, where live-in care arrangements were commonplace. Victoria – who founded an association of migrant care workers – explained, for instance, how they were able to provide support to migrant care workers who had been dismissed by the family they were working for, in some cases after having been insulted and abused:

> We had colleagues for whom it was very tough. They were told, 'What are you doing here? Go back to your country'. (…) They left their jobs and they were very depressed. We've been helping, I tell you, many women who came and whose situation was 'Look, they treated me like this, they told this or that'. Us, 'No, you have to cheer up, you're not like this and you have to carry on'. And we've worked, because we always had the luck to work with professional colleagues, we have a colleague who's a psychologist, others who used to be psychologists. So they've helped us with the women to make them realise that things are not as we're told (Victoria, 54, Ecuador, Madrid).

Mayra, also of Ecuadorian origin, joined a group of domestic workers in Madrid who met twice a month. She described how these contacts provided a powerful form of support:

> We have an association, a group of women where we say we empower ourselves because we learn techniques and tricks to be able to endure the situation. It's not that it's to teach us but it's the experience of each one of us, amongst ourselves we've constructed a method to take care of ourselves for things that affect us at work (Mayra, 52, Ecuador, Madrid).

These forms of support were crucial for workers' well-being and, though they sometimes ushered in support for judicial proceedings, this was not their primary function. While unions could theoretically play that role, they were rarely mentioned by respondents in Madrid and did not act as a significant source of support in cases of harassment. Members of the association mentioned by Mayra were, for instance, rather critical of the role of unions, which they perceived as out-dated organisations unable to address the specific challenges of the highly feminised care and domestic-work sectors. One respondent, a victim of harassment in Madrid, thought of involving a union but her story shows that she was discouraged by the union itself from initiating a legal action:

> NS: Were you thinking in this situation of seeking support, for example, from a union?
> Rita: Yes, yes.
> NS: What could they do in this situation?
> Rita: I said I was about to denounce her for harassment because I knew that the union had to back me up. What happens is – and this is what the union told me – that if I go to court I need to be courageous. They told me 'If you go to court you need to be courageous because you go to court and this woman, she'll harass you even more than you can imagine, she'll harass you and harass you until she can prove that you're arrogant and, instead of you winning, she'll be the one winning. Do you take the risk of going to court?' Because the trial will take years, he told me. 'You might have left the care home but the trial will be going on for one, two, three or more years'. So I said: 'No, it's not like I got to the point that … I'm not starving as much as to go to court' I said (Rita, 54, Ecuador, Madrid).

This story illustrates that cases of racist harassment are particularly difficult to challenge legally, even for unions. The mere existence of anti-discrimination legislation does not empower racialised workers because the path to employment tribunals is fraught with pitfalls. The reluctance of the union to start judicial proceedings seems to reflect its awareness of their limited effectiveness. At the same time it highlights again that most cases remain unchallenged (at least in legal terms) and thus unsanctioned.

In London, unions were described as potentially supportive institutions, even though no respondent actually resorted to a union for help – in some cases despite having joined a union following problems at work. Isabel, the Filipina care worker who experienced abuse in her first workplace in the UK, thought unions could have effectively supported her had she asked for help:

> Because here in this country racism and bullying is a really big issue – they don't really allow it. It's not a crime but it's really a big issue for them. (…) I can get a big support from the union if I were a union member (…) because what I have experienced there is really racism, bullying, abuse (Isabel, 37, the Philippines, London).

However, in practice, the unions faced difficulties similar to those in Madrid, in spite of the stronger regulatory framework in the UK. Workers felt that it was difficult to prove discrimination, especially in cases of covert forms of racism. Furthermore, it was common amongst respondents in the UK to fear that joining a union would be perceived negatively by the management. When cases of discrimination did arise and the potential for confrontation through mediation by a union increased, this fear grew as well. Worry that making an allegation of discrimination would make the situation worse in the future discouraged Sameera from seeking the union's support:

> NS: And did you get in touch with the union?
> Sameera: No, I didn't because I was thinking if I have not resolved that problem, but thank God it was fine and I don't want to involve the union for anything because then there might be a grudge against me. If something which can't be resolved at all then I involve them, if not…but at the moment it's ok (Sameera, 32, Mauritius, London).

The commercialisation of unions' services, notably in the UK, also played a role in diminishing the trust which workers could place in unions: if union membership was a cost/benefit calculation for unions (and for workers), then the likelihood of obtaining the union's support for a costly and uncertain procedure was perceived as low. This paradox may be the most prominent in the UK; despite the existence of well-developed anti-discrimination legislation encompassing a wide range of possible forms of discrimination, the possibility of lodging a complaint with an employment tribunal is hampered by a series of structural characteristics of the UK employment regime. These include low levels of employment protection compared to other European countries, costly judicial procedures and a low probability of obtaining union support, given that the chances of winning discrimination cases are generally low and that unions take that variable into account. Willing to support her care assistant colleagues who were harassed by the manager of the care home she worked in, Grace did not assess positively the potential role of unions:

> Everybody is making money, even unions sometimes they're making money, they collect all the membership and they don't support you when you need them, they're collecting money, everything is business nowadays. So when it comes to litigations, when it comes to spending so much money to fight your case, goodbye to you, they don't want to know. (…) Unless you're a strong person who can go through this hassle and this trouble, forget it, because it's

a very lengthy procedure and you need a lot of evidence to prove that (Grace, 61, the
Philippines, London).

It thus appears that, when discrimination and abuse do happen, these rights are often
barely accessible, notwithstanding the level of development of the regulatory framework. Existing power relationships make it difficult for workers to challenge their
managers and employers. The difficulty of proving discrimination and harassment
adds to the problem and to the fear of starting a procedure in vain, thus risking exposure to more abuse.

5.6   Conclusion

My analysis of various forms of racism and discrimination and of the consequent
coping strategies revealed how these are in fact interrelated and are symptomatic of
broader institutional racism. Exploring situations of harassment and abuse by colleagues highlighted common manifestations of racism and discrimination and
exposed some of their implications for workers' well-being. This chapter pointed
out how these experiences were embedded in workplace power relationships and
identified the role played by managers and employers in different situations. In none
of the cases analysed here did bullying and harassment by colleagues usher in disciplinary procedures or legal cases. The second aspect – that of direct discrimination
or harassment by managers   highlighted how intersecting migration, care and
employment regimes fostered abuse at the workplace level by exacerbating precariousness. Migrant workers were the most exposed to direct harassment by managers.
Against the background of disempowering processes fostered by labour market
fragmentation, racialised care workers are left with limited options to challenge racist discrimination by employers or racist remarks by colleagues. The institutional
indifference to care workers' experiences of racism not only fosters disintegration
but also undermines the effectiveness of anti-discrimination legislation.

This chapter argues in this regard that experiencing racism on a daily basis, with
little leverage to challenge it, constitutes a disintegrating mechanism. The chapter
demonstrated that anti-discrimination legislation often remains out of reach for
racialised precarious workers and that anti-racism is too often reduced to the legal
framework of anti-discrimination policies, falling short of analysing the structural
dynamics that foster racism at multiple levels. By defining migrant workers' rights,
employment and migration regimes shape the conditions for workers' exposure to
racist discrimination, harassment and abuse. Challenging these situations is complex and no single framework can improve workers' experiences from all these
perspectives. Anti-discrimination legislation appears to be of very limited efficacy
for precarious workers: in spite of the numerous experiences related by respondents
in this research, no one actually resorted to anti-discrimination legislation. The great
majority of cases remain unchallenged, which suggests that it is difficult to fix structurally unequal power relationships through individual legal action. Moreover, most

abusive situations are created or exacerbated by the space for arbitrariness derived from the articulation of migration and employment policies. Therefore, overstating the relevance of anti-discrimination legislation, and its potentially integrative effects, runs the risk of equating anti-racism with anti-discrimination policies, instead of conducting a political economy analysis of the material conditions under which racism and discrimination thrive. As argued in the introduction to this volume (Collyer et al. 2020) integration and disintegration are deeply entangled; this chapter demonstrated in this regard that anti-discrimination legislation fulfils a discursive purpose but is of limited relevance to the experiences of racialised workers and thus comes to play an ambiguous role in the politics of (dis)integration. Challenging racism and racist discrimination cannot rely solely on an anti-discrimination legislative framework. Low levels of employment protection weaken migrants' possibilities for denouncing an employer for harassment, due to the unfavourable power relationship thus established. Support mechanisms at the workplace level can include greater presence of trade unions and support organisations as well as protective whistleblowing policies. Overall, migrant and minority-ethnic workers' inclusion crucially depends on empowering workers through employment protection, reducing the precariousness of their migration statuses and improving their access to the judicial system through administrative and financial support. As long as legal protections do not effectively challenge the marginalisation of racialised care workers and the neglect of their experiences of racism they will continue to feed into the politics of (dis)integration.

References

Anderson, B. (2010). Migration, immigration controls and the fashioning of precarious workers. *Work, Employment and Society, 24*(2), 300–317.

Anthias, F., & Yuval-Davis, N. (1992). *Racialized boundaries: Race, nation, gender, colour and class and the anti-racist struggle*. London: Routledge.

Aspinall, P. J. (2002). Collective terminology to describe the minority ethnic population: The persistence of confusion and ambiguity in usage. *Sociology, 36*(4), 803–816.

Balibar, E., & Wallerstein, I. M. (1988). *Race, Nation, Classe: Les Identités Ambiguës*. Paris: Ed. La Découverte.

Boyatzis, R. E. (1998). *Transforming qualitative information: Thematic analysis and code development*. London: Sage.

Byrd, C. (2011). Conflating apples and oranges: Understanding modern forms of racism. *Sociology Compass, 5*(11), 1005–1017.

Cangiano, A., Shutes, I., Spencer, S., & Leeson, G. (2009). *Migrant care workers in ageing societies: Research findings in the United Kingdom*. Oxford: University of Oxford, COMPAS Report.

Carlmicheal, S., & Hamilton, C. V. (1967/1992). *Black power. The politics of liberation*. New York: Vintage Books.

Colectivo Ioé. (2003). *Experiencias de Discriminación de Minorías Étnicas en España*. Retrieved in August 2018 from https://www.colectivoioe.org/uploads/edb969a5b5bb4f6aaf3f9afb-865cf396533d9315.pdf

Collyer, M., Hinger, S., & Schweitzer, R. (2020). Politics of (dis)integration – An introduction. In S. Hinger & R. Schweitzer (Eds.), *Politics of (dis)integration* (pp. 1–18). Cham: Springer VS.

De Genova, N. (2013). Spectacles of migrant 'illegality': The scene of exclusion, the obscene of inclusion. *Ethnic and Racial Studies, 36*(7), 1180–1198.

Department for Business Innovation and Skills. (2014). *Findings from the survey of tribunal employment applications* 2013. Research series no. 177. Retrieved in August 2018 from https://assets.publishing.service.gov.uk/government/uploads/system/uploads/attachment_data/file/316704/bis-14-708-survey-of-employment-tribunal-applications-2013.pdf

Duggan, L. (2003). *The twilight of equality. Neoliberalism, cultural politics and the attack on democracy.* Boston: Beacon Press Books.

Ehrenreich, B., & Hochschild, A. R. (2002). *Global woman: Nannies, maids, and sex workers in the new economy.* New York: Holt Press.

Foucault, M. (2004). *Naissance de la Biopolitique. Cours au Collège de France, 1978–1979.* Paris: Seuil/Gallimard.

Fraser, N. (2016). Contradictions of capital and care. *New Left Review, 100*, 99–117.

Gawronski, B., Peters, K. R., Brochu, P. M., & Strack, F. (2008). Understanding the relations between different forms of racial prejudice: A cognitive consistency perspective. *Personality and Social Psychology Bulletin, 34*(5), 648–665.

Gilroy, P. (1987/2002). *There ain't no black in the Union Jack.* London: Routledge.

Guillaumin, C. (1972/2002). *L'idéologie raciste.* Paris: Editions Folios Essais.

HALDE. (2010). *Rapport annuel HALDE 2010.* Paris: La Documention Française. Retrieved in August 2018 from http://www.ladocumentationfrancaise.fr/var/storage/rapports-publics/114000234.pdf

Hall, S. (1978). Racism and reaction. In BBC TV/Commission for Racial Equality (Ed.), *Five views of multi-racial Britain* (pp. 23–35). London: Commission for Racial Equality.

Headley, C. (2000). Philosophical approaches to racism: A critique of the individualistic perspective. *Journal of Social Philosophy, 31*(2), 223–257.

Ikuenobe, P. (2010). Conceptualizing racism and its subtle forms. *Journal for the Theory of Social Behaviour, 41*(2), 161–181.

Lentin, A., & Titley, G. (2011). *The crises of multiculturalism: Racism in a neoliberal age.* New York: Zed Books.

MacQuarie, J.-C. (2018). *Invisible migrants: Glocturnal cities' 'other workers' in the post-circadian capitalist era.* PhD thesis. Budapest: Central European University. Retrieved 1 April 2019 from https://bit.ly/2FCMkFX

McCall, L. (2005). The complexity of intersectionality. *Journal of Women and Culture in Society, 30*(3), 1771–1800.

Ministerio de Sanidad, Política Social e Igualdad. (2011). *Informe anual sobre la situación de la discriminación y la aplicación del principio de igualdad de trato por origen racial o étnico en España.* Madrid: Ministerio de Sanidad, Politica Social e Igualdad. Retrieved in August 2018 from http://www.mscbs.gob.es/ssi/igualdadOportunidades/docs/2010_Informe_Anual_Consejoigualdad_Accesible.pdf.

Ministry of Justice. (2012). *Employment tribunals and EAT statistics, 2011–12.* London: Ministry of Justice. Retrieved in August 2018 from https://assets.publishing.service.gov.uk/government/uploads/system/uploads/attachment_data/file/218497/employment-trib-stats-april-march-2011-12.pdf.

Nimführ, S., Otto, L., & Samateh, G. (2020). Denying, while demanding integration: An analysis of the integration paradox in Malta and refugees' coping strategies. In S. Hinger & R. Schweitzer (Eds.), *Politics of (dis)integration* (pp. 161–181). Cham: Springer VS.

Parreñas, R. (2000). Migrant Filipina domestic workers and the international division of reproductive labor. *Gender & Society, 14*(4), 560–580.

Rass, C., & Wolff, F. (2018). What is in a migration regime? Genealogical approach and methodological proposal. In A. Pott, C. Rass, & F. Wolff (Eds.), *Was ist ein Migrationsregime?* (What is a migration regime?) (pp. 19–64). Osnabrück: Springer.

Rattansi, A. (2011). *Multiculturalism: A very short introduction.* Oxford: Oxford University Press.

Renton, D. (2013). *Culture of disbelief? Why race discrimination claims fail in the employment tribunal*. London: Institute of Race Relations. Retrieved in August 2018 from http://www.irr.org.uk/news/culture-of-disbelief-why-race-discrimination-claims-fail-in-the-employment-tribunal/.

Sahraoui, N. (forthcoming). *Racialised workers and European older-age care from care labour to care ethics*. London: Palgrave Macmillan.

Schweitzer, R. (2020). How inclusive institutions enforce exclusive immigration rules: Mainstream public service provision and the implementation of a hostile environment for irregular migrants living in Britain. In S. Hinger & R. Schweitzer (Eds.), *Politics of (dis)integration* (pp. 121–140). Cham: Springer VS.

Sivanandan, A. (1985). RAT and the degradation of black struggle. *Race & Class, 26*(4), 1–33.

Smith, D. E. (2005). *Institutional ethnography: A sociology for people*. Oxford: Altamira Press.

Spitálszky, A. (2013). *Racism and related discriminatory practices in employment in Spain*. Brussels: European Network Against Racism. Retrieved in August 2018 from http://www.enar-eu.org/IMG/pdf/spain.pdf.

Standing, G. (2011). *The precariat: The new dangerous class*. London: Bloomsbury Academic.

Thelwell, E. (2015, March 12). Are race discrimination laws still needed in the workplace? *BBC News Online*. Retrieved in August 2018 from http://www.bbc.com/news/uk-31856147

Williams, F. (2012). Converging variations in migrant care work in Europe. *Journal of European Social Policy, 22*(4), 363–376.

Williams, F. (2014). Making connections across the transnational political economy of care. In B. Anderson & I. Shutes (Eds.), *Migration and care labour: Theory, policy and politics* (pp. 11–30). Hampshire: Palgrave Macmillan.

Chapter 6
Returning for (Dis)Integration in the Labour Market? The Careers of Labour Migrants Returning to Poland from the United Kingdom

Mateusz Karolak

6.1 Introduction[1]

Since the 2004 and 2007 enlargements of the European Union (EU), return migration from Western to Eastern EU member-states has become a relevant topic on political and research agendas. The new migration patterns and the increasing number of returnees raised questions regarding migrants' (re)integration into their society of origin. Although return migration occurs in supposedly more integration-friendly circumstances – the returnees do not lack the foundations of integration such as rights and citizenship, nor facilitators such as language and other cultural knowledge (Ager and Strang 2008) – some returnees still encounter problems in the core domains of integration, including those crucial for their social position and integration on the labour market. Existing research points out that, regarding the labour market situation, the population of returnees is very heterogeneous and its structure resembles that of the society of origin (except for the excessive growth in the number of self-employed among the returnees). It openly challenges the discourse of the universal profitability of labour mobility and return. The so-called 'triple win scenario' (Sinatti 2015) assumes that migrants, after fulfilling the temporary demand for labour in the receiving country, return to their country of origin and work, making efficient use of the skills and knowledge accumulated abroad (cf. Samuk 2020). In this way, they help to solve the problems of their country's economy (e.g. filling the demand for labour, easing skills shortages and boosting the innovation level) and demography.

---

[1] The work on this chapter was possible thanks to a doctoral scholarship received from the National Science Center Poland (NCN) (UMO-2016/20/T/HS6/00479).

M. Karolak (✉)
University of Wrocław, Wrocław, Poland
e-mail: mateusz.karolak@uwr.edu.pl

S. Hinger, R. Schweitzer (eds.), *Politics of (Dis)Integration*,
IMISCOE Research Series, https://doi.org/10.1007/978-3-030-25089-8_6

101

As observed by various sociologists (e.g. Bauman 2000; Sennett 1998; Urry 2000), spatial mobility became perceived in advanced economies as a key element of a successful occupational career. Spatial flexibility – one of the critical dimensions of the transition from a Fordist to a post-Fordist economy – went from being just an option into a social expectation deriving from the logic of late capitalism. As pointed out by Jesse Potter (2015, p. 7): 'The primary attribute of successful new economy workers is their mobile and flexible approach to their productive lives'. Jane Wills et al. (2010, p. 6) observe that, in the eyes of many, the migrant became 'the world's paradigmatic worker', praised for their hard work, ability to adjust to the market and readiness to move once they are no longer needed. Thomas Faist (2013, p. 1644), in turn, notes that

> [t]his shift towards a positive evaluation of movement is deeply problematic because it usually does not reflect underlying trends that aim to build a flexible, docile and politically abstinent global workforce – processes sometimes discussed under the label 'neoliberalism'.

The discrepancy between the praising discourse of mobility and the much more ambiguous realities experienced by returning labour migrants has still not been sufficiently explained and the mechanisms contributing to both the returnees' integration and their disintegration require further examination. Therefore the main task of this chapter is to contribute to this emerging discussion and to analyse the practices and labour market (dis)integration paths of intra-EU return migrants, taking as an example the experiences of Polish post-accession migrants returning to Poland from the United Kingdom.

On a theoretical level, the chapter argues that, in the context of the growing precarisation of work (Standing 2011), it is necessary to rethink the rigid integration–exclusion discourse, which considers as integrated into labour market all those in employment, regardless of its quality and stability.

Instead, drawing inspiration from labour-market segmentation theories, it is argued that tracing the course of migrants' occupational careers on the multi-segmented labour market enables us to go beyond a dichotomous understanding of labour market integration and to account for the varieties of change in employment patterns and condtions. In this way, this chapter reveals the labour-related layer of the politics of (dis)integration.

My case study of return migration from the UK to Poland will serve as a specific laboratory for looking at ongoing global changes. Firstly, intra-EU mobility, with its East–West–East migration, is a significant part of the global division of labour, with all its inequalities (Favell 2008; Wills et al. 2010). Secondly, the abolition of national borders within the Schengen area might be seen not so much as a sign of borders' disappearance but, rather, of their proliferation and displacement into other than spatial dimensions of life (Mezzadra and Neilson 2013). These changes brought out new forms of intra-EU labour mobility control, well described by the theory of governmentality (Foucault 2008; Mezzadra and Neilson 2013). The traditional control exercised externally, usually by legal means and state forces (e.g. visas, temporary work schemes, employer-sponsored migration, physical borders), has been gradually replaced by the emergence of mobile subjects who deeply internalise the rules of the market game and whose footloose mobility becomes functional to the workings of contemporary capitalism (cf. Foucault 2008, p. 230).

The chapter is structured as followed: first, I shed light on the specificity of intra-EU movement and post-accession migration between Poland and the UK. Second, I examine the state policies, or lack thereof, with regard to return migration. Next, I look at the pitfals of a simplified understanding of labour market integration and introduce the theory of multi-segmented labour markets. Finally, after the methodological note, the four main types of returning migrants' transitions between labour markets are presented.

6.2 Migration and Return Migration – The Case of Poland and the UK

The opening of EU borders in 2004 and 2007 and the gradual withdrawing of labour market restrictions for EU citizens affected the whole of Europe. As summed up by Drinkwater and Garapich (2013, p. 2), 'EU enlargement resulted in the biggest demographic change in Europe since the devastation and flux experienced at the end of the Second World War (…), with the UK at the centre of that movement'.

At the end of 2017, of the 2.5 million Poles living abroad, 2.1 million resided in the EU. In the UK, the number of Poles skyrocketed from 24,000 in 2004 to 690,000 in 2007 and reached 793,000 by 2017 (GUS 2018). Simultaneously, the number of Polish returnees from the UK between 2004 and 2014 is estimated to be at least 587,000 (Karolak 2016).

Besides the unexpected growth in migration flows, patterns of migration have also changed. In addition to the settlement, circular or incomplete forms of migrations observed in the 1990s (Okólski 2001), researchers noted the importance of a new phenomenon known as 'liquid migration' (Engbersen et al. 2010 Engbersen and Snel 2013). It is characterised by individualisation, lesser attachment to the family and multidimensional temporariness, leading to an increasing number of returnees. '[Liquid] migrants try their luck in new and multiple countries of destination, benefiting from open borders and labour markets' (Engbersen et al. 2013, pp. 960–961). The 'liquid migrants' were clearly present in the post-2004 EU accession migration from Poland to the UK. As shown by John Eade and his collaborators (2007), the undecided migrants – called in the study the 'searchers' – accounted for 42% of all Polish migrants in the UK.

For 73% of Poles, work was the main reason for their emigration (GUS 2013). However, as shown in various qualitative studies (e.g. Grabowska 2016a; Kaźmierska et al. 2011; Polkowski 2017), non-economic reasons were equally important for some migrants. For young Central and Eastern Europeans, migration is often treated as a relevant life experience and rite of passage into adulthood (Grabowska 2016a) – the journey which teaches cultural independence and offers a chance to gain economic independence, seen by young people as unachievable in their country of origin (Polkowski 2017). Finally, the Polish National Census (GUS 2013, p. 70) showed that 50% of Polish citizens abroad plan to return 1 day to Poland, whereas 38% were still undecided and only 12% did not want to return at all. However, initial declarations about migration plans usually do not correspond with the future course of migration – as was shown in the case of Poles in the UK (Drinkwater and Garapich 2013).

The existing research provides mixed evidence regarding the labour market situation of those who eventually decide to return. Moreover, there is, unfortunately, a lack of representative data regarding Polish return migrants from the UK. Nevertheless, it has been suggested that, thus far, migratory experience is not perceived as an advantage in the Polish labour market, in contrast to a knowledge of foreign languages and other soft skills (Kaczmarczyk and Lesińska 2012, p. 31).

After analysis of the 1999–2009 Labour Force Survey, Anacka and Fihel (2013, p. 68) conclude that: '(…) in comparison with non-migrants, migrants are clearly less likely to find employment in Poland'. How, then can we account for these differences and explain them in the context of individual biographies? Do returnees face problems with integration and what quality of employment can they expect? Which role do the migration episode(s) and state's policy play in shaping returnees' career paths?

Before I attempt to answer these questions, it is, however, necessary to analyse the very concept of integration, with a particular focus on integration into the labour market which – as I argue – requires re-conceptualisation in times of a growing precarisation of labour and expanding inequalities among employees.

6.3   Return Migrants' (Dis)Integration, the Role of the State and the Conceptual Framework

The conceptual framework of the core domains of integration introduced by Alastair Ager and Alison Strang (2008) proved helpful in understanding the theoretical challenge posed by the concept of returning migrants' integration. Ager and Strang proposed to differentiate between foundations (rights and citizenship), facilitators (language and cultural knowledge), social connection (social bridges, bonds and links) as well as markers and means of integration such as employment, housing, education and health (for a more detailed discussion of Ager and Strang's integration framework see the chapter by Tina Magazzini in this volume. From this perspective, returning migrants do not lack the essential foundations of integration – citizenship and rights. Furthermore, almost all of them dispose of the critical facilitators of integration which are language and cultural knowledge.

When it comes to other domains of integration identified by Ager and Strang, the situation of returning migrants, including the first generation, is more ambiguous. They might lack safety and stability which, in conjunction with weaker social connections, may have an impact on their life situation in the spheres of employment, housing, education and health.

The state, with its institutions, could be an important actor in the process of creating both favourable and unfavourable conditions for returnees' integration. Its actual role depends, however, on the particular constellation of return mobility. The state can either treat returnees on an equal footing with all other citizens, providing them with the same access to institutional support regardless of their migration experience or it can recognise returning migrants as a separate group of citizens in need of support, drawing up particular policies for such situations. In this case, policies for returnees could take either a reactive or an active form (Lesińska 2013). The former is merely a state response to already existing processes of return which have occurred independently of the state's actions. The latter, in turn, aims to 'encourage nationals to return. When returns are recognised as a positive and desirable process (…), then policy-makers act to stimulate migrants' decision to return and to facilitate the process of coming back to the home country' (*Ibid.*, p. 79). What is important to note is that active policies for returnees are often selective and aimed at bringing back a particular occupational group of migrants who are perceived as valuable for society (e.g. schemes encouraging the return of doctors, entrepreneurs or scholars); however, such a move might be treated as a symptom of the increasingly utilitarian approach of the state towards its citizens (Sahraoui et al. 2018). Whereas encouraging return migration often appears on political agendas and in discourses, support for the integration of returning migrants is less often perceived as an issue of state policy.

In Poland, an evolution of state policies addressing Poles abroad is observable. Just after the EU enlargement of 2004, the state initiated an educational campaign focusing on the rights of Polish labour migrants aborad and aimed at 'protecting Polish citizens against dangers and threats related to the often unprepared labour emigration' (Lesińska 2013, p. 84). Among many activities, the state planned not only to improve the image of Poland among potential returnees but also to introduce tax relief, reduce their social insurance and pension contribution rate and organise job fairs abroad, designed to match employers with potential employees and ensure that the latter can return directly into the Polish labour market.

These policies, however, were never implemented due to the change of government in 2008, which shifted towards a reactive type of policy. It was assumed that 'the main aim of the State policy is not to influence individual migrants' decisions to return, but to provide them with a tool enabling them to make a rational choice' (Lesińska 2013, p. 85). The main instrument disseminated via various information channels was potentially helpful in organising migrants' return (e.g. how to avoid double taxation or how to change a child's school).

Crucially, reintegration, in these policies, was understood as the mere fact of being active in the labour market, which points to the broader phenomenon of equating labour-market integration with finding employment. Therefore, in the next section, I highlight the limitations of the debate on labour market integration and propose to examine returning labour migrants' experiences not through the binary opposition of integration–exclusion but, rather, through the theoretical lens of the multi-segmented labour market and the concept of (dis)integration, as proposed in the introduction to this volume (Collyer et al. 2020). I argue that the combination of theories of the multi-segmented labour market and the sociological concept of career helps to account for the diversity of returnees' experiences of (dis)integration.

6.4   Integration, Inclusion and Exclusion and Their Limitations

Despite some advantages in explaining inequalities, the dominant approaches to integration have several pitfalls. First, they implicitly assume and generalise a particular view on society and its desirable values. Beyond each approach about integration, there is an underlying moral meta-narration. It is assumed that 'social inclusion or integration, as the opposite of social exclusion, is inherently good and desirable' (Fangen et al. 2011, p. 2). Such an assumption, in turn, leads to a situation whereby attempts to integrate those perceived as socially excluded might turn out to be 'problematic, disempowering or inequitable' (2011, p. 2). To be more specific, the contemporary European policies of integration tend to narrow themselves to the issue of employment, reflecting the shift from welfare to 'workfare' policies, as shown, for example, by Sophie Hinger (2020).

Ruth Levitas (2005) argues that, despite differences in understanding what it means to be socially excluded or included (thus, integrated), the underlying assumptions of integration discourses stem from Durkheim's understanding of society as organised around organic solidarity, with cohesion as its natural state (Durkheim 1997 [1893]). Both Durkheim and dominant discourses of integration share the assumption that 'the individual identity as well as individual integration into society is primarily constituted through work' (Levitas 2005, p. 181). Importantly, in both cases, work is understood narrowly as paid employment. Such a narrow understanding of work leads to the situation in which all those who exercise unpaid reproductive work are left aside or labelled as reluctant to work.

Second, the dichotomous view imposed by the basic opposition between the integrated and the excluded oversimplifies a very complex social reality and obscures the differences between those perceived as integrated. This has one further connotation, namely the language of exclusion shifts away from sight the class perspective and undermines the divergent, or sometimes even conflicting, interests of various groups.

Last but not least, the discussed approaches essentialise social reality, skipping the relational and processual aspects of the social position. This leads to the overlooking of both the life trajectories of individuals and the dynamic structural changes (e.g. in the employment patterns) which might shift the social position of entire groups.

From this perspective, exploring returning migrants' experiences in terms of traditionally understood labour market integration would bring few results, as the analysis would boil down to the question of whether the returnee is employed or not. Therefore, bearing in mind the above-mentioned limitations of the integration discourse, yet acknowledging the possibility of returning migrants encountering various disadvantages on the labour market, the following issue arises: How should we approach and map the returnees' labour experiences without imposing moral meta-narration, ignoring the spectre of individual and group (class) inequalities as well as essentialising?

In this chapter I propose to look at the returnees' labour market (dis)integration through the lense of multi-segemented labour market theory (Loveridge and Mok 1979). According to this theory, the labour market is not homogenous and its model could be built around two continuous axes – the vertical or 'social axis' covers the field of industrial relations and shows the 'differentiation of jobs and people in terms of their rewards (and punishments), working conditions, responsibility, autonomy and job security' (1979, p. 123) and the horizontal or 'bureaucratic'/'technical' axis reflects the differences in skills, training required and place in the hierarchy. In this way, by underlining the varieties of employment (for example, starting with the bank manager in a secure and very well paid job, through the less secure but still well paid free-lancer, to the precarious waiter on the zero-hours contract) this model reflects the continuum of returning migrants' positions not only within but also outside the labour market.

After my methodological note, the last sections are devoted to the application of the proposed theoretical framework and the exploration of differences in returning migrants' transitions between the British and Polish labour markets.

6.5 Research Design and Methodology

Following the methodologies established in the biographical tradition (Schütze 2016), 30 biographical narrative interviews with Polish returnees from the UK and with re-emigrants to the UK were carried out between November 2013 and June 2016, as part of my PhD research. The interviews included biographical issues, explored the motives and motivations for migration, return and re-emigration, and addressed returnees' post-migration experiences on the labour market.

The choice of the informants, as well as the analysis of the collected interviews, followed the procedures of grounded theory methodology or GTM (Glaser and Strauss 1967). The fieldwork began with a purposive sampling of long-term labour migrants who had worked in the UK for at least 1 year and who, after their return, lived in Poland for at least 6 months, irrespective of their reasons for migration, return and re-emigration (if this occurred). The relatively broad criteria of the initial sample were aimed at grasping the variety of labour migrants motivations for return. It was also assumed that irrespective of the explicitly declared reason for return the biographical narrative interviews could also reveal the configurations of individual and structural factors, which influence the process of return and subsequent returnees' situation in the labour market.

The respondents were initially recruited through snowball sampling, mailings and migrant Internet forums. At the first stage of the fieldwork, I reached mainly migrants with secondary or higher education, younger than 35 years of age. Over time, following the prescriptions of the GTM, I began comparison and open coding of the already conducted interviews, while still collecting new narratives. At this stage of the research, the sampling became theoretical and aimed at saturating the themes and categories emerging from the initial analysis. Since the objective of the theoretical sampling lies in 'simultaneous maximization and minimization of both differences and similarities of data that bear on categories being studied' (Glaser and Strauss 1967, p. 55) I interviewed migrants with lower education levels and/or older than 35. Moreover, initially I talked to people who either returned to Lower Silesia region of Poland or after return left Poland for Scotland, yet over time the sample was extended to migrants living in Warsaw and London, the capitals that attract return migrants (Anacka and Fihel 2013) and, as it turned out in a course of the research, some of the double return migrants.

Of the interviewees, 16 were women and 14 were men. The biggest group of the informants (16) was between 25 and 30 years old; 4 of them were under 25 years old and the remaining 10 were over 30 years old. The majority of the informants (23) had at the moment of the interview (not necessarily during migration) some form of tertiary education, that is: 16 informants had obtained a Master's degree (13 MA and 3 MSc) and 6 informants held a Bachelor's degree (5 BA, and 1 BSc). Moreover, 6 informants had completed secondary education (3 general and 3 technical) and 2 others had an elementary level of education.

It needs to be underlined that 'Unlike statistical sampling, theoretical sampling [does] not aim at statistical representativeness, but at the development of an empirically grounded understanding of the substantive field of study.' (Mrozowicki 2011, p. 88) Thus the research results presented in the next section, although not representative, reveal the variety of returnees' experiences in the labour market as well as some of the mechanisms contributing to the returning migrants' disintegration.

6.6   Returning Migrants' Labour Market Transitions Shaped by the Politics of (Dis)Integration

Analysis of the interview narratives revealed four main types of return migrant transitions between the British and the Polish labour markets – the effortless, the unforeseen, the failed and the postponed.

6.6.1   The Effortless Transition

The first type, the effortless transition between the labour markets, describes the situation in which returning migrants not only had no trouble finding employment in Poland but also worked in accordance with their expectations. Understandably, this was typically the case of returnees keen to enhance their career and who found an interesting job in Poland before leaving the UK and only then decided to move back there. However, crucial for this type of transition were structural circumstances enabling an efficient use of migrants' capital – such as a diploma from a British university – which, by some employers, was perceived as an advantage and which singled some migrants out, as it did for Patrycja:

> It seems to me that, as I had a university degree from the UK…, on not such a typical field of study in Poland, it really mattered and it meant that I even got the chance of a job interview, and in the end I got this job. Well, my boss later liked to sell it so nicely that the team in our organisation consists of people from all over Europe. Well, because I came from Scotland, as later he was putting it so nicely, he liked to boast about such things – that people are from all over Poland and even Europe. (Interview 1)

The experience of study abroad was perceived by some employers as something prestigious and was interpreted through the lens of the cosmopolitism, which provided returnees with a symbolic advantage as they make the institution more international. In international corporations non-institutionalised forms of cultural capital also acted as leverage. For Krystian, who returned to 'find a Polish wife' (Interview 2), his foreign diploma in law, his language skills and his knowledge of the international context helped him not only in finding a job but enabled him to consciously choose the nature and content of his future employment:

> But I just came back with the idea not to work a lot, because I worked a lot [in England]. (…) And I thought I would be really chilled when it came to my future job. You know such a calm job in a corporation, it's cool. I also get along with people quite well so I'm good at it. A corporation is OK, I can handle it really well, and that's it and here I am. I first got to the complaints department and of course they really liked that I had been in England, that I knew the language and local customs.

Returnees' social capital was also significant when searching for an adequate job. However, here, the ties established during their migration appeared not to be as relevant as the primary links with family. Thus the successful translation of social capital into employment required emotional work and the maintenance of transnational relations with significant others. For example, once Tomek's wife became pregnant she wanted to return to Poland and Tomek – although he was very pleased with his job in the UK as a truck driver – went back with her. He used his family ties and, because of his experience of working abroad, it did not take him long to find employment. This is how he remembers his first job interview after returning to Poland:

> A friend of my father's gave me the tip-off that there would be vacancies in a certain company and that I should try there. And I wrote my CV, in half an hour, it was terrible… I went there and they already had two piles with those resumés – one for those who were turned down and one for those to ask who sent you. So he looks at me… and the drivers there knew my father so I had it a lot easier, so to say. ((Tomek imitates the interviewer)) 'You are the son of this man, it's good… you were on the [British] island, you'll get along well in English, you won't have a problem somewhere abroad'. Well, that is how it started, because it was just my luck. (Interview 3)

The effortless transition between British and Polish labour markets depends on many factors. Nevertheless, possession of the sought-after skills appeared to be crucial in securing employment after return which, in turn, leads to the maintenance of a coherent career model. This model consists of a sequence of jobs that transcend the national borders yet are still related to each other in terms of the tasks and skills required or that are performed in the same sector of the economy. Moreover, the coherent careers are in line with migrants' expectations and typically they are situated in the relatively stable and well-paid segments of the labour market.

Importantly, this type of the transition is also effortless from the perspective of the state, which took a *laissez-faire* stance on returnees' integration. In the narratives of migrants who easily found satisfactory work on their return, the successful integration was perceived as a result of their personal merits, sometimes combined with a bit of luck. In the collected accounts the state institutions and policies played no role.

However, the withdrawal of the state strengthened effectively the disintegration of some other returnees, since the valuation and successful deployment of the different capitals possessed by them is largely limited by structural circumstances and the specificity of certain occupations, as will be shown in the next sections.

6.6.2   The Unforseen Transition

Characteristic for the unforseen type of transition is a career course other than that initially expected by the returnees. Despite their specific plans and ideas regarding a professional career in Poland, returnees encountered difficulties and eventually found employment – though not what they were expecting and in worse conditions than they had initially envisioned. Many migrants returned with the hope of professional advancement, which was supposed not only to compensate for their lower earnings – compared to those accessible to them in the UK – but also to be a sign of adult life. In terms of the sequence of events, migrants first returned and only later started looking for employment.

In the initial period after their return, migrants' accumulated savings also enabled them to be more picky regarding employment, as Anna, a 24-year-old waitress with a BA who was aiming for a managerial position, recalled:

> Well, they called me, I don't think they liked it very much that I had some conditions, that I negotiated. I should beg them and kiss them and I don't know … to get this job, and … and finally I just said that the holidays had ended. (Interview 4)

Despite their higher ambitions and search for a job commensurate with their formal qualifications, some returnees could not find satisfactory employment. They explained that this was due to the extremely high competition and to job requirements which were impossible to meet. Women pointed also at gender discrimination, as Anna goes on to say:

> I was supposed to be the deputy manager of a children's centre – you know, at these large, covered playgrounds. I even reached the second round of the recruitment but, unfortunately, in my opinion my fault was that I am 26 years old, so I will get pregnant right away, I will certainly give birth to four children and I won't work or something like that (ironically).

Certainly, the age is a reason, that I am a woman is a reason. So they didn't call me and they still aren't calling.

Moreover, according to some narratives, the work experience from abroad was perceived either negatively as the returnees were deemed to now have higher financial demands, or at least irrelevant. As explained by Zofia, 31, a female quality controller holding an MSc:

You think it's going to be fantastic and how it [the labour experience from abroad] will open all doors for you, will break all ceilings. Well, it's not true because, in most places, they treat you as if you're just starting from scratch. It's as if, you know, 'You've been working somewhere abroad for a long time, but we don't care about it, it's different here', you know, that's how it works. (Interview 5)

Eventually, facing shrinking savings and unexpected expenditure, these returnees started searching for any job, lowering their expectations. This time, the work experience gained abroad – usually in services in the UK – appeared to be helpful in finding employment analogous in terms of job content and usually in catering or the hospitality sector. As explained by Krzysztof (29, M, hotel receptionist/student), 'It is true that maybe this experience abroad makes them choose your CV from the pile of other resumés, isn't it?' (Interview 6). Their new positions were characterised by the high work insecurity, a feature which they were already familiar with in the UK. This time, however, the unstable jobs were not compensated for by higher earnings, which often led to more general frustration, as was the case for 26-year-old freelance copywriter Maja (who has a degree):

So now it's OK, even though, after return to Poland, I lost hope. I was quite depressed since I didn't want to be a waitress. I knew that my references from England would certainly give me work in Poland, because I used to work there [in England] for Hilton and Marriott. (…) So they employed me very willingly and I must admit that, when I was looking for a job in Poland – between my fourth and fifth year of study – I finally decided to work in a hotel. I only chose where they pay better and where is closer to a place where I lived. (Interview 11)

In this way some returning migrants have fallen into the experience trap, which means the impossibility of obtaining the employment they wanted and being channelled instead, by the precarious work experience from abroad, into the sectors of the economy which the returnees wanted to leave behind. This process is particularly evident among those whose return was motivated by reasons not directly related to work – for instance, family reunion or breaking up with a partner in the UK. On the other hand the 'experience trap' might also turn into an 'experience path' – a situation whereby a low-skilled job, accepted unexpectedly and incompatible with the person's qualifications, turns into a passion developed back in Poland (cf. Grabowska 2016b).

Other aspects of the unforeseen transition underlined in the narratives are the insufficiency of social ties and the unexpected hostility of the state institutions, reflected for example by the attitude of civil servants. As a result of a stay abroad returnees redefine their perception of normality in the various areas of social life, including the functioning of the state and its institutions (Karolak 2016). Usually returnees have higher than before migration expectations towards the transparency of the state institutions, what ends with the 'harsh collision with reality', as described by Maja. Another interviewee, Kasia (27, F, a freelance musician with a BA) compares her experiences from Scotland and Poland:

> You know what, [in Poland] it's not really about the employers. I'm a freelancer and I create a job for myself. So, it's more about the civil servants, I'm talking more about the civil servants who you can't reach if you don't know right people. And even if you get in, you have to 'market yourself' and you have to lie. (…) Scotland has changed me a lot. It created my vision of the world, tolerance, openness and gave me access, you know, to the support… to the whole social system, to all these benefits, the education system, subsidies for education. It was easy to communicate with police or social welfare authorities, well… The social welfare system, the social system in general, the system of society is a paradise in comparison with Poland. It is so easy to find oneself in it and…. and to feel part of it. (Interview 7)

Kasia's self-confidence and expectations regarding life in Poland have clashed with the reality. Although one cannot judge to what extent her skills fit labour market demand, it is undeniable that she feels disintegrated, mainly due to her weak social contacts, lack of credentials as well as lack of sufficient assistance of the state. Knowing 'the right people' appears to returnees to be crucial in a successful search for work in Poland. Moreover, many of them complain about the passivity and even hostility of the state institutions, which were supposed to support them. It needs to be noticed that the interviewees do not claim that they were discriminated because they were returning migrants, they rather have realised that the institutions could operate differently, what in some cases contributed to the 'feeling of being unwanted in Poland' and enhanced the disintegration process, as described in the next section.

6.6.3   The Failed Transition

The third type of transition refers to a failed one. It indicates a situation in which the returnee, despite attempts to find employment in Poland, eventually leaves the labour market and either decides to migrate yet again or becomes economically inactive. There is no one single reason for a failed transition since its generative mechanisms are very complex and include both structural and agential powers.

To better understand the difficulties faced by returnees, let us analyse in depth the case of Zofia, whom we met above, a 31-year-old woman from a town of 40,000 inhabitants. After graduating she made use of contacts in Wales and started working in a meat-processing plant. She was employed in accordance with her education as a quality controller; however, after 3 months she lost her job and the plant closed in the wake of the financial crisis. She found another job, also consistent with her education and experience, but needed to move 300 kilometres away. She felt isolated and concentrated mainly on her work, but she did not feel accepted by her colleagues. Finally, after two and half years spend abroad, Zofia stated:

> I returned to Poland and decided to do this because it was supposed to be good, it was supposed to be so, uh… colourful and in general the work was supposed to be there, and it was supposed to be 'oh' and 'ah'. Because Europe is in crisis, but in Poland, nothing happens, supposedly nothing happens. (Interview 5)

In terms of human capital, Zofia was well prepared to return. She did not experience skills mismatch, she had learned the technical language and gathered relevant experience in three different workplaces. Yet, she could not find a job that would satisfy her. Because she returned to her hometown, where there were few job opportunities, she considered moving to a bigger city. However, Zofia realised that the relationship between the wages offered and living costs, especially rent, were unacceptable:

> The closest big city is 80 kilometres away, so to commute every day to work in which the earnings were so great (ironically) that the costs of commuting or cost of renting an apartment … well, it was pointless. It was better to stay at home, really, and do nothing, because [working would be] doing something for nothing, since anyway you need to spend everything to, so to speak, survive, so you will end up with nothing. (Interview 5)

After a while she found a paid internship programme which guaranteed free accommodation. However, the programme was unexpectedly terminated and she needed to start looking for a job again. The following, longer excerpt from the interview with Zofia illustrates her hesitations and reflexive attempts to overcome the structural constraints:

> And then it turned out again that you had to search for something, look for something, so I started looking for something and my sister said that maybe I would like to come to Warsaw and just live there. I thought about it, I admit frankly, that I thought about it, but… again the vision of moving, and then, I don't know what… It just wasn't fun for me. (…) but it was not only the vision of moving that was at stake. It was also about how old I was then – 27? And I thought, OK, well, I would go to my sister, I would live with her, I would look for a job, but she has a husband, she has a child, I will find a job and then what? So will I live with her for the rest of my life? Well, while staying at my parents' home there was no other solution than to commute and still live with them. Because if you earn, I don't know, 1,500 *zlotys* gross ((*ca. 350 Euros*)), it is quite hard to save anything, it's hard to do anything about it at all. (…) but at some point you just want to become independent, you know… And especially since I was always … like I was always curious about the world. I wanted to be such a free spirit, independent… and I already was independent before, because I lived alone and I managed it very well and so coming back to my parents was a bit like a backward step. Apart from the fact that they are really great people and … it's well known that nobody wants to live with their parents for the rest of their lives, no matter how wonderful they are. (…) So I started thinking about going abroad again, but I knew I didn't want to go back to Wales. (Interview 5)

Zofia's narration reveals several important aspects. First, although after return she did not have any relevant institutional support, she was not left alone with her problems in the labour market. Even with the anticipated low wages, she could count on help from her parents and sister. For precarious young workers in Poland, the support of the family often replaces that from the ineffective welfare state and became a common way of coping with the uncertainties of life (Karolak and Mrozowicki 2017). Moving back in with parents was a common practice among young returnees – nine of our interviewees had lived with their parents at one time or another after return. However, only those whose parents lived in major Polish cities with more job opportunities could take advantage of it. In the smaller towns, the need for independence from parents, in combination with the impossibility of paying all living costs from the offered wage, often leads to tensions and, in the end, re-emigration, perceived by young people as the only reasonable solution.

As noted by Cassarino (2004, p. 271), the situation of return migrants (also in the labour market) depends on 'the extent to which they have provided for the preparation of their return'. Preparation requires time, resources and willingness and ends in a certain level of readiness to return which, in turn, influences returnees' employment prospects. It is however also necessary to examine the structural situation in the country to which one returns. In Poland, structural constraints (the precarious work offered to young Poles, the high cost of city living, the lack of cheap and efficient public transport and exploitation during internships), together with workings of institutions confronted with returnees' expectations co-shaped by their previous experiences abroad, make some of them feel unwanted in and by their country of origin. It is well ilustrated in the narration of Agnieszka, a 26 years old cartographer, who after return to Poland opened with her husband a family busines, but after 2 years re-emigrated to the UK:

> It was killing us, because we realised in what country we were living. We are two well-educated persons and we returned here [to Poland] from abroad with money. We bought a flat – a new one. We spent here a ton of money earned in another country, we established a company, the company was working, we paid taxes, we both wanted to work in this company, we want to have a child, supposedly there was a need for children in Poland and supposedly the pro-family policy should work. But it turned out, that on each of these paths … in each of these sphere the state instead of encouraging us in any way… instead of saying in any way 'you are cool, you are young, ambitious, you want to have children and you even give work', we had an impression that they [the institutions] were bulling us in every possible situation and they were just trying to make it difficult for us ((laughs)). So we came to a very sad conclusions, that well, maybe the state doesn't want us to live here, it doesn't want us to earn money here, it doesn't want us to have children. (Interview 12)

Wheras the structural conditions make it impossible for some of returnees to successfully make use of their skills, also the returnees' subjective perception of 'being unwanted' by their country of origin contributes to their disintegration. It is not a deliberate mechanism; nevertheless, it *de facto* leads to the returnees' decision to leave Poland again (cf. White 2014). All in all, the facilitated intra-EU mobility and the individualised, transnational strategies employed by migrating workers effectively decrease the pressure on collective attempts to change the situation in their native land (cf. Meardi 2012).

6.6.4   The Postponed Transition

The final identified form of transition between the British and the Polish labour markets is the postponed transition. It refers to the situation in which a migrant who was economically active abroad but who, after return, did not even attempt to enter the Polish labour market and instead took a long break from employment. During this break from work, returnees typically re-entered or began academic education. Note that, of 11 cases in which return migrants undertake further education, six postponed their transition whereas five returnees studied and worked in Poland from the start.

This 'holiday from work' was possible because returnees' social income consisted of, on the one hand, their savings and, on the other, family support – typically accommodation but also financial transfer. As explained by Joanna who, at 36 and with an MA, was not working:

> I had savings and later… I lived with my mother, so we… my mom helped, I had an apartment for free, etc. so there was no problem with that. So I could have calmly sacrificed myself… I don't hide the fact that I just took a holiday. I really rested, relaxed and, as I say, I worked on myself. (Interview 8)

Joanna, unlike Zofia, did not find it difficult to live with her mother. On the contrary, she perceived it as her duty to help her mother in a painful moment of divorce. Nevertheless, in other cases young returnees found themselves in an ambivalent situation, on the one hand being closer to the loving family, on the other suffering from the loss of economic independence, as put by Eryka, a 28-year-old female plant worker in Czechia who has an MA:

> Interviewer: How did it happen that you decided to return and go to college?
> Eryka: I mean, firstly, I missed my family; secondly, as I say … my dad said that he won't keep a sponger at his home, so I have to go back to Poland and start studying. As long as my parents live and have the money, they'll educate me. (…) I was certainly happy that I came back, yes, especially to my mother, because I'm very close to her. I'm the youngest one. It certainly was… it was hard that I didn't have my money, yes, there was no money, so it wasn't like there [in the UK], when there was a payout every week, so every week you could go shopping. There was no such thing in Poland, it was also hard to find a job. (Interview 9)

Although inconvenient, returnees accepted this economic support, treating it as a temporary measure enabling them to improve their education, which eventually was supposed to help them to find employment in a primary segment of the labour market. From this perspective, the biographical experience of migration appears as trial adulthood, during which young people, within a biographical action scheme, experienced the mundane reality of life with jobs, taxes, incurrences as well as rented and usually shared apartments, but also could enjoy personal and economic freedom (cf. King et al. 2016). For them, return to Poland meant giving up all this and equalled a return to institutional patterns of expectation.

The question which arises is what happens to these returning migrants once they finish higher education. Do they remain on the occupational path and act like those graduates who have never migrated, or does the experience of life and work abroad still play a role in their decisions? To answer it exhaustively would require separate research focused on this particular type of transition; however a look at the six identified cases of postponed transition gives us a few hints already. After graduating, three of the participants migrated again, one to work in Czechia and commuting every day from Poland, the two others remaining in Poland, although they do not rule out the possibility of moving abroad. Asked why she decided to leave Poland after obtaining a brilliant BA degree from Jagiellonian University, Weronika (25, a tourist guide) answers:

Well, my reason was probably… it was financial, wasn't it? When we were in Cracow I studied, I worked. My boyfriend also studied in absentia and had a good position at work. I also had a good job. We earned good money, well, maybe normal. But in fact, with renting a flat, with travelling home, for example, every three months, etc., it wasn't enough to live on, was it? And it wasn't enough to start saving money for some future purposes, for some longer holidays, etc. So let's say that, by doing less here, whether in England or Scotland, we are earning more money and actually we can put this money aside for the future and we can visit more and so on… Well, I think that was my reason. (Interview 10)

For Weronika and her boyfriend, the re-migration was to enable them to achieve greater economic stability. From their perspective, they already had relatively good jobs in Poland but still felt that they could only live day-to-day, so migration appeared as an opportunity to make future plans. In this type of transition the role of the state and its institutions remained ambivalent. On the one hand the state gave those young returnees the opportunity to study for free. On the other hand, similarly to other types of transition, it did not provide any significant support, especially at the moment of transition from the school to work. This led to the situation in which the individual labour migration started replacing the role of the malfunctioning labour market institutions.

6.7   Conclusions

This chapter has discussed the labour market transitions and experiences of Polish migrants returning from the United Kingdom through the conceptual lens of (dis) integration. Analysis of the life stories of these mobile EU citizens revealed the heterogeneity of their career patterns. Contrary to the dominant discourse about spatial mobility being a career boost, supposedly contributing to upward mobility in society, return migration in many cases was linked with the fragmentation of careers and difficulties on the labour market.

After abandoning the rigid conceptual division between labour market integration and exclusion and employing the concept of the multi-segmented labour market, it became apparent that, although returnees usually found employment once back in Poland – and thus could be formally perceived as integrated in the labour market – the quality of their employment often deviated from their expectations and qualifications. Returning migrants often found themselves in vulnerable and precarious occupational positions, which highlights the fact that neither formal belonging nor experience from abroad can guarantee successful integration, the latter being always intertwined with certain processes of disintegration. The feeling of permanent temporariness while abroad as well as the feeling of 'being unwanted' and the 'experience trap' after return were recognised as relevant mechanisms contributing to the migrants' disintegration in Poland. Structural factors also turned out to be important, as they effectively hampered returnees' attempts to get the job they wanted. Note, however, that the structural constraints did not concern returnees as such but, rather, certain socio-economic groups to which the returnees belonged (sometimes simultaneously), be they youth, women or residents of small towns. What turned out to be specific for returnees, was their perception of the Polish state and its institutions as rather passive or in some cases even hostile. Although there is no evidence that such attitudes were aimed particularly against returning migrants it discouraged them from staying in Poland.

Nevertheless, there was a group of returnees who, after return, not only maintained their occupational status but also managed to climb the career ladder. They were able to actively manage, accumulate and exchange resources (most of all cultural and social capital) across borders, thus gaining an advantage on the Polish labour market. Importantly, analysis of their entire life stories revealed that the process of capital accumulation had already started before their migration, so they entered the UK with a decent knowledge of English and skills that were in demand. Moreover, the return of this group was usually directly related to work and was preceded by a search for employment from abroad.

The general conclusion which can be drawn from this chapter is that, in order to better understand the return migrants' labour market transitions, one should not consider the migration episode as an exclusive cause of returnees' positions in the labour market. Instead, the migration episode should be perceived as a catalyst or inhibitor of certain biographical trajectories deriving from the intersection of migrants' origins, gender, age, class, education as well as structural settings and politics of (dis)integration.

Annex 1: Interviewees' Characteristics

Interview	Age	Gender	Job or, if return migrating, last job before leaving	Education	Country of residence
1	25	Female	NGO employee	Tertiary (MA)	UK
2	28	Male	Lawyer	Tertiary (MA)	Poland
3	30	Male	Truck driver	Secondary technical	UK
4	25	Female	Waitress	Tertiary (BA)	Poland
5	31	Female	Quality controller	Tertiary (MSc)	UK
6	29	Male	Hotel receptionist/student	Tertiary (BA)	Poland
7	29	Female	Freelance musician	Tertiary (BA)	Poland
8	36	Female	Economically inactive	Tertiary (MA)	Poland
9	28	Female	Plant worker in Czechia	Tertiary (MA)	Poland
10	25	Female	Tourist guide	Tertiary (MA)	UK
11	26	Female	Freelance copywriter	Tertiary (MA)	Poland
12	26	Female	Cartographer	Tertiary (BA)	UK

References

Ager, A., & Strang, A. (2008). Understanding integration: A conceptual framework. *Journal of Refugee Studies, 21*(2), 166–191.

Anacka, M., & Fihel, A. (2013). Charakterystyka migrantów powracających do polski oraz ich aktywność zawodowa na rodzimym rynku pracy. *Studia Migracyjne – Przegląd Polonijny, 4*, 57–71.

Bauman, Z. (2000). *Liquid modernity*. Cambridge: Polity Press.

Cassarino, J.-P. (2004). Theorising return migration: The conceptual approach to return migrants revisited. *International Journal on Multicultural Societies, 6*(2), 253–279.

Collyer, M., Hinger, S., & Schweitzer, R. (2020). Politics of (dis)integration – An introduction. In S. Hinger & R. Schweitzer (Eds.), *Politics of (dis)integration* (pp. 1–18). Cham: Springer VS.

Drinkwater, S., & Garapich, M. P. (2013). *Migration plans and strategies of recent polish migrants to England and Wales: Do they have any and how do they change?* (Norface Discussion Paper Series No. 2013–23). London: NORFACE.

Durkheim, E. (1997 [1893]). *Division of labour in society*. New York: Free Press.

Eade, J., Drinkwater, S., & Garapich, M. P. (2007). *Class and ethnicity: Polish migrant workers in London* (Full research report, RES-000-22-1294). Swindon: ESRC.

Engbersen, G., & Snel, E. (2013). Dynamic and fluid patterns of post-accession migration flows. In B. Glorius, I. Grabowska-Lusińska, & A. Kuvik (Eds.), *Mobility in transition. Migration patterns after EU enlargement* (pp. 21–40). Amsterdam: Amsterdam University Press.

Engbersen, G., Snel, E., & De Boom, J. (2010). "A Van full of poles": Liquid migration from central and Eastern Europe. In R. Black, G. Engbersen, M. Okólski, & C. Pantîru (Eds.), *A continent moving west?: EU Enlargement and labour migration from central and Eastern Europe* (pp. 115–140). Amsterdam University Press.

Engbersen, G., Leerkes, A., Grabowska-Lusinska, I., Snel, E., & Burgers, J. (2013). On the differential attachments of migrants from Central and Eastern Europe: A typology of labour migration. *Journal of Ethnic and Migration Studies, 39*(6), 959–981.

Faist, T. (2013). The mobility turn: A new paradigm for the social sciences? *Ethnic and Racial Studies, 36*(11), 1637–1646.

Fangen, K., Johansson, T., & Hammarén, N. (2011). *Young migrants: Exclusion and belonging in Europe*. Basingstoke: Palgrave Macmillan.

Favell, A. (2008). The new face of east–west migration in Europe. *Journal of Ethnic and Migration Studies, 34*(5), 701–716.

Foucault, M. (2008). *The birth of biopolitics: Lectures at the Collège de France, 1978–79*. Basingstoke: Palgrave Macmillan.

Glaser, B., & Strauss, A. (1967). *The discovery of grounded theory: Strategies for qualitative research*. Chicago: Aldine.

Grabowska, I. (2016a). The transition from education to employment abroad: The experiences of young people from Poland. *Europe-Asia Studies, 68*(8), 1421–1440.

Grabowska, I. (2016b). *Movers and stayers: Social mobility, migration and skills*. Frankfurt am Main: Peter Lang.

GUS. (2013). *Migracje zagraniczne ludności. Narodowy Spis Powszechny Ludności i Mieszkań 2011*. Warsaw: National Population and Housing Census 2011.

GUS. (2018). *Informacja o rozmiarach i kierunkack czasowej emigracji z Polski w latach 2004–2017*. Warsaw: Statistics Poland.

Hinger, S. (2020). Integration through disintegration? The distinction between deserving and undeserving refugees in national and local integration policies in Germany. In S. Hinger & R. Schweitzer (Eds.), *Politics of (dis)integration* (pp. 19–39). Cham: Springer VS.

Kaczmarczyk, P., & Lesińska, M. (2012). Return migration, state policy and integration of return-ees. In M. L. Butterworth (Ed.), *Welcome home? Challenges and chances of return migration* (pp. 29–37). Washington, DC: Transatlantic Forum on Migration and Integration.

Karolak, M. (2016). From potential to actual social remittances? Exploring how Polish return migrants cope with difficult employment conditions. *Central and Eastern European Migration Review, 5*(2), 21–39.

Karolak, M., & Mrozowicki, A. (2017). Between normalisation and resistance. Life strategies of young precarious workers. *Warsaw Forum of Economic Sociology, 1*(15), 7–32.

Kaźmierska, K., Piotrowski, A., & Waniek, K. (2011). Biographical consequences of working abroad in the context of European mental space construction. *The Sociological Review, 60*(1), 139–158.

King, R., Lulle, A., Morosanu, L., & Williams, A. (2016). *International youth mobility and life transitions in Europe: Questions, definitions, typologies and theoretical approaches* (Working Paper No. 86). Brighton: University of Sussex, Sussex Centre for Migration Research.

Lesińska, M. (2013). The dilemmas of policy towards return migration. The case of Poland after the EU accession. *Central and Eastern European Migration Review, 2*(1), 77–90.

Levitas, R. (2005). *The inclusive society? Social exclusion and new labour.* Basingstoke: Palgrave Macmillan.

Loveridge, R., & Mok, A. (1979). *Theories of labour market segmentation: A critique.* The Hague: M. Nijhoff.

Meardi, G. (2012). *Social failures of EU enlargement: A case of workers voting with their feet.* London: Routledge.

Mezzadra, S., & Neilson, B. (2013). *Border as method, or the multiplication of labor.* Durham/London: Duke University Press.

Mrozowicki, A. (2011). *Coping with social change: Life strategies of workers in Poland's new capitalism.* Leuven: University Press Leuven.

Okólski, M. (2001). Incomplete migration: A new form of mobility in Central and Eastern Europe. The case of Polish and Ukrainian migrants. In C. Wallace & D. Stola (Eds.), *Patterns of migration in Central Europe* (pp. 105–128). Basingstoke: Palgrave.

Polkowski, R. (2017). Normality unpacked: Migration, ethnicity and local structure of feeling among Polish migrant workers in Northern Ireland with a comparative perspective on Scotland. *Journal of Ethnic and Migration Studies, 43*(15), 2519–2535.

Potter, J. (2015). *Crisis at work: Identity and the end of career.* Basingstoke: Palgrave Macmillan.

Sahraoui, N., Polkowski, R., & Karolak, M. (2018). Migration policies and their underlying threats: Going beyond the polarization of EU versus non-EU migration policies. In O. Fedyuk & P. Stewart (Eds.), *Inclusion and exclusion in Europe: Migration, work and employment perspectives* (pp. 57–78). Colchester: ECPR Press.

Samuk, Ş. (2020). Can integration be temporary? The (dis)integration of temporary migrant workers in Canada and the UK. In S. Hinger & R. Schweitzer (Eds.), *Politics of (dis)integration* (pp. 61–79). Cham: Springer VS.

Schütze, F. (2016). Biography analysis on the empirical base of autobiographical narratives: How to analyse autobiographical narrative interviews. In F. Schütze, W. Fiedler, & H. Krüger (Eds.), *Sozialwissenschaftliche Prozessanalyse: Grundlagen der qualitativen Sozialforschung* (pp. 75–116). Opladen/Berlin/Toronto: Verlag Barbara Budrich.

Sennett, R. (1998). *The corrosion of character: The personal consequences of work in the new capitalism.* New York/London: W. W. Norton.

Sinatti, G. (2015). Return migration as a win-win-win scenario? Visions of return among Senegalese migrants, the state of origin and receiving countries. *Ethnic and Racial Studies, 38*(2), 275–291.

Standing, G. (2011). *The precariat: The new dangerous class.* London: Bloomsbury Academic.

Urry, J. (2000). *Sociology beyond societies: Mobilities for the twenty-first century*. London/New York: Routledge.

White, A. (2014). Polish return and double return migration. *Europe-Asia Studies, 66*(1), 25–49.

Wills, J., Datta, K., Evans, Y., Herbert, J., May, J., & McIlwaine, C. (2010). *Global cities at work: New migrant divisions of labour*. New York: Pluto Press.

Chapter 7
How Inclusive Institutions Enforce Exclusive Immigration Rules: Mainstream Public Service Provision and the Implementation of a Hostile Environment for Irregular Migrants Living in Britain

Reinhard Schweitzer

7.1 Introduction

Migrant irregularity is not a new phenomenon but has long characterised the mobility or residence of many people coming to Europe in search of better employment opportunities or after fleeing violence and persecution elsewhere (Black 2003). What changed are the regulatory measures through which the governments of receiving states try to undermine irregular migration and residence. Control and surveillance have not only been intensified but also gradually extended from the external boundaries to the interior of the state and society (Balibar 1998). In order to effectively constrain irregular migrants'[1] opportunities for participation and their access to various rights and services, immigration law and policy penetrate ever more spheres of everyday life and social interaction (Broeders and Engbersen 2007; Cvajner and Sciortino 2010; Garcés-Mascareñas 2015; Schweitzer 2018a; Spencer and Hughes 2015; Van der Leun 2006). This policy trend towards a selective prevention of integration is particularly visible in the UK, where the government officially aims to 'create here in Britain a really hostile environment for illegal migration' (Kirkup and Winnett 2012).

In this chapter I am particularly interested in the implementation of such policies, which hinges on the capacity and willingness of a growing number and variety of actors to effectively exclude certain categories of foreigner (Guiraudon and Lahav 2000; Jordan et al. 2003). In everyday practice, this often entails the formal

---

[1] I use the terms 'irregular migrants' and 'migrants in irregular situations' interchangeably; both refer to foreigners who currently lack a formal right of residence in the country where they live.

R. Schweitzer (✉)
University of Vienna, Vienna, Austria
e-mail: reinhard.schweitzer@univie.ac.at

S. Hinger, R. Schweitzer (eds.), *Politics of (Dis)Integration*,
IMISCOE Research Series, https://doi.org/10.1007/978-3-030-25089-8_7

121

or informal consolidation of an external logic that demands the exclusion of a person – *qua* irregular immigrant – with various internal logics that require his or her (partial) inclusion – as a local resident, worker, patient, student, service recipient and so on. Much of this constant renegotiation of irregular migrants' inclusion and exclusion takes place within the institutions of the liberal welfare state (Bommes and Geddes 2000), which face and often struggle to meet the most fundamental needs and legitimate claims of irregular and regular residents.

Protecting the welfare state against proclaimed 'health tourists' and 'benefit-scrounging foreigners' has become a routine justification for restrictive policies towards actual or potential newcomers. Their exclusion is thereby argued to be necessary in order to ensure adequate service delivery for the deserving, which is also critically discussed by Hinger (2020) in this volume. At the same time, public welfare is also 'a major factor driving the incorporation of immigrants [...] because it follows a logic of inclusion: failure to grant social rights to any group of residents leads to social divisions, and can undermine the rights of the majority' (Castles 2004, p. 216). The provision of mainstream public services to irregular migrants thus involves the intertwining of integration and disintegration policies, and its analysis highlights the fact that the very concept of 'integration' comprises two empirically different but intrinsically related aspects: not only the 'integration' of a particular individual or group *into* society but also the 'integration' (or cohesion) *of* that same society (Treibel 2015). What remains unacknowledged in most public, political and scholarly debates around integration is that both of these aspects ultimately hinge on the same connections and interactions between people and institutions, and thus cannot be regulated as if they were two entirely separate processes (Schweitzer 2017a). As argued in the introduction to this volume (Collyer et al. 2020), policies aimed at preventing the integration of certain individuals thus also contribute to the *dis*integration of society as a whole. One way of doing this is by undermining the inclusiveness of mainstream welfare provision.

Among the institutional and individual actors who participate in the everyday negotiation of irregular migrants' (dis)integration are *street-level bureaucrats* who work within public welfare systems (Lipsky 1980). As doctors, school administrators or welfare officers, they increasingly (have to) implement certain aspects of the immigration rules and are thereby 'often placed in the awkward position of triggering the law's force when they come face to face with an 'unlawful' person' (Park 2013, p. 12). At the same time, their individual agency and decisions must also be seen as structurally embedded; within not only a political environment that can encourage hostility towards certain groups but also the much more specific institutional contexts within which they work.

Drawing on key theoretical insights from organisation studies, this chapter looks at how various local institutions providing different kinds of mainstream public services in London have responded to the external demand for their participation in immigration control. One crucial component and apparent commonality within these organisational responses is the rather spontaneous emergence of specialised subdivisions that deal specifically with migrant irregularity. My analysis shows that it is through them, that the politics of (dis)integration becomes institutionalised within the British welfare system. On the one hand, this modification allows the organisation to more effectively fulfil its actual function for society by shielding its core professional staff from contradictory logics and demands (e.g. doctors from checking the passports of their patients). On the other hand, however, the structural adjustments have also helped to systematically undermine the necessary firewall between immigration enforcement and public service provision and rendered this overlap less visible to the general public and less exposed to internal and external resistance or contestation.

7.2   A 'Hostile Environment' for Just One Category of Residents?

Many Western states increasingly address the issue of irregular migration through policies of *internal control*, often by restricting the access of unlawful residents to employment, housing, healthcare or other services (Broeders and Engbersen 2007; Guiraudon and Lahav 2000; Lahav and Guiraudon 2006; Spencer and Hughes 2015; Squire 2011; Van der Leun 2006). Facing a growing permeability of its external borders, it is argued, the state 'raises a protective wall of legal and documentary requirements around the key institutions of the welfare state' (Broeders and Engbersen 2007, p. 1595). As a way to regain control and increase the effectiveness of these policies, governments thereby partly shift the burden of enforcing immigration regulations to a range of actors beyond the level of the nation-state and hitherto detached from its immigration regime. This includes not only employers and transport companies but also local authorities and mainstream welfare services. The British government's effort to create an 'environment' that will 'make it [...] more difficult for illegal immigrants to live in the UK' (Home Office 2013, p. 2) also critically depends on the participation of such actors. Concrete policy measures include an obligation for private landlords and certain National Health Service (NHS) staff to check the immigration status of their tenants and patients, a prohibition on banks opening accounts for irregular migrants and new powers to check driving licence applicants' immigration status and revoke the licences of those who have overstayed their visa. This criminalisation of ordinary interactions with unlawful residents generates uncertainty among public servants and furthers discrimination against non-European (–looking) immigrants and even citizens (MRN 2015; Spencer and Hughes 2015).

Walsh (2014, p. 242) has described this development as *deputisation*, which he generally defines as 'the activation and empowerment of certain individuals to participate in preventing and controlling legal transgressions'. He thereby distinguishes *deputisation* from *responsibilisation* – whereby such participation is encouraged but voluntary – and *autonomisation* – which happens spontaneously or even against the will of the authority. As I will show, some welfare workers are obliged or encouraged to base their actions or decisions regarding a client on the immigration status of the latter, while others are being specifically prevented or discouraged from doing so (which I will refer to as *shielding*).

In practice, only those actors who are not shielded from the logic of immigration control can be expected to exclude irregular migrants from a particular site or service. If the same actors are also required or encouraged to share their knowledge of someone's irregularity with the responsible state authority – in this case the Home Office (HO) – they effectively become part of the deportation regime. Such information sharing, whether systematic or sporadic, indicates the lack of a *firewall*, i.e. any mechanism or rule that prevents individuals or organisations from passing this kind of information to the immigration authorities, thereby effectively limiting the reach of internal immigration control (Carens 2013; FRA 2013; OHCHR 2014). Seen from a system-theoretical perspective, a firewall constitutes one way of ensuring the independent and thus effective performance of the various (other) subsystems which, together, make up a modern, functionally differentiated, society (Luhmann 1982, 1995; Walzer 1983).

An understanding of society as 'a plurality of specialized subsystems that have their own set of symbolic codes, leading values, operational programs and regulative means' (Cvajner and Sciortino 2010, p. 392; see also Sciortino 2000) thus helps the analysis of how immigration policies work (or not) within specific institutional spheres. It means taking into account the different organisational cultures and logics, shared norms, professional identities, values and codes of conduct that guide the actions and shape the interests of the people working in these societal subsystems, which are only recently becoming part of the immigration regime (Jordan et al 2003). It is thereby very suitable to identify the various challenges that arise where the logic of (internalised) immigration control – fundamentally based on the distinction between regular and irregular status – intersects with other logics, such as those according to which doctors treat their patients, social workers try to protect vulnerable clients against destitution, or universities select prospective students.

It has been shown that policies of internal control encounter both support and resistance on the part of other local residents, the wider public, specific interest groups and civil society organisations, as well as individual professionals, civil servants and local government officials (Broeders and Engbersen 2007; Ellermann 2006; Guiraudon and Lahav 2000; Van der Leun 2006). Coinciding *and* conflicting interests can even be present simultaneously within the same institution, and a lot depends on individual motivations and perceptions (Perna 2018). Particularly where rigorous exclusion would create significant costs or contradictions, however, migrant irregularity is often more or less routinely accommodated within existing organisational structures and institutional logics (Schweitzer 2018b). Conceptually but also empirically, this implies a certain level of recognition and incorporation of formally irregular migrants and can thus not only make visible but also further their claims for social membership (Chauvin and Garcés-Mascareñas 2014; Hellgren 2014; Schweitzer 2017b). The next section theorises the underlying negotiation processes in more detail to better understand the crucial role that local institutions and individual street-level bureaucrats (can) play within the broader politics of (dis) integration.

7.3 Public Sector Organisations and Street-Level Bureaucrats as Local Mediators of Competing Institutional Logics

The provision and allocation of public services in general and their extension to irregular migrants in particular, always involves a series of political decisions regarding the exact circumstances under which to offer, deny or require payment for particular services. These political decisions are then translated into legal frameworks and policies which, in turn, have to be implemented 'on the ground'. As argued by Boswell (2007, p. 83), neo-institutional theories make two crucial assumptions in relation to the role that liberal institutions (can) play for policy implementation – firstly, that they 'have sufficient independence from the political system and rival administrative agencies' and, secondly, that 'the actors within these institutions operate according to interests and norms that are at variance with those predominating politics or rival agencies'. As I will show, both assumptions are highly relevant for understanding the involvement of public welfare institutions in the implementation of immigration control or even enforcement.

Access to services depends not only on the more or less explicit laws and regulations that circumscribe formal eligibility but often also on a case-by-case assessment by individuals who either administer or provide them to the population. In trying to control immigration through these local actors, the government is exploiting the fact that their role often already involves some form of gate-keeping. As famously argued by Lipsky (1980, 1987), this requires a significant level of discretion on the part of street-level bureaucrats, who have to be able to deal with the irregularities that more or less routinely arise in their daily encounters with service users and often require customised solutions. According to him, it is thus their particular position within certain organisations – characterised by 'relatively high degrees of discretion and relative autonomy from organizational authority' – that 'regularly permits them to make policy' (Lipsky 1987, p. 121). While these micro-level decisions can have a significant impact on individual lives, they are difficult to control by state authorities.

This highlights the ambivalent relationship of street-level bureaucrats with the state (which employs them) and the local population (for whom they work). As bureaucrats, they have to adhere to a set of official rules, follow formal procedures and apply established criteria, all of which circumscribe their possible actions towards their clients. As professionals, they are 'expected to exercise discretionary judgement in their field [of expertise]' and to be able to deal with a broad range of individual cases and human circumstances (Lipsky 1987, p. 121). The balance between these two aspects of their job depends on their position within the organisation (as well as that of the organisation *vis-à-vis* other agencies) and whether their specific role mainly involves administrative or professionalised tasks. In modern bureaucracies, the various organisational roles are generally separated from the person who performs them, which 'has resulted in a capacity to constitute agency and identity in more segmented and piecemeal ways, according to the demands of distinct institutional realms' (Webb 2006, p. 34).

Lipsky (1987) has also shown that street-level bureaucrats tend to refuse to comply with rules which they perceive as contrary to their own professional or organisational role. A particularly strong professional status – like that of a doctor or teacher – and the absence or inefficiency of sanctioning mechanisms thereby make non-compliance even more likely. This not only enables bureaucrats to effectively deal with exceptional cases and irregular situations but also allows them to exercise political agency by contesting or circumventing the implementation of a particular policy or at least re-interpreting certain aspects of it. All this does not mean, however, that their decisions are taken in some sort of vacuum.

Another important insight stemming from organisation studies is that organisational actors and their actions are always embedded within certain (although sometimes multiple) *institutional logics* (Besharov and Smith 2013; Lindberg 2014; Meyer and Rowan 1977; Reay and Hinings 2009; Scott 2001). These provide 'a coherent set of organizing principles for a particular realm of social life' (Besharov and Smith 2013, p. 366) and underpin 'the belief systems and related practices that predominate in an organizational field' (Scott 2001, p. 139), such as healthcare or social work. While organisational action within any such field is normally guided by only one institutional logic, several other logics constantly tend to coexist, compete with and sometimes replace the dominant one as the guiding principle – a process that also helps to explain institutional change (Lindberg 2014; Scott et al. 2000). Besharov and Smith (2013, p. 365) have argued that the concrete 'implications of logic multiplicity depend on how logics are instantiated within organizations'.

What is particularly crucial to my analysis here is that organisations can actively reduce the risk of competing logics generating internal conflict through structural adjustments that either make compliance with a new set of rules more likely or non-compliance less visible. According to Besharov & Smith (2013, p. 376), this can be achieved 'by developing a cadre of organizational members who are less strongly attached to particular logics or by buffering members from the influence of those logics'. In contrast to this, Reay & Hinings (2009, p. 645) posit that 'actors guided by different logics may manage the rivalry by forming collaborations that maintain independence but support the accomplishment of mutual goals'.

On the one hand, both of these accounts recognise that, in order to have an actual effect on organisational practice, institutional logics have to be *enacted* by individual actors working within the organisation (Lindberg 2014). On the other, they reflect one of the central premises of neo-institutionalism, which posits that organisations constantly strive for legitimacy and, in order to be seen as legitimate by their environment, need to effectively fulfil their ascribed function (Meyer and Rowan 1977; Scott 2001). Some structural elements are thereby incorporated because of their resonance with certain *institutionalised myths* that reflect what their environment sees as proper functioning and successful performance, even if, in practice, they do not help or even hinder the efficient realisation of the central goals of the organisation (Meyer and Rowan 1977).

Under this premise it can be argued that, from the perspective of public service providers, the supposedly clear-cut and binary distinction between regular and irregular migrants represents such an institutionalised myth. It is incorporated into their organisational field not because it makes practical sense but because providing services to unlawful residents would undermine the sovereignty of the state or at least the efficiency of its immigration system. Where this logic requires irregular migrants to be denied access to a particular service, some members of the organisations that provide it will become responsible for exercising a form of immigration control and thereby enact a new institutional logic within these organisations. While probably seen as legitimate or even necessary by a majority of the population, this may, for various reasons, contradict service providers' own individual interests, professional ethics or the particular logic that dominates the institutional setting in which their actions and decisions are embedded. The underlying moral and political conflicts are thus not solved but merely delegated to the implementing agency, where they have to be managed through 'the actions of micro-level actors […] developing localized structures and systems that [enable] day-to-day work', as Reay & Hinings (2009, p. 630) have shown.

In the following section, I use these theoretical insights to explain a crucial aspect of how different organisations (namely hospitals, universities and local welfare departments) have responded to the increasing pressure to incorporate the exclusionary logic of immigration control into their own organisational structures and operations. The empirical data were collected between July 2014 and February 2015 as part of my PhD research in London, where I conducted a total of 46 semi-structured interviews with migrants in irregular situations, NGO practitioners and street-level bureaucrats working in organisations that provide public healthcare, education and social assistance to local residents. All interviews were audio-recorded, fully transcribed and anonymised, and then thematically coded using the software *NVivo*; details of those quoted here are provided at the end of the chapter.

7.4   Organisational Responses to Everyday Bordering Within Different Institutions

7.4.1   Everyday Bordering Within the Hospital

Since 2004, when the UK government introduced the *Overseas Visitors Hospital Charging Regulations*, all foreigners who are not 'ordinarily resident'[2] are categorised as 'Overseas Visitors' and as such, in principle, should be charged the full cost of any NHS hospital treatment they incur[3] (da Lomba 2011; DoH 2013a). However,

---

[2] A status not explicitly defined in law but conditional, among other things, on lawful residence.

[3] Until 2004 they were entitled to free treatment after 12 months of, even irregular, residence in the country. The general charging regulations do not apply to Accident & Emergency (A&E) services, nor to the diagnosis and treatment of certain communicable diseases.

the Department of Health (DoH) (2013b, p. 55) also makes very clear that, where treatments are considered 'urgent' or 'immediately necessary', they cannot 'be delayed or withheld pending payment', which gives significant weight to the medical assessment of the patient's condition. The discretion in taking these decisions comes with the very nature of the medical profession and unavoidably plays a significant role within every healthcare system. In the British case, however, where the treatment of 'Overseas Visitors' is officially defined as 'urgent' if it 'cannot wait until the person can be reasonably expected to return home' (DoH 2013a, p. 43), clinicians are also required to take into consideration the likelihood and possible duration of a patient's stay in the country (da Lomba 2011). Both directly depend on immigration status and are particularly difficult to assess in the case of irregular migrants, who are estimated to represent more than 60 per cent of the total 'chargeable population'[4] (DoH 2012, 2013a).

Upon registration with a family doctor – to which they are legally entitled – 'Overseas Visitors' hold exactly the same NHS card as any other NHS patient. This lack of specification of the holder's entitlement beyond primary and emergency care is a remainder of the system's universalistic origins and makes it difficult for hospitals to comply with their legal obligation 'to determine whether the Charging Regulations apply to any overseas visitor they treat' (DoH 2013a, p. 16) and recover the costs of any services they have delivered. At the hospital level, this discrepancy has created the need for a particular kind of administrative personnel – that is, a new organisational role – responsible for identifying who is chargeable. It is not surprising that, from the perspective of these so-called *Overseas Visitors Managers* (OVMs), one of the major problems of the NHS is that people too easily slip through the system, as the head of the responsible department at a medium-sized London hospital, explained to me:

> the reason why they can slip through the system [...] is that anybody can obtain a national health number. [...] All they do, actually, is go to a GP, ask the GP to register them, and the GP therefore registers them and gives them an NHS number (Interview 2).

This reflects what according to one of the GPs I interviewed has become a common view within the NHS – that GP registration is seen 'as an underground route to secondary care' (Interview 3). But the OVM also acknowledged that even though 'by law, we have to check every new patient that comes into the hospital, [...] that is physically impossible, and it would cost an absolute fortune' (Interview 2), which is why, in practice, her department focuses mainly on the areas of women's health and orthopaedic care. Asked for the reasons behind this selection, she explained that it was 'principally because a lot of people come over here to give birth, and orthopaedic because it is quite an expensive area'; however, she also mentioned that 'we also have good staff who we could encourage to participate in those sections' (Interview 2). The exact meaning of this comment became clear to me when she later received

---

[4]The remaining 40 per cent are temporary visitors who notably include British citizens residing in another country.

a phone call from the hospital's maternity ward notifying her about the arrival of a new patient, after which she explained to me:

> In that case I would be very, very surprised if that person is entitled to NHS care, so we will go up to see her; we will ask her to see her documentation. I mean, she is on the labour ward, so I don't think that's the right time to ask, personally, so I will probably leave that and go after she has given birth. [...] It could be that she has got Leave to Remain. It may have been that she just came to see her family and just came down... you know, we cannot guarantee that. But this case we would class as suspicious (Interview 2).

Her account is a good example of how 'NHS staff often have to make assumptions about government [immigration] policy in their work', as Wind-Cowie and Wood (2014, p. 55) have noted; however, it also highlights the level of direct implication of her role in the actual enforcement of this policy, as well as the very subtle kind of discretion (as to who, when and how to check) that she employs in carrying out this function. Asked what happens in case a patient is unable to prove their entitlement or to produce a valid passport, my interviewee replied that

> [t]hey *have to* produce their passport, which [...] will have a stamp in it, so that will show whether that person is entitled or not. From there, once we have identified her, we will raise an invoice. If she doesn't pay... again, we have to treat this patient but, if she doesn't pay then, in three months' time, that invoice will be going over to... we will inform the DoH [...] who then filter it and would let the HO know (Interview 2).

She thereby refers to a formal mechanism that very explicitly institutionalises the overlap between the interest of the hospital (in recovering the costs) and that of the immigration authority (in controlling immigration), by allowing

> NHS bodies [... to] share non-medical information with the Home Office, via the Department of Health, on those with a debt of £1,000 or more once that debt has been outstanding for three months, with a view to better collect debts owed. The Home Office can then use that information to deny any future immigration application to enter or remain in the UK that the person with the debt might make (DoH 2013a, p. 63).

Notably, this information exchange does not require patients' explicit consent although they 'should' be made 'aware of the potential immigration consequences of not paying' (*ibid.*) which, for Wind-Cowie and Wood (2014, p. 13) 'poses an enormous ethical challenge for healthcare professionals and the NHS as a whole'. While the OVM I interviewed clearly perceived her role within the hospital and the NHS as one of control, she did not readily acknowledge that what she is controlling is immigration. Instead, when I asked her how she felt about 'quasi' acting as an immigration officer, her answer was ambiguous:

> I don't think we do. I mean, if you were an immigration officer you would be informing immigration [authorities], you would be informing the borders agency. And we will work with the borders agency, and we will let the... DoH know of patients who owe us money. Now, it's the DoH that then would possibly pass that information to the HO, and it would then put it on a system so that perhaps these people... but they are not traced here! It's normally the people who try to get back [into the UK] whom we are stopping. [...] So personally, I don't think that we work as an immigration officer... maybe wrongly, perhaps we do (Interview 2).

She clearly emphasises that she and her team are not targeting immigration offenders but patients who owe the hospital money. At the same time, however, she is aware that her role – together with the mechanism of letting the HO know – plays a decisive part in the government's broader efforts to limit irregular residence – and unwanted immigration more generally:

> I believe that that is a deterrent and I think what it is doing is stopping a lot of people getting their Leave to Remain. What we are also finding is that some of the patients that have gone home, wherever that might be… the Caribbean, Africa, Asia… you know; they have gone home with a debt but when they apply for another visa they are being told that they can't get it (Interview 2).

Importantly, such outstanding NHS debt can thereby also function as an effective barrier to regularisation, even where the applicants would otherwise meet all the legal requirements for their residence to be legalised under the immigration rules.

7.4.2   Everyday Bordering Within the University

Like access to free secondary healthcare, the admission to study at a UK university is also strictly contingent on legal residence in the country; universities themselves have to play a fundamental role in determining a foreigner's eligibility for a student visa. Before international students can even make such an application to the HO, they have to request a *Confirmation of Acceptance for Studies* (CAS) statement from their prospective university, which thereby officially confirms its intention to 'sponsor' the student's visa application. Only institutions holding a sponsor licence – which has to be renewed annually and can be revoked by the HO – can issue CAS statements and thus recruit international students. In principle, the issuing of a CAS statement is at the university's discretion, but it should be refused if a student is (or has previously been) in breach of immigration rules or if the university deems any of the documents submitted or declarations made by the student to be fraudulent. According to the *Immigration Policy and Guidance Manager* of a medium-sized university in London, this puts a lot of pressure on institutions as well as on individual members of staff:

> So we have to… get that balance right; and we won't always get it right. There will be instances where… you know, we would have said 'no' to the student when actually we might have been able to be a little bit more flexible with them. […] So it is very difficult, and I think also the guidance that comes from the HO to education providers […] about who you can and can't accept isn't always helpful. And therefore, there is a lot interpretation, and a lot of discretion, and of discrepancy across the education sector in particular, [with] people like myself having to say what this or that particular rule means (Interview 4).

She also highlights the unequal power relations between the government and public universities and thereby hints at the increasing neoliberalisation of the latter, which explains why education providers have accepted this responsibility in the first place:

We, as a sector, are responding to the HO because we have to, because we need international students because it's such a big financial incentive. We have to have those students to operate, and that's the same for most universities in the UK, and so in a way any changes they make, while we will complain about them across the sector, and we will lobby for them to be slightly different, ultimately those changes will go ahead […] and we will have to respond to them (Interview 4).

Also here, the external logic of (internalised) immigration control not only conflicts but also partly overlaps with the university's own functional logic and imperatives, as my interviewee pinpoints in the following statement:

We don't have that many obligations that are border-control-like. We just need to know that the students we have got here should be here, and everything else is what you would expect to do as a normal university anyway; you know, check whether your students are attending classes… that's not about immigration control, that's about your students getting what they are paying for. […] They have the right that, if they are not attending classes, somebody knows that and somebody is asking why and so that kind of overlap between good pastoral care and regulating university life and HO intelligence is… you know, there is a bit of a blurred line with that, I think (Interview 4).

From her perspective, this only becomes problematic where immigration rules are in direct conflict with the academic assessment of a prospective student's suitability for a particular course: 'The academic department might say 'we really want that student', but we then have to say whether or not we are able to sponsor them for a visa, and if we can't then obviously we can't go ahead with the process'. She also noted that such situations are 'often difficult for students to understand, and academic colleagues as well, because they are only interested in the academic situation' (Interview 4). This ultimately reflects the fact that academic staff are much more shielded from any control responsibility beyond the academic, as a lecturer of another university emphasised:

The government is outsourcing immigration control to a whole variety of people […and that] certainly increases the workload, which is why […] it's now all being done by bureaucrats; because they have to do it like that, it has to be centralised, and that makes sense to me because otherwise that would be just a pain in the neck (Interview 5).

In order for academics to do their job, somebody else has to deal with students' immigration issues in a systematic way – if not the central government then at least specially trained bureaucrats working within the university. In fact, most UK universities have already established dedicated teams of advisors who check all foreign students' eligibility and assist them with any visa issues. While these advisors are usually certified (to give immigration advice) by the *Office of the Immigration Services Commissioner* (OISC), they are less attached to some of the logics that otherwise dominate organisational action within universities. The way the Immigration Policy and Guidance Manager justified the role of her own team clearly indicates this:

Before my team existed, these decisions might have been taken by different colleagues depending on who is involved, so it might have been the academic department even… And so there was room for different decisions based on personalities, and there was no record of those decisions, it was a bit… of a mess […because] there is not so much awareness of the actual technicalities and the rules and so on, you know. [...] I wouldn't expect admissions to understand that necessarily, because their job is to process an application and an academic's job is to teach (Interview 4).

Crucial to my analysis is that also here, one side-effect of this organisational adjustment is that part of the university administration works much more closely with the immigration authority. As my interviewee explained, her team

[h]as names and contacts at the HO [and] where we are concerned about a student's status [or] if the student is telling us things and we need more information, with the student's consent we can actually contact the HO for what's called a Student Eligibility Check (Interview 4).

What she initially describes as a mechanism through which the HO 'helps' the university to deal with complex cases, however, also puts a legal obligation on individual student advisors to inform the HO 'if we categorically know that somebody is in breach of their visa condition' (Interview 4). The way in which she and her team tend to handle such encounters with (potential) irregularity in practice suggests that they often struggle with this obligation:

If I'm completely honest, where we suspect that, we would, from an advisory point of view, make the student aware [...] that we would have a legal obligation... But we wouldn't... just say 'We think you are in breach' and tell the HO. We would kind of engage with the individual to try and encourage them to stop doing what we think they are doing; but ultimately, we wouldn't want to kind of police that because that puts an unrealistic kind of burden on us. [...] We did have an application once from a student who... was a failed asylum-seeker and had gone kind of underground, so to speak, and so obviously if we would have suddenly sent this student's eligibility check to the HO we would be flagging up that this student is here, that we have their address, we had all that information... And that doesn't... that's not what we are there to do, we are there to assess a student's ability to study with us, not to say to the HO 'we found this failed asylum-seeker and here is where they are' (Interview 4).

Ultimately, this reflects her awareness of the consequences that such information exchange with the immigration authority could potentially have for a student's stay in the country, and that immigration enforcement as such lies beyond what she perceives to be her responsibility as a university employee.

7.4.3   Everyday Bordering Within the Local Welfare Office

Irregular migrants living in the UK generally also have *No Recourse to Public Funds* (*NRPF*). This condition is defined under immigration legislation[5] and renders them ineligible to receive any public support or benefit, including those services administered at the local level[6] (NRPF Network 2018; Stephens et al. 2010). The

---

[5] In Section 115 of the Immigration and Asylum Act 1999.

[6] Notably, neither primary and emergency healthcare nor compulsory education are classified as 'public funds' in this respect.

national legal framework only acknowledges very few and narrowly defined situations in which unlawful residents can avail themselves of publicly funded measures of social assistance and protection. One of them is where they have minor children who are assessed as destitute (or about to become destitute) and thus become eligible for support from the local authority (LA) which, under Section 17 of the *Children Act 1989*, has a duty to ensure the welfare of every child in need within its jurisdiction (Dorling et al. 2013; NRPF Network 2018). It is important to note that LAs are only allowed to support unlawful residents where withholding such support would result in a breach of the child's human rights. In addition, immigration law places a legal duty on LAs to inform the HO when unlawful residents request support from social services (NRPF Network 2018).

Where the statutory case-assessment by the LA establishes such responsibility towards a particular family, however, this usually implies a substantial financial burden. Data collected by Price & Spencer (2015, p. 51) suggest that more than one third of accepted NRPF cases remain in LA support for between one and 3 years. Nor can LAs refuse support on the basis of insufficient municipal funds or be reimbursed by the state for these additional expenditures (NRPF Network 2018). Particularly in areas of high immigration and in the context of substantial cuts to LA budgets, this has created significant financial pressure and triggered organisational adjustments that clearly parallel what is happening in hospitals and universities: In order to deal more effectively with irregular migrants' claims, many local welfare departments established specific teams who are responsible for doing just that.

For Price & Spencer (2015), the existence of a dedicated NRPF team constitutes one of three crucial factors that explain the significant variation in how the different LAs respond to claims for support under Section 17 of the Children Act. Specifically tasked to deal with clients identified as having No Recourse to Public Funds, these teams are particularly common within London, where the majority of families receiving so-called *Section-17 support* live.[7] From the perspective of LAs, having such a team not only seems to favour a more consistent application of the rules and more efficient referral procedures but also allows for more effective gate-keeping, as the manager of an NRPF team was keen to emphasise:

> They will only be able to get support […] through my team, and it's only provided conditional on various other things… they have to be able to show that they are territorially the responsibility of [this borough], that they are destitute, and that they have either an on-going application with the HO or are imminently about to make one […] And that's the point about having the dedicated team: that, when this function was spread across the authority's social care and health services, applicants could come in repeatedly, and […] it was impossible to identify a scenario that had been heard before. When you have a small discrete team, you can spot patterns very, very quickly. And one of the things we do is pick up patterns of information that is out in the community [about] what worked and so other people would then come in repeating [the same story]. And we spot that much more quickly now (Interview 6.1).

---

[7] According to a countrywide survey, 1632 of 2679 families who received support during the financial year 2012/13 were registered in one of the 33 London boroughs, at least 16 of which already had established NRPF teams (Price and Spencer 2015, p. 25).

That NRPF teams tend to perceive their role mainly in terms of gate-keeping rather than safeguarding and providing social care to vulnerable residents reflects the conditions under which they are being introduced. In one borough, the combined annual cost of NRPF support reached more than six million pounds by 2014 (compared to around £150,000 in the years before 2008). A review of how the council had been dealing with such cases found the overall approach to be ambiguous and ineffective. Part of the identified problem was that 'the assessment by social workers prioritises safeguarding, [...] not NRPF eligibility criteria', as stated in the official minutes of a meeting where the review results were discussed in November 2014. In order to address this deficit, a dedicated team of five specialist case-workers and one 'embedded' HO worker was set up in order to deal with all NRPF cases – about 80 per cent of which concern migrant families in irregular situations – in a more consistent way. In a background paper presented at the same meeting, this 'robust front door approach' was praised for having already 'started to have significant impact on managing spend in this area'. Whereas, prior to the new approach, more than half of all cases had been accepted for support, only one of the 96 applications that have been made since then has been successful, while eight were being supported temporarily pending full assessment. Based on the average acceptance rates of 9.7 (prior to the pilot) and 1.3 cases per month (during the pilot), another internal document calculates the annual saving to the LA at 2.2 million pounds. Quite clearly, shifting the responsibility of carrying out initial case assessments from social workers to administrative staff (who, in this case, are directly supported by a HO worker) has altered the dominant logic driving the assessment itself. As one NGO practitioner put it, within NRPF teams

> there can be a bit of a culture of looking at the immigration status first, or looking at the adults and I think, because it's not part of social services, you don't get such a child-centred approach, so they are not really looking at 'Is this child in need and what are the needs of this child?'; they are looking at 'Well this adult overstayed their visa or this adult is somehow to blame' and, you know, trying to allocate blame or deciding who is deserving is not the correct test (Interview 1).

Also Price and Spencer's (2015, p. 47) study suggests that those NRPF teams which consist mainly of case-workers rather than social workers 'tended to conceive of their duties to these families as administrative tasks'. One such administrative function of NRPF teams precisely consists in linking local social service departments even closer to the HO which – in the eyes of a social worker I interviewed (together with the NRPF manager) – reflects the overlapping interests of both organisations:

> I do think that there has been, over the last few months, a change from the HO as well, and I don't know whether or not that's the work that the No Recourse Team has been doing, because they are much more open to us. We had a visit, [...] they are coming and doing some training for us and we have a point of contact if we have concerns over any person, which actually is something that is practically unheard of. [...] They didn't have an open-door-approach at all. And I think that has changed because they have seen the value of actually working much more in partnership; and we hope to build on that as well (Interview 6.2).

Once again, another benefit of having a specially trained team dealing with all these cases centrally is that 'normal' social workers are thereby effectively shielded from having to apply the logic of immigration control, as the same interviewee indicated:

> If we see people where we think there is some issue around their status, then actually we refer it to [the NRPF team] for them to investigate; that's where the expertise around migration is [...]. We don't have to make those judgements (Interview 6.2).

At the same time, the fact that more and more social service departments are starting to also rely on HO case-workers 'embedded' within their NRPF teams shows that this development is not just about expertise but also about access to certain information that social services – as well as the HO – would otherwise lack, as the NRPF team manager noted:

> What we found is that having an embedded [HO] worker is much more effective; because the embedded worker goes straight onto the system, is able to do a forensic analysis of what's happening. So when we have walk-ins we get the answer that minute, this person has a claim, this person doesn't have a claim, they have a long history, it has been refused so many times, or they have an outstanding appeal, or whatever. [...] And likewise, the reason the HO agreed to this and the reason they are now extending these options to other boroughs is because they have learned that, actually, the quality of intelligence that they get from us, about patterns more than to do with individuals, is much greater than you will get from just that kind of exchange around individual cases (Interview 6.1).

While this cooperation again seems to be driven by a mutual interest of the LA and the HO, for applicants who are not only destitute but also in an irregular situation it means an almost total overlap of both parts of the administration – the one that might be legally obliged to help them and the one that threatens to deport them. The way in which a destitute migrant mother spoke about an appointment with social services, exemplifies this:

> I have to call and ask my lawyer now, because they said that... they normally would invite immigration so that immigration will threaten people... that they will take them back home... so now I have to call my lawyer to let her know...
> *Interviewer*: So on Monday you are going to meet with your social worker and you think there will also be an immigration officer?
> Yes, immigration officers. That's what they do. That's what they do to threaten... they will say that it's better for them to take you back to your country than just to leave you here without support. [...] But once I have sent the application and I have the copy of the proof of the posting, that way they can't... (Interview 7).

Her reluctance to even meet her social worker without prior advice from a lawyer says a lot about the level of trust she has in the former. Notably, the invention of NRPF teams has been crucial for establishing the intimate institutional relationship between social work and immigration enforcement that ultimately triggers this reluctance. Like other services that were originally set up as means of integration – of individuals and society as a whole – social service departments now also contribute to the disintegration of irregular migrants.

7.5 Conclusion

In this chapter I have discussed the role of public service provision as a site where integration and disintegration policies and practices intersect, and the resulting conflicts must be dealt with on an everyday basis. Specifically, I have looked at the implementation of explicit disintegration policies within three concrete institutions that otherwise fulfil integrative functions – namely hospitals, universities and social service departments. By becoming more or less actively involved in this implementation, these institutions and (at least some of) the individuals working within them participate in the broader politics of (dis)integration. As set out in the introduction to this volume, the latter involves the intertwining of apparently contradictory processes and thus requires a constant renegotiation of conflicting (policy) aims and related institutional logics.

The main contribution of the chapter is to show that the politics of (dis)integration can also trigger institutional change. As my analysis shows, an important structural feature that accompanies the extension of everyday bordering practices into different spheres of public service provision has been the emergence of specialised sub-units within the very organisations that provide these services to the local population. I have argued that it is precisely through OVMs, Student Immigration Advisors and NRPF teams that the state has been able to not only raise but also effectively patrol 'a protective wall [...] around the key institutions of the welfare state', as Broeders & Engbersen (2007, p. 1595) have argued. In fact, this wall no longer merely surrounds these institutions but now runs right through them. It is important to note, however, that although these sub-divisions have come to play an important role within the 'hostile environment' approach, their creation has not been explicitly demanded by central government. Instead, it was the need to ensure their own (cost-) effective functioning that encouraged the various organisations themselves to introduce a certain element of immigration control into their institutional structures and operations. Rather than (legally enforced) deputisation, the underlying processes are thus better described as what Walsh (2014) defined as (encouraged but voluntary) responsibilisation or even (spontaneous) autonomisation.

From the perspective of organisation theory, such structural adjustments to a new set of external requirements represent a common way for organisations to avoid internal conflicts between the dominant and other logics that compete to guide their actions. Where individual actors perceive these logics as incompatible, they will struggle to incorporate the new demands into their work, which renders their deputisation inherently difficult. This is particularly true for professionals who are trained to work *within* a particular field and thus become the most attached to its dominant logic. Doctors, social workers or academics, for example, are more difficult to convince than reception staff that access to the service they deliver should be based on immigration status rather than medical need, apparent destitution or intellectual potential.

Arguably, this is precisely why it makes sense (from the point of view of the organisation) to develop what Besharov & Smith (2013, p. 376) have called 'a cadre of organisational members who are less strongly attached to particular logics' in order to more effectively deal with contradictory external demands. While this helps to buffer professionals from having to deal with these uncomfortable demands, it also means that crucial gate-keeping responsibilities are transferred from trained professionals to untrained administrators or even very differently trained immigration officers. These insights hopefully contribute to a better understanding of how internal immigration control works within the different spheres of public welfare and why the pressure to exclude irregular residents will not necessarily reduce their number but the ability of public institutions to fulfil their primary function for society as a whole.

7.6   List of Interviews

Interview 1:   Case-worker and lawyer working for the organisation *Project 17*, 22 October 2014.

Interview 2:   Head of the Overseas Department of a medium-sized NHS hospital, 31 October 2014.

Interview 3:   General Practitioner (GP) at a health centre in North London, 10 November 2014.

Interview 4:   Immigration Policy and Guidance Manager at a university in South London, 24 February 2015.

Interview 5:   University lecturer at a university in central London, 4 February 2015.

Interview 6:   NRPF service manager (6.1) and social worker (6.2), both working for the same local council in London, 26 February 2015.

Interview 7:   Single mother from Nigeria, living in London since 2013, 17 February 2015.

References

Balibar, E. (1998). The borders of Europe. In P. Cheah & B. Robbins (Eds.), *Cosmopolitics: Thinking and feeling beyond the nation* (pp. 216–233). Minneapolis: University of Minnesota Press.

Besharov, M. L., & Smith, W. K. (2013). Multiple institutional logics in organizations: Explaining their varied nature and implications. *Academy of Management Review, 39*(3), 364–381.

Black, R. (2003). Breaking the convention: Researching the 'illegal' migration of refugees to Europe. *Antipode, 35*(1), 34–54.

Bommes, M., & Geddes, A. (Eds.). (2000). *Immigration and welfare: Challenging the Borders of the welfare state*. London/New York: Routledge.

Boswell, C. (2007). Theorizing migration policy: Is there a third way? *International Migration Review, 41*(1), 75–100.

Broeders, D., & Engbersen, G. (2007). The fight against illegal migration: Identification policies and immigrants' counterstrategies. *American Behavioral Scientist, 50*(12), 1592–1609.

Carens, J. (2013). *The ethics of immigration*. New York: Oxford University Press.

Castles, S. (2004). Why migration policies fail. *Ethnic and Racial Studies, 27*(2), 205–227.

Chauvin, S., & Garcés-Mascareñas, B. (2014). Becoming less illegal: Deservingness frames and undocumented migrant incorporation. *Sociology Compass, 8*(4), 422–432.

Collyer, M., Hinger, S., & Schweitzer, R. (2020). Politics of (Dis)Integration – An Introduction. In S. Hinger, & R. Schweitzer (Eds.), *Politics of (Dis)Integration* (pp. 1–18). Cham: Springer VS.

Cvajner, M., & Sciortino, G. (2010). Theorizing irregular migration: The control of spatial mobility in differentiated societies. *European Journal of Social Theory, 13*(3), 389–404.

Da Lomba, S. (2011). Irregular migrants and the human right to health care: A case-study of health-care provision for irregular migrants in France and the UK. *International Journal of Law in Context, 7*(3), 357–374.

DoH. (2012). *2012 Review of Overseas Visitors Charging Policy*. London: Department of Health. Retrieved 05 July 2018 from: https://www.gov.uk/government/uploads/system/uploads/attachment_data/file/210439/Overseas_Visitors_Charging_Review_2012_-_Summary_document.pdf.

DoH. (2013a). *Guidance on implementing the overseas vvisitors hospital charging regulations*. London: Department of Health. Retrieved 05 July 2018 from: https://www.gov.uk/government/publications/guidance-on-overseas-visitors-hospital-charging-regulations.

DoH. (2013b). *Sustaining Services, Ensuring Fairness. A Consultation on Migrant Access and their Financial Contribution to NHS Provision in England*. London: Department of Health. Retrieved 05 July 2018 from: https://assets.publishing.service.gov.uk/government/uploads/system/uploads/attachment_data/file/210438/Sustaining_services__ensuring_fairness_consultation_document.pdf.

Dorling, K., Bolton, S., Barrett, J., Compton, R., East, A., Freeman, S., Hurrell, A., Smallwood, D., & Brzezina, D. (2013). *Growing up in a hostile environment: The rights of undocumented migrant children in the UK*. Colchester: Children's Legal Centre (CORAM). Retrieved 05 July 2018 from: https://www.childrenslegalcentre.com/growing-hostile-environment/.

Ellermann, A. (2006). Street-level democracy: How immigration bureaucrats manage public opposition. *West European Politics, 29*(2), 293–309.

FRA. (2013). *Apprehension of migrants in an irregular situation: Fundamental rights considerations*. Vienna: European Union Agency for Fundamental Rights.

Garcés-Mascareñas, B. (2015). Revisiting bordering practices: Irregular migration, borders, and citizenship in Malaysia. *International Political Sociology, 9*(2), 128–142.

Guiraudon, V., & Lahav, G. (2000). A reappraisal of the state sovereignty debate: The case of migration control. *Comparative Political Studies, 33*(2), 163–195.

Hellgren, Z. (2014). Negotiating the boundaries of social membership: Undocumented migrant claims-making in Sweden and Spain. *Journal of Ethnic and Migration Studies, 40*(8), 1175–1191.

Hinger, S. (2020). Integration through disintegration? The distinction between deserving and undeserving refugees in national and local integration policies in Germany. In S. Hinger, & R. Schweitzer (Eds.), *Politics of (Dis)Integration* (pp. 19–39). Cham: Springer VS.

Home Office. (2013). *Immigration bill factsheet: Overview of the bill*. London: Home Office. Retrieved 05 July 2018 from: https://www.gov.uk/government/uploads/system/uploads/attachment_data/file/249251/Overview_Immigration_Bill_Factsheet.pdf.

Jordan, B., Stråth, B., & Triandafyllidou, A. (2003). Contextualising immigration policy implementation in Europe. *Journal of Ethnic and Migration Studies, 29*(2), 195–224.

Kirkup, J., & Winnett, R. (2012). Theresa may interview: 'We're going to give illegal migrants a really hostile reception', *The Telegraph*, 25 May. Retrieved 05 July 2018 from: http://www.

telegraph.co.uk/news/uknews/immigration/9291483/Theresa-May-interview-Were-going-to-give-illegal-migrants-a-really-hostile-reception.html.

Lahav, G., & Guiraudon, V. (2006). Actors and venues in immigration control: Closing the gap between political demands and policy outcomes. *West European Politics, 29*(2), 201–223.

Lindberg, K. (2014). Performing multiple logics in practice. *Scandinavian Journal of Management, 30*(4), 485–497.

Lipsky, M. (1980). *Street-level bureaucracy: The dilemmas of the individual in public service.* New York: Russell Sage Foundation.

Lipsky, M. (1987). Street-level bureaucrats as policy makers. In D. L. Yarwood (Ed.), *Public administration, politics, and the people: Selected readings for managers, employees, and citizens* (pp. 121–127). London: Longman.

Luhmann, N. (1982). *The differentiation of society.* Columbia: Columbia University Press.

Luhmann, N. (1995). *Social systems.* Stanford: Stanford University Press.

Meyer, J. W., & Rowan, B. (1977). Institutionalized organizations: Formal structure as myth and ceremony. *American Journal of Sociology, 83*(2), 340–362.

MRN. (2015). *Briefing on the proposed immigration bill 2015–16.* London: Migrants' Rights Network. Retrieved 05 July 2018 from: https://www.migrantsrights.org.uk/wp-content/uploads/publications/MRN_Immigration_Bill_Briefing_2015-v1.pdf.

NRPF Network (2018). *Assessing and supporting children and families who have no recourse to public funds (NRPF).* Practice Guidance for Local Authorities. Retrieved 05 July 2018 from: http://guidance.nrpfnetwork.org.uk/reader/practice-guidance-families/.

OHCHR. (2014). The economic, social and cultural rights of migrants in an irregular situation. In *Office of the United Nations High Commissioner for Human Rights.* New York/Geneva.

Park, J. S. W. (2013). *Illegal migrations and the huckleberry Finn problem.* Philadelphia: Temple University Press.

Perna, R. (2018). Bound between care and control: Institutional contradictions and daily practices of healthcare for migrants in an irregular situation in Italy. *Ethnic and Racial Studies (online first)*, 1–20. https://doi.org/10.1080/01419870.2018.1533645.

Price, J., & Spencer, S. (2015). *Safeguarding children from destitution: Local authority responses to families with 'no recourse to public funds.* Oxford: University of Oxford, COMPAS Report. Retrieved 05 July 2018 from: www.compas.ox.ac.uk/research/welfare/nrpf/.

Reay, T., & Hinings, C. R. (2009). Managing the rivalry of competing institutional logics. *Organization Studies, 30*(6), 629–652.

Schweitzer, R. (2017a). *Integration against the state – The state against integration?* Politics blog. Retrieved 05 July 2018 from: http://politicsblog.ac.uk/2017/02/05/integration-state-state-integration/.

Schweitzer, R. (2017b). Integration against the state: Irregular migrants' agency between deportation and regularisation in the United Kingdom. *Politics, 37*(3), 317–331.

Schweitzer, R. (2018a). *The micro-Management of Migrant Irregularity and its control : A qualitative study of the intersection of public service provision with immigration enforcement in London and Barcelona.* Brighton: University of Sussex, PhD thesis.

Schweitzer, R. (2018b). Health care versus border care: Justification and hypocrisy in the multi-level negotiation of irregular migrants' access to fundamental rights and services. *Journal of Immigrant and Refugee Studies (online first), 17*, 61–76. https://doi.org/10.1080/15562948.2018.1489088.

Sciortino, G. (2000). Toward a political sociology of entry policies: Conceptual problems and theoretical proposals. *Journal of Ethnic and Migration Studies, 26*(2), 213–228.

Scott, W. R. (2001). *Institutions and organizations.* Los Angeles: Sage.

Scott, W. R., Ruef, M., Mendel, P. J., & Caronna, C. A. (2000). *Institutional change and healthcare organizations: From professional dominance to managed care.* Chicago: University of Chicago Press.

Spencer, S., & Hughes, V. (2015). *Outside and in: Legal entitlements to health care and education for migrants with irregular status in Europe.* Oxford: University of Oxford, COMPAS Report.

Squire, V. (2011). The contested politics of mobility. Politicizing mobility, mobilizing politics. In V. Squire (Ed.), *The contested politics of mobility. Borderzones and irregularity* (pp. 1–25). London: Routledge.

Stephens, M., Fitzpatrick, S., Elsinga, M., van Steen, G., & Chzhen, Y. (2010). *Study on housing exclusion: Welfare policies, labour market and housing provision*. Brussels: European Commission.

Treibel, A. (2015). *Integriert Euch! Plädoyer für ein selbstbewusstes Einwanderungsland*. Frankfurt/New York: Campus Verlag.

Van der Leun, J. (2006). Excluding illegal migrants in the Netherlands: Between national policies and local implementation. *West European Politics, 29*(2), 310–326.

Walsh, J. P. (2014). Watchful citizens: Immigration control, surveillance and societal participation. *Social and Legal Studies, 23*(2), 237–259.

Walzer, M. (1983). *Spheres of justice: A defense of pluralism and equality*. New York: Basic Books.

Webb, J. (2006). *Organisations, identities and the self*. Basingstoke: Palgrave Macmillan.

Wind-Cowie, M., & Wood, C. (2014). *Do no harm. Ensuring fair use of the NHS efficiently and effectively*. London: DEMOS. Retrieved 05 July 2018 from: http://demos.co.uk/files/Demos_DoNoHarmREPORT.pdf?1413823102.

Chapter 8
Jewish Immigrants in Israel: Disintegration Within Integration?

Amandine Desille

8.1 Introduction

In Europe and North America, boundaries of belonging—the abstract lines that define the limit of an 'imagined community' (Anderson 1983) – seem to be drawn through new frames of *deservingness* (Chauvin and Garcés-Mascareñas 2014; Faist 2013; Soysal 2012). Recent research shows that the country of origin becomes secondary in the determination of whether or not an individual can become part of society and is gradually being replaced by his or her perceived economic utility and ability to actively participate in society.

While the main debate around this issue takes place in North America and Europe today, the reframing of the categories of immigrant settling in Israel is relatively absent in the scientific immigration debate. Indeed, the strong ethnonational ideology underlying the Law of Return – Israel's national immigration policy – and the stability of this policy over time, leaves questions of belonging unchallenged. However, I argue that several changes have taken place since the Law of Return was promulgated in 1950 and I scrutinise their impact on immigrant integration frames in this chapter.

First of all, Israel's immigration landscape is beginning to resemble that of certain post-industrial countries (Berthomière 1996, 2004; Elias and Kemp 2010). The beneficiaries of the Law of Return have become more ethnically diverse and the large immigration flows from the former Soviet Union and Ethiopia, in particular, have raised new questions of race and religion (Yonah 2005). The globalisation of Israel's economy has led to the entry of a non-Jewish workforce from Asia and Eastern Europe, within the frame of a policy that resembles the guest-worker programmes implemented by several European countries after World War

A. Desille (✉)
University of Lisbon, Lisboa, Portugal
e-mail: amandine.desille@campus.ul.pt

© The Author(s) 2020
S. Hinger, R. Schweitzer (eds.), *Politics of (Dis)Integration*,
IMISCOE Research Series, https://doi.org/10.1007/978-3-030-25089-8_8

II. Additionally, Israel has seen an increase in the number of asylum-seekers whose presence is criminalised by the Government.[1]

Secondly, Israel's semi-socialist economy has experienced a drastic shift towards neoliberalism, as exemplified by deregulation, privatisation and the increasing withdrawal of the welfare state, in parallel with the adoption of a free market economy, the growing prestige of business careers and so on. Although Israel is still characterised by a somewhat centralised administration, municipalities take on more and more responsibilities towards their residents and the future development of the local economy.

In this context, I focus on one type of immigration – Jewish immigration as framed by the Law of Return – and the growing role of municipalities in their integration. This chapter aims to determine the extent to which urban logics under neoliberal reforms reframe immigrant 'deservingness' (Chauvin and Garcés-Mascareñas 2014). Has the 'economic utility' (Faist 2013) of Jewish immigrants become a new criterion determining the efforts which local governments put into attracting certain new immigrants while dissuading others?

The main objective is therefore to unpack the immigrant policies of Israel, as they are interpreted and adapted at the municipal level. A substantial aspect of the changes I detail below lies in the tensions between new frames of deservingness and persisting ethnonational state logics. It is not the first time in history that Israel has limited the immigration of Jews in favour of categories perceived as more desirable. However, the political and socioeconomic context has seen the emergence of new frames through which these categories are justified. This chapter contributes to the developing scholarship on deservingness by reconnecting neoliberalisation processes at the global level with national identity politics and micro-processes of change produced at the local level. Confronting global, national and local frames therefore sheds light on how *disintegration*, as a process of latent (or sometimes even intentional) exclusion of certain groups, takes place and affects society as a whole (see Collyer et al. 2020).

The chapter is based on a research conducted in four peripheral cities in Israel from 2013 to 2017. It is organised as follows: firstly, I define the concepts of *desirability* and *deservingness* that underlie immigrant policies. Secondly, I address the history of the 'absorption' of Jewish immigrants, concomitant to nation-building in Israel. Immigrant absorption has changed, together with the neoliberalisation of the country, which has introduced tensions between the state, the city and the immigrants. Focusing on local immigration and integration policies formed by Israeli cities' municipalities, I show how ethnonational and neoliberal logics are intertwined – in fact, my enquiry reveals the tensions resulting from national ethnic preference on the one hand and economic desirability as pushed forward at municipal level on the other. To conclude, I compare my empirical results with the desirable versus deserving debate, observed under neoliberalisation processes.

---

[1] In this chapter, Government with a capital letter refers to the central administration, including its elected officials and its managerial and technical agents.

8.2   Immigrant Integration: Desirability Versus Deservingness

Immigration and citizenship policies are the set of rules that fix access to a national territory and its formal membership. Therefore, scholars who attempt to unpack immigration policies often focus on the underlying logics determining who can be part of the national community and who cannot. While some nation-states prevent access to formal membership entirely if the applicant cannot prove ethnic ascendency (*jus sanguinis*), others permit access to formal membership to any individual born within the boundaries of the country (*jus solis*), even when s/he cannot prove his or her ethnic ascendency. In the second case, membership may be granted with the condition of quick assimilation into the polity or following a more pluralist attitude.

However, over recent decades, the entangled processes of globalisation, expanded free market economy and rescaling of governance have greatly challenged nation-states' management of these issues (Glick Schiller and Salazar 2013; Sassen 2005). The heterogeneity of immigrant situations and the concomitant heterogeneity of regulations and policies have led to a rather fragmented management of immigration, which even includes the deliberate undermining of integration processes (Collyer et al. 2020). Additionally, economic criteria have gained substantial weight in determining the desirability of certain individuals (immigrants or not) over others. Immigration becomes an important stake for the globalised market economy, and 'immigration policy – the power of the state to exclude, admit, and expel – is productively deployed not only as a tool of statecraft but as a tool for neoliberal capital accumulation via the constitution of neoliberal subjects' (Varsanyi 2008, p. 883).

Whereas 'migrants contribute to neoliberal governance by encouraging a form of subjectivity that reinforces the ethos of the self-reliant, enterprising individual' (Glick Schiller and Çağlar 2010, p. 16), they face the increasing requirement that they take responsibility for their own integration, including continuous training and proactive integration in the labour market, in order to be recognised as 'active, participatory and productive citizens' (Soysal 2012). This injunction falls particularly on immigrants but is also increasingly true for all citizens (see also Karolak 2020; Samuk 2020). As Thomas Faist points out: 'It is not only the categorization of people along nationality/citizenship and thus the accident of birthplace, but also their distinction with respect to economic utility and social adaptation that make a difference to the life chances of many individuals' (Faist 2013, p. 1644).

In this context of tensions between globalisation and neoliberalisation on the one hand and the trends of nationalism and the militarisation of borders on the other, the tendency of nation-states is to 'leav[e] the messy and costly details of servicing and policing expanding noncitizen populations to state[2] and local governments' (Varsanyi 2008, p. 879). Indeed, local governments – such as municipalities – have

---

[2] In this case, regional and not federal state.

been recognised as emerging actors in the governance of immigration. More than a merely pragmatic response to immigrants' settlement in their cities, municipalities are forced to respond to the demographic changes. As Neil Brenner argues, post-Keynesian competition states mobilise diverse institutional realignments and regulatory strategies to '[enhance] fiscal constraints and competitive pressures upon cities and regions, impelling their regulatory institutions to privilege the goals of local economic development and territorial competitiveness over traditional welfarist, redistributive priorities' (Brenner 2004, p. 176).

Sometimes, 'interlocality competition' (Brenner 2004) has permitted a more positive embracing of the settlement of foreign-born populations in cities. In fact, municipalities increasingly tend to consider immigration as a potential catalyst for city development. Immigrants are seen as potential members of the 'creative class' (Florida 2003) or – formulated from a more critical perspective – as the neoliberal agents of urban restructuring (Glick Schiller and Çağlar 2010). Municipalities engaged in 'remaking, reimagining and marketing' their city (*ibid.*, p. 2) favour immigrants whom they perceive as having more to contribute. Martin Jorgensen, when studying this issue in Denmark, states: 'Cities compete to attract the most skilled and creative migrants, and the [rural] municipalities are responsible for poorly skilled and less resourceful immigrants and descendants' (Jørgensen 2012, p. 245).

However, empirically, municipal policies include immigrants with very heterogeneous social and human capital and therefore very differently perceived probabilities of succeeding in integrating autonomously into the various institutions of the host country. 'Sanctuary cities' (see Hinger 2020) have developed access to local membership and sets of integration policies for immigrants of all backgrounds, including those with precarious or no legal status. An interesting contribution to our understanding of who is perceived as deserving is that of Sébastien Chauvin and Blanca Garcés-Mascareñas (2012, 2014). In their analyses, immigrants gain the attention of policymakers when their economic performance is positive, when they actively participate in the community or when they fall into the category of vulnerability. The last category, vulnerability, is often offered by the state in exchange for the migrant's renunciation of agency in the process of proving his vulnerability. In other words, the denial of agency is artificial and, on the contrary, produces self-narratives that respond to the state's expectations of passive victims.

This chapter brings empirical grounding to this debate: the case of Israel presents a strong ethnonational definition of belonging and access to citizenship. However, with the recent involvement of municipalities, new tensions appear which may lead to further instability in immigration policymaking. My objective is to analyse the role of Israeli municipalities in producing or reproducing frames of access to community membership.

8.3 The Absorption of Jewish Immigrants and Nation-Building

The Law of Return, ratified by the Israeli parliament in 1950, is Israel's only immigration policy. It is conceived not only as a return migration policy but also as an immigrant settlement policy. Indeed, it states that every Jew who expresses the desire to immigrate to Israel, identified as the 'ancestral homeland', can do so. As the Israeli sociologists Gershon Shafir and Yoav Peled state, '[The Law of Return] became the most important legal expression of Israel's self-definition as a Jewish state. It established an ethno-nationalist citizenship that, in principle, encompassed all Jews, and only Jews, by virtue of their ethnic descent' (Shafir and Peled 2004). In 1952, the state ratified a second law, the Nationality Law, granting beneficiaries of the Law of Return immediate access to Israeli citizenship.

From the beginning and despite the all-encompassing framing of the Law of Return, immigration to Israel and integration after settlement never included all Jews equally. The first waves of immigrants who settled in Ottoman Palestine had to prove their capacity to sustain themselves, without the support of Zionist institutions (Shilo 1994). 'Penniless Jews' were prevented from immigrating and the ideal newcomer was young, able to work and had at least a small amount of capital. Zionist organisations revised the rescuing/refuge purpose of the settlement in Palestine and advised the careful, organised building of the settlement (*ibid.*). The first organised immigration of 'penniless' Yemenite Jews occurred in 1911 but was of equal 'economic value' (*ibid.*, p. 611) since their settlement was meant to replace that of Arab labourers and provide a cheap Jewish labour force in Palestine (*ibid.*).

In 1948, Israel declared itself open to the mass migration of Jews in the Diaspora but, following the arrival of more than 687,000 Jewish immigrants between the second half of 1948 and the end of 1951 (CBS 2016), the Government and its operative arm, the Jewish Agency, had to rethink their plan. In 1952, the Government and the Jewish Agency both stopped supporting immigration unless applicants were under 35 or were refugees in immediate danger (Sitton 1962). Candidates for immigration who were not 'desirable' as workers nor 'deserving' in the context of the establishment of Israel as a haven for threatened Jews in the Diaspora had to bear the cost of their immigration and settlement themselves.

For those who made it to the country, equal integration into the new nation was far from a reality. In fact, the absorption policy – the set of policies governing immigrants' settlement in Israel – was conceived along a two-path ethnicised integration approach. Shmuel Noah Eisenstadt, founder of the Israeli School of Sociology and its leader until the 1970s, had developed the basis of the state immigration policy. As stated in the introduction to this volume, the role of academia in influencing politics of (dis)integration is clear to see (Collyer et al. 2020). Hence, Eisenstadt (1954) suggests that: 'To each *aliya*[3] is assigned a specific functional contribution in the nation-building process and a consequent location on the centre-periphery

---

[3] A Hebrew term meaning ascent and referring to Jewish immigration to Israel.

continuum' (Ram 1995, p. 31). In Eisenstadt's model, immigration from the end of the nineteenth century represents the core of the 'social system' necessary for modernisation, while the mass migration of the 1950s represents the periphery. The 'centre' is ethnically Russian and Polish and bears the universal interests of society at large whereas the periphery is mostly made up of non-European Jews from Africa and Asia. As such, the latter has a marginal role in nation-building: its members are meant to be assimilated within the core culture in order to create a 'unified and homogeneous nation' (Frankenstein 1953, cited by Ram 1995, p. 38).

Eisenstadt (1954) viewed three aspects of the successful transformation of 'traditional' immigrants into 'modern Jews':

> Acculturation – learning of the various norms, roles, and customs of the absorbing society; personal adjustment – strengthening of the mental makeup of the immigrants, building confidence and satisfaction in them; and institutional dispersion – the proportional dispersion of immigrants in the various institutional spheres, residential locations, and so forth (Eisenstadt 1954, pp. 10, 15).

Absorption was designated in terms of the 'diffusion' of values, norms, and roles, from the modern absorbing society to the traditional immigrants, until they were entirely immersed (ibid., p. 38).

'The proportional dispersion of immigrants in the various institutional spheres, residential locations, and so forth' (Eisenstadt 1954, pp. 10, 15) refers to an actual geographical dispersion of immigrants (Lipshitz 1991). In fact, the central administration planned the establishment of new cities called development towns, located at the frontiers of the new state. With the saturation of older urban centres, new immigrants from Africa and Asia[4] were forced to settle in development towns.

Non-European Jews were therefore doubly excluded from the core of the new nation. Socio-culturally, they were considered as peripheral and needing to integrate within Ashkenazi[5] modern society in order to differentiate themselves from the Arab culture[6] (Chetrit 2000; Ram 2000; Smooha and Peretz 1982; Tzfadia and Yacobi 2011; Yiftachel 2000). Geographically, they were directed to the borders, where they suffered effective segregation on the part of the state (Khazzoom 2005; Lipshitz 1991, 1998; Shama and Iris 1977; Tzfadia 2006; Yiftachel 2000).

The resentment of African and Asian immigrants from development towns and peripheral neighbourhoods in larger cities grew when Soviet Jews entered Israel in the 1970s. Associated with national political crises (which I describe in the next section), the preferential treatment given to these new immigrants exacerbated the divide and led to social unrest. A socio-political movement emerged in that period and African and Asian immigrants gathered around a Mizrahi[7] identity. The

---

[4] Immigrants from Central and Eastern Europe were also directed towards development towns; however, due to their better social networks and higher levels of capital, they could re-emigrate to the centre quite shortly after their arrival.

[5] *Ashkenazi* means Jew of European origin.

[6] Even though I refer to 'African and Asian Jews", the majority of these immigrants came from North Africa and the Middle East, where they had co-habited with Muslim and Christian Arabs in Morocco, Yemen, Libya, Egypt and Lebanon etc. – a minority came from India, for instance.

[7] A Hebrew term meaning Easterner.

Ashkenazi–Mizrahi divide was reinforced again 20 years later with the fall of the USSR, when more than 800,000 Former Soviet Union immigrants made their way to Israel between 1989 and 2000 (Berthomière 2004).

The 'Russians' were not the only ones who alimented the Ashkenazi–Mizrahi gap. At the other end of the spectrum, Israel received a new group of racialised immigrants: Ethiopian Jews (Anteby 1998; Djerrahian 2015; Elias and Kemp 2010). Thirty years after Governmental operations to bring them to Israel, Ethiopian Jews[8] still suffer from high rates of poverty, lower achievement in the education system and the labour market, institutional racism and more. At the time of my fieldwork (2015–2016), as European Jewish communities were increasingly afraid of becoming the target of terrorist attacks, following those in France and beyond, the state once more privileged Western immigrants over the settlement of new Ethiopian immigrants, triggering protests among Ethiopian Israelis (Lior 2016; Lis 2016).

Whether it be the prevention of 'penniless Jews' from settling during the pre-state period, the differentiated immigration possibilities of (perceived) non-productive, non-refugee Jews in the 1950s or the preferential immigration of 'Western' Ashkenazi immigrants over 'Eastern' Mizrahi immigrants today, Jews who should have benefitted from the support of the state have been categorised either as economically useful or as vulnerable refugees for more than a century. However, this distinction has taken a new turn since the late 1970s and the neoliberalisation at work in Israel.

8.4 Towards Neoliberalisation: Tensions Between the State, the City and the Immigrants

The 1970s represented an important rupture for the state and the beginning of the progressive liberalisation of Israel's economy and politics. In the 1970s, Israel saw the infiltration of a 'new right' ideology from the UK and the USA (Kay 2012). In 1977, Likud rose to power in the Israeli parliament and Menachem Begin became Prime Minister. In fact, the 1973 war and the growing resentment among African and Asian immigrants led to the delegitimation of the Mapai (Labour) camp.[9] This

---

[8] Between November 1984 and January 1985, 7000 Beta Israel or Ethiopian Jews were transferred to Israel during the so-called 'Moses operation'. Even though 6000 Ethiopian Jews had already made it to Israel before them, this first operation heralds the symbolic start of Ethiopian immigration to Israel. 11,000 new Ethiopian immigrants arrived in Israel after this operation. Lastly, in May 1991, Israel conducted the second operation, the 'Solomon operation'', an airlift which brought 14,300 Ethiopian Jews to Israel in 36 h (Anteby 1998; Berthomière 1996).

[9] The Mapai (an acronym for the Party of Eretz Israel Workers), led by David Ben-Gurion, dominated Israeli politics from 1949 to 1968 and instituted a semi-socialist economy in Israel, characterised by a centralised planned economy, the monopoly of state corporations such as the construction company Solel Bone, the housing company Amidar and the national Union *Histadrut*, collective settlements such as the *kibbutz* and state-planned immigration settlement, etc. Mapai then became *Avoda* (Labour).

election initiated the shift from a founding Labour Zionist bloc to the more neoZionist, neoliberal Likud party (Shafir and Peled 2004) – and a more complex stratification of Israel society along socioeconomic, political, ethnic and religious divisions (Berthomière 2004). Yet the real neoliberal turn, which led to the actual withdrawal of the state and reduced public expenditure, occurred in 1985, under pressure from the US Government (Kay 2012).

The country's shift to a more neoliberal approach to government and the economy still holds today. The elections that took place when I started my doctoral research in 2013 confirmed this trend. The winning coalition was made up of parties that all believed in a free market, the reduction of taxes, the cutting of welfare subsidies, the weakening labour unions and, in general, supporting the withdrawal of the state (Rubin et al. 2014). However, the neoliberalisation of Israel does not mean that other ideologies do not subsist.

The impact of these reforms on Israel's immigration policy has been two-fold: first, since the 1980s, immigrant integration shifted from being the responsibility of the state to self-responsibility through the implementation of 'direct absorption' (Doron and Kargar 1993); second, *de facto* decentralisation meant an increased role of cities in different planning domains (Ben-Elia 2006; Razin 2003).

The direct absorption policy stipulates that new immigrants receive a six-month allocation from the state, as well as different discounts for residential, local and income taxes, the purchase of cars or electric appliances, and university fees; these various entitlements are known as the 'absorption basket'. Most immigrants are no longer directed to state housing nor employed in state enterprises but are free to choose where to settle and must rely on their own networks to find a job. In that context, the Government had to find new incentives – notably through housing projects – to attract newcomers to the peripheral cities suffering from out-migration (Berthomière 2002). The direct absorption policy mostly concerns Western immigrants –those from Ethiopia or India, for instance, are still directed to absorption centres and receive support for access to housing in specific neighbourhoods listed by the Government (Anteby 1998).

Decentralisation has meant that municipalities, including those in development towns, increased their autonomy when it came to immigrant settlement (Auerbach 2001, 2011; Desille 2017; Tzfadia 2005, 2006; Yacobi and Tzfadia 2009). In this sense, municipal immigrant integration policies are the result of three types of logics which are in tension: state logics, immigrant logics (represented by certain political parties such as Shas[10] and Israel Beitenu[11] for instance) and the interests of the cities themselves (Desille 2017).

---

[10] 'Shas (Sephardic Guardians of the Torah) was originally formed in Jerusalem in 1983 with the support of Rabbi Schach, and led by Rabbis Ovadia Yosef and Aryeh Deri. Shas aimed at representing Sephardic Jews in Israel, as well as facilitating their access to resources to carry out their activities. It has a social agenda, particularly successful in a context of welfare vacuum. Their success surprised the leaders themselves. But Shas has been extremely resilient and has managed to secure a diverse base of voters up to today" (Desille 2017, p. 138).

[11] 'In 1995, *refuznik* and Soviet immigrant from the 1970s Natan Sharansky founded the Russian right-wing party *Israel beAliyah* (a pun meaning 'Israel on the rise' as well as 'Israel in immigration'). At the 1996 elections, half of FSU immigrants voted for this party, securing seven seats in

8.5 Description of the Study

To understand the underlying logics leading to the development and framing of local immigrant integration policies, I have selected four development towns (established or expanded in the 1950s to absorb new immigrants and secure the new borders of the state): Acre, Arad, Kiryat Gat and Kiryat Shmona, located on the map in Fig. 8.1.

The four cities belong to the same urban hierarchy: they are middle-sized cities (20,000 to 50,000 residents), remote from the Tel Aviv–Jerusalem axis, economically depressed (with an indicator of 4 or 5 on a scale of 10),[12] and have some regional function, notably in terms of service delivery. Second, the local political landscape of each city is quite similar, with the same political parties dominating local politics: Likud, national religious and religious parties, and Israel Beitenu party (Israel Beitenu council members are usually in charge of immigration issues). Finally, the cities residential bases are similar, constituted, as they are, mostly of African and Asian immigrants and their descendants from the 1950s onwards' waves of immigration, as well as a large group of former-USSR immigrants (between 16 and 40%).

However, their planning and development followed different rationales. Acre is not explicitly a city established for immigration settlement purposes, since it is a very ancient site and was a Palestinian settlement until 1948. However, it has been greatly expanded to receive immigrants from the 1950s onwards. Today, it represents the most proactive city among the four under scrutiny when it comes to immigration settlement issues. Kiryat Shmona was established in 1949 and Kiryat Gat in 1955 for the settlement of new immigrants. Both development towns were established on the sites of Palestinian villages which were entirely destroyed; however, unlike Acre, there are no Palestinian residents in these cities. Arad, a second-generation new town, was established in 1962, with new planning criteria to overcome the socioeconomic issues that quickly surfaced in development towns such as Kiryat Gat and Kiryat Shmona. Although Kiryat Gat and Arad have formulated

---

the parliament. Following political conflicts, *Israel beAliyah* was to disappear to leave *Israel Beitenu* (Israel our house) to enter the political scene. The Moldavian immigrant Avigdor Lieberman founded *Israel Beitenu* in 1999. It represents Russian-speaking immigrants and is primarily secular, nationalist, Zionist and adopts a hawkish position with regard to the conflict" (Desille 2017, p. 139).

[12] The socio-economic rank is calculated for each city depending on the financial resources of the residents (from work, benefits etc.). These are housing (the density, quality, and other components of this aspect), home appliances (e.g. air conditioners, personal computers and VCRs), the motorisation level (quantitative and qualitative), schooling and education, employment and unemployment profile, various types of socio-economic distress and and demographic characteristics. 1/10 indicates cities in distress while 10/10 indicates well-off one. Based on these indicators, budgets, national transfers and staff decisions impacting on local governments are taken by the Ministry of the Interior.

Fig. 8.1 Map of Israel

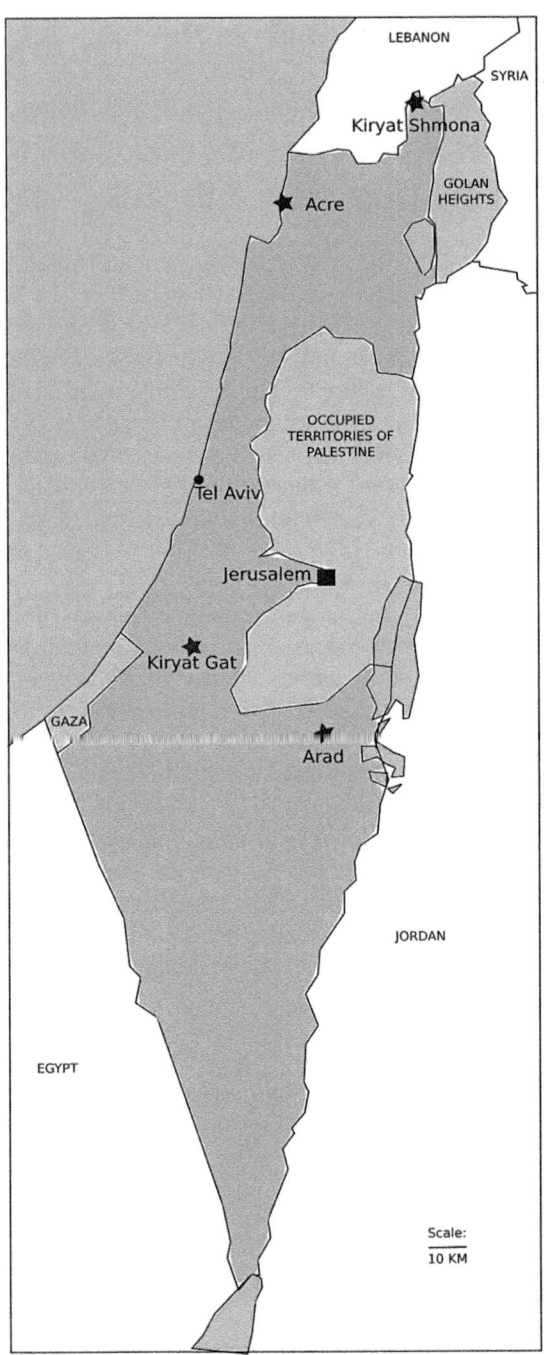

some local immigration policies, Kiryat Shmona remains reluctant to direct its limited municipal resources towards new immigrants.

Additionally, their leadership, in the sense of the political style of the mayor and the city council (administrative bureaucracy, New Public Management, intermediary/hybrid), is also different. Acre and Kiryat Gat have adopted a more managerial approach, characterised by partnerships with the private sector and the business-like management of several public issues. Both the history of the places as well as the motivation and management style of their leaders are major causes leading local immigration policies to diverge (Desille 2017).

Whether they were involved or not in immigration settlement, political representatives and technical staff in all four cities formulated some definition of integration during our encounters. Based on 60 interviews, I analysed the narratives and discourses underlying the concept of immigrant integration, with the aim of providing a grounded theory to this loaded concept. As Rinus Penninx (2013, p. 18) suggests:

> The essence of policies is their intention to guide and steer processes in society – in our case processes of immigrant integration. Explicit policies are part of a political process of a normative nature in which the topic of integration is formulated as problem. The problem is given a normative framing (What do we want to be the outcome of the integration process?) and concrete actions are designed and developed to reach the desired outcome. Therefore, the systematic study of policies should investigate the framing and normative elements as well as practice and what relation these have (or do not have) with the process of integration as empirically measured. Ideally, this should be done using a terminology that is independent of policy concepts.

Through in-depth encounters, I sought to reveal the ideas and beliefs that framed municipal immigrant integration policies in the cities, aside from the definition provided by the more explicit national policies I have mentioned in the earlier sections (the Law of Return, the direct absorption policy and the community absorption policy). My results show that ethnonational frames of citizenship, elaborated at the national level, persist and are reproduced at the local level. However, the rescaling of integration policies also has two effects; it permits local governments to have a wider margin for manœuvre to include a multicultural agenda whereby immigrants are given more freedom to preserve their sociocultural practices while, at the same time, privileging the settlement of immigrants who are perceived as more contributing or desirable based on their so-called economic utility (a process similar to that in certain European countries, shown by Hinger 2020).

8.6   The Ethnicisation of Integration Paths: Between Moral Obligations and Economic Development Imperatives

On the topic of immigrant integration, participants in my research identified several opportunities linked with immigration. First and foremost – and based on a Zionist ideology – the incoming of Jewish individuals is associated with an ideal of territorial and community regeneration. For these depressed cities, immigrants hold the promise of 'new blood', a 'revolution'. This promise is concretely operationalised through five ideas: (1) they not only enable socioeconomic development, (2) a demographic boost in areas suffering from out-migration and (3) cultural diversity but also (4) increase the political weight of previous immigrant groups and (5) provide new channels for public funds.

The active involvement of certain municipalities in reaching out to potential Jewish immigrants allows these cities to gain a degree of control over the profile of those who settle there. In particular and in order to contribute to the various aspects I have cited above (economic development, demographics, cultural diversity), immigrants targeted by these policies are expected to have a high level of education, to be of working age and to bring 'culture' (which implies the dual meaning of Western liberal attitudes and knowledge of the arts – music, literature, theatre and so on). In this context, the best-suited candidates are usually 'Western' *Ashkenazi* immigrants and, more particularly here, Former Soviet Union (FSU) immigrants (since these cities already host large numbers of the latter).

FSU immigration is highly correlated with educational credentials. Interviewees mentioned a wide array of topics in which FSU immigrants are believed to excel: the sciences, university teaching and research, but also applied technology, maths, chemistry and physics. As the director of the municipal economic corporation of Kiryat Shmona argues: 'All the teachers of maths, music, chemistry and physics are immigrants. They did something great to Kiryat Shmona'.[13] They are perceived as having higher numbers of trained individuals in the fields of medicine, computing and engineering. It is, in fact, true that FSU immigrants are relatively better educated: the Central Bureau of Statistics reports that 50 per cent of the FSU immigrants who arrived after 1990 hold academic degrees (CBS 2013). Nevertheless, many degrees are not automatically recognised and their holders have to sit equivalent exams on arrival in Israel, leading many of them to give up on their previous career. Similarly, some professions are absent from the Israeli labour market, including types of engineering (forestry, heavy metal) which are virtually non-existent in Israel. Altogether, it is estimated that only 34 per cent of newcomers continue to work in the same profession as in their home countries (CBS 2013). In this sense, Jewish immigration to Israel meets similar challenges to those confronted by other types of return migration, such as those discussed by Karolak in this volume.

The second dimension associated with FSU immigrants, and Western immigrants in general, is culture, including music, literature, cinema and even sport. In the 1990s, FSU immigrants, particularly the *intelligentsia* (understood as members of a cultural and literary elite back in Russia) and supported by state institutions, therefore invested considerable efforts in fostering a vibrant cultural environment, which was usually segregated and Russian-speaking (Remennick 2003; Storper-Perez 1998). Daniele Storper-Perez has documented these initiatives in Jerusalem and, while large cities were certainly hosting more of these initiatives than the small

---

[13] Interview conducted on 21 January 2015 with the director of the economic corporation, Kiryat Shmona.

cities of the periphery, I have met members of the *intelligentsia* who have invested time and effort in activating their contacts with Russian-speaking artists and recreating their homeland cultural life in Israeli development towns (including the organisation of weekly salons, from the 1990s onwards, dedicated to poetry recitals, concerts and other cultural events). Nowadays, providing cultural activities in their native tongue to Russian-speaking immigrants is one of the main tasks which municipal departments for immigration and integration take upon themselves and for which they can easily obtain state funding. Arad's community worker explains:

> If you want to attract more immigrants, you organise lectures that are not in Hebrew. Most of the immigrants here are FSU immigrants, from Russia, who are Russian-speakers. If you want to attract them, you need something in their language. Among all these immigrants, there are many elderly people who don't even speak Hebrew. They speak only Russian. So for the Golden Age month, we organise activities that target this population.[14]

Closely concomitant with the pressure on individuals to be productive, their ability and willingness to participate in the workforce was highly appreciated by my interviewees. FSU immigrants are perceived as possessing such attributes – they are hard workers with a serious work ethic who do not mind the downward mobility often experienced by immigrants on arrival. Acre's deputy mayor argues:

> They taught us what it is to come to work or not to come to work. People used to come to work, just to be at work. They came to work. They jumped on every job. They worked in everything to keep going.[15]

Nevertheless, the capacity of FSU immigrants to enter the labour market – compared to previous waves of immigration – seems to be concomitant not with a so-called natural inclination for hard work but with the accession of Israel to the circle of industrialised countries. The Israeli economy of the 1990s offered better opportunities than that of the 1950s and 1960s. Secondly, FSU immigrants benefited from the direct absorption policy, whereby they could, at least in theory, choose where to live and move closer to economic centres. Thirdly, family structure was also a factor, as FSU immigrants belong to smaller, usually multigenerational families in which the elderly can take care of the children, providing more possibilities for parents to participate in the labour market (Lewin-Epstein et al. 2003; Lipshitz 1998; Tzfadia 2006).

Although there are considerable differences between FSU immigrants in terms of their geographic origin (ranging from Ukraine to Uzbekistan), their education, their previous occupations etc., the 'Russians' have a fairly stereotyped profile and are perceived to be educated, consumers of cultural activities, hardworking, 'people of the system' with high representation in the politics of Israel etc. In short, the 'Russians' are idealised as 'active, participatory and productive individuals' (Soysal 2012, p. 11). In a world that promotes lifelong education, employment at any cost and self-involvement in civil society (*ibid.*), such individuals could ultimately replace the state where it has withdrawn. As Glick Schiller and Çağlar (2010, p. 17)

---

[14] Interview conducted on 02 June 2015 with a community worker, Arad municipality.

[15] Interview 3 conducted on 07 January 2015 with the Deputy Mayor, Acre municipality.

state: 'Local authorities upheld migrants as models of self-reliant survival without support from state services and programmes'.

What is striking, though, and strongly differs from the narratives collected, is that local governments do not put in place specific mechanisms, infrastructure or support systems to enabling them to benefit from immigration (such as providing efficient entrepreneurship training (only available in Hebrew today), making available commercial spaces, easing bureaucratic processes, etc.). A naïve belief in an 'in-place economy'[16] persists in which immigrants are mere taxpayers. On top of paying taxes, immigrants constitute a demographic boost in those 'shrinking cities' suffering from out-migration. Their presence enables the maintenance of public services and the channelling of new resources for the municipality.

However, the cities also host quite considerable numbers of Jews who immigrated recently from Africa and Asia, especially Ethiopian and Indian Jews and FSU immigrants from Azerbaijan, Georgia and Uzbekistan. In Acre – and in Kiryat Gat in particular – interviews with the Mayor, the Deputy Mayor and the city's spokesperson show that these cities are open to Jewish immigrants from the Global South. For instance, the Mayor of Acre is proud of the achievements of the population of Mountain Jews — immigrants from Azerbaijan who, in other cities, usually fall into the category of undesirable immigrants. He confirms that the mechanisms set up to facilitate their participation in the various city institutions have worked: pupils excel in schools and adults participate in the workforce.[17] However, this type of immigration is usually associated with the moral obligation incumbent upon the Jewish people: cities must provide for those residents, based on solidarity which stems from their belonging to 'one people'. Here, the vulnerability narrative that I exposed in the first section of this chapter becomes more prominent.

At the policy level, the integration of immigrants from the Global South is conceived of somewhat differently: instead of direct absorption, these immigrants have to settle in absorption centres before they can rent a home or access property. They usually undergo a conversion to Orthodox Judaism if their practice is not considered proper by the religious authorities. In general, they are the objects of an assimilationist approach, with the absorption of the group rather than the individual and with similar logics of renunciation of agency which I described earlier. Finally, the immigrant status is 'inherited' and second-generation immigrants continue to benefit from special entitlements (discounts in education and enrolment in special units in the army in particular). In addition to the variation in the absorption approach, when it comes to discourses, the perceived benefits of these immigrants are linked to the potential funding which local governments can obtain to serve these populations.

In general, there is a trade-off between economic performance and multiculturalism – understood as individual choice over socio-cultural life. In fact, individuals

---

[16] Coined by French geographers Christophe Terrier and Laurent Davezies in the expression 'économie présentielle" or 'économie résidentielle" which we translated as 'in-place economy", the approach implies focusing on the area's residents, who produce and consume, rather than on the industrial economy.

[17] Interview conducted on 10 February 2015 with Shimon Lancry, Mayor of Acre.

perceived as economically useful can 'buy' their cultural freedom, whereas groups from the Global South accepted by the cities are framed according to their potential vulnerability and strongly racialised. It is precisely this vulnerability that makes them deserving but it also means that the assimilationist injunction is stronger. In this sense, it seems to fit Chauvin and Garcés-Mascareñas' (2014) concept of deservingness. Moreover, it points to a certain neoliberalisation of Israel's integration frames, such as Will Kimlycka's 'neoliberal multiculturalism' (2015) in which immigration is seen as positive for groups who do not threaten the redistributive systems of the states hosting them.

By actively categorising African and Asian Jewish immigrants as vulnerable, these policies and the discourses they are based on participate in their continuous exclusion from a new model of integration in Israel. Ethiopian and Indian new immigrants undergo a similar process of disintegration as the *Mizrahi* did some decades earlier. This fragmented integration governance has effects on urban society as a whole. For instance, police violence and limited immigration quotas have triggered important protests in Tel Aviv, in Jerusalem and in cities with a significant group of Ethiopian Israelis (such as Kiryat Gat) in 2016. In parallel, the criminalisation of other racialised groups, such as asylum-seekers from Sudan and Eritrea, has again encouraged debates on ethnicisation and integration.

8.7 Conclusion: Reframing of the Deserving vs Desirable Dichotomy under Neoliberalisation Processes

Israel's immigration policy and the concomitant integration policies elaborated by the state since the 1950s, have always borne exclusion mechanisms. Firstly, it completely excludes non-Jewish immigrants from access to the national community. Even the goal of the 'encompassing of all Jews' has always been restricted to individuals who could prove that they would quickly participate in building the 'Jewish home'. Individuals who were not perceived to be economically useful could enter the country if they were under immediate threat – thereby fitting instead the definition of refugee – and were accepted because of their very vulnerability and obliged to assimilate with the European *Ashkenazi* model. This was true before the establishment of Israel – when the first groups of Jews arranged to reach mandatory Palestine at the establishment of the state – and is still true today. However, what makes the last decade different is the justification of this limitation: the rationale behind this *disintegration within inclusion* is increasingly linked to neoliberal reforms of governance.

Although Berthomière (2002) suggests that the FSU immigration in the 1990s, after Israel had shifted to a free market economy, would reveal the tensions between state logics and immigrant logics, I argue that the devolution of responsibilities to the city level, and the rescaling of power, had an equally important weight on the reframing of the integration paradigm. The logics at work are therefore threefold:

the state, the city and the immigrants. In fact, the development imperative that falls on municipalities, in a context of 'interlocality competition' (Brenner 2004) for resources, residents and more, has sanctioned immigration as a potential lever for development. The ethnicisation of Israel's integration policies is dissimulated under an injunction to local economic development, where municipalities privilege certain immigrants because of their perceived economic utility. More insidious still, the neoliberal approach to integration participates in the reinforcement of ethnicisation, rather than its transformation. As Collyer et al. (2020) argue in the introduction of this volume, 'the perception and practices of integration depend on the dominant perception of nationhood. […] this also works the other way around – integration policies that officially target only specific groups or individuals often serve as an arena in which the broader issue of belonging (or not) to the nation is (re)negotiated' (p. 12).

With this in mind, some local governments proactively design programmes to reach out to immigrants whom they perceive as 'desirable' and able to integrate better and faster in the local community and the local economy. In this sense, the Law of Return, when interpreted at the local level, includes a criterion of economic performance and self-responsibility for integration, whereby immigrants rely on their own capacity to learn the language (Hebrew courses are still subsidised) and look for housing and employment (including being involved in professional retraining if necessary). Western immigrants, and particularly, here, FSU immigrants, are believed to have sufficient social and human capital to deal effectively with their settlement and contribute to the city's growth.

However, this does not mean that the ethnonational frame of integration, the belonging to the Jewish people, is no longer a fundamental aspect of immigrant integration: ethnonationalist frames persist. In this context, at the national level, all Jewish candidates for immigration are legitimate but the less they are perceived as net contributors – and therefore the more they are seen as vulnerable – the more they are subjected to an assimilationist injunction. There is still an economic aspect to welcoming groups from Ethiopia or India for instance: municipalities are assured of receiving substantial funds to support the groups' integration, thereby effectively gaining money. However, the ministry officers and the municipal agents I interviewed adopt a much less pluralist attitude towards them. The national ideological frame of integration is more prevalent for groups who go through absorption centres and do not benefit from direct absorption.

The case of Israel's development towns brings some elements to the understanding of *politics of (dis)integration*, as addressed in this collective volume. Firstly, new actors in the governance of immigrant integration – here local government's officials and public service workers – actively participate in reframing integration. Secondly, even in the conception of a return policy, strongly justified by ethnonational criteria, integration is conceived differently based on country of origin and assumed economic utility. Ethnicity, and the strong stereotyping associated with it, is the only determinant for the Jewish Agency, the ministry in charge of immigration matters and the municipalities to decide whether or not an immigrant is 'desirable' and will therefore benefit from 'direct absorption' – which ensures the migrant's free choice of sociocultural practice, geographical settlement and employment – or 'deserving' and hence subject to community absorption, often associated with religious coercion, group professional retraining and job placement, as well as restricted choice of residence.

References

Anderson, B. R. O. (1983). *Imagined communities: Reflections on the origin and spread of nationalism*. London/New York: Verso (revised edition).

Anteby, L. (1998). Post-sionisme et Aliyah. *Bulletin du Centre de Recherche Français à Jérusalem, 3*, 19–31.

Auerbach. (2001). *Central-Local Government Relations: The Case of Temporary Housing for Immigrants 1990–1992*. Jerusalem: The Floersheimer Institute for Policy Studies.

Auerbach, G. (2011). Local autonomy in action: Mobile homes for immigrants in Israel. *Applied Geography, 31*(2), 556–563.

Ben-Elia, N. (2006). *The fourth generation: New local government for Israel*. Jerusalem: The Floersheimer Institute for Policy Studies.

Berthomière, W. (1996). De l'aliya à l'immigration ou la lecture d'un continuum migratoire. *Revue Européenne des Migrations Internationales, 12*(3), 33–60.

Berthomière, W. (2002). Logiques de migrants versus logiques d'état: Quels impacts sur la stratégie territoriale d'Israël? *Espace, Populations, Sociétés, 20*(1), 37–52.

Berthomière, W. (2004). Sionisme et immigration en Israël. *Mouvements, 33–34*(3), 30–35.

Brenner, N. (2004). *New state spaces*. Oxford: Oxford University Press.

CBS. (2013). Immigration absorption survey 2010–2011, selected findings. Jerusalem: Central Bureau of Statistics. Retrieved from 1 Nov 2016 http://www.cbs.gov.il/webpub/pub/text_page_eng.html?publ=101&CYear=2011&CMonth=1

CBS. (2016). *Statistical Abstract of Israel 2016*. Jerusalem: Central Bureau of Statistics. Retrieved from 20 Nov 2016 http://www.cbs.gov.il/reader/shnatonenew_site.htm

Chauvin, S., & Garcés-Mascareñas, B. (2012). Beyond informal citizenship: The new moral economy of migrant illegality. *International Political Sociology, 6*(3), 241–259.

Chauvin, S., & Garcés-Mascareñas, B. (2014). Becoming less illegal: Deservingness frames and undocumented migrant incorporation. *Sociology Compass, 8*(4), 422–432.

Chetrit, S. S. (2000). Mizrahi politics in Israel: Between integration and alternative. *Journal of Palestine Studies, 29*(4), 51–65.

Collyer, M., Hinger, S. & Schweitzer, R. (2020). Politics of (dis)integration – an introduction. In S. Hinger & R. Schweitzer (Eds.), *Politics of (Dis)Integration* (pp. 1–18). Cham: Springer VS.

Desille, A. (2017). *Governing or being governed? A scalar approach of the transformations of state power and authority through the case of immigration and integration policies of four frontier towns in Israel*. Poitiers: University of Poitiers.

Djerrahian, G. (2015). Le discours sur la *blackness* en Israël. Évolution et chevauchements. *Ethnologie Française, 45*(2), 333.

Doron, A., & Kargar, H. J. (1993). The politics of immigration policy in Israel. *International Migration, 31*(4), 497–512.

Eisenstadt, S. N. (1954). *Absorption of immigrants*. London: Routledge & Kegan Paul.

Elias, N., & Kemp, A. (2010). The new second generation: Non-Jewish olim, black Jews and children of migrant workers in Israel. *Israel Studies, 15*(1), 73–94.

Faist, T. (2013). The mobility turn: A new paradigm for the social sciences? *Ethnic and Racial Studies, 36*(11), 1637–1646.

Florida, R. (2003). Cities and the creative class. *City and Community, 2*(1), 3–19.

Frankenstein, C. (1953). *Between past and future: Essays and studies on aspects of immigrant absorption in Israel*. Jerusalem: Henrietta Szold Foundation for Child and Youth Welfare.

Glick Schiller, N., & Çağlar, A. (Eds.). (2010). *Locating migration: Rescaling cities and migrants.* Ithaca: Cornell University Press.

Glick Schiller, N., & Salazar, N. B. (2013). Regimes of mobility across the globe. *Journal of Ethnic and Migration Studies, 39*(2), 183–200.

Hinger, S. (2020). Integration through disintegration? The distinction between deserving and undeserving refugees in national and local integration policies in Germany. In S. Hinger & R. Schweitzer (Eds.), *Politics of (Dis)Integration* (pp. 19–39). Cham: Springer VS.

Jørgensen, M. B. (2012). The diverging logics of integration policy making at national and city level. *International Migration Review, 46*(1), 244–278.

Karolak, M. (2020). Returning for (Dis)Integration in the Labour Market? The Careers of Labour Migrants Returning to Poland from the United Kingdom. In S. Hinger & R. Schweitzer (Eds.), *Politics of (Dis)Integration* (pp. 101–120). Cham: Springer VS.

Kay, A. (2012). *From Altneuland to the new promised land: A study of the evolution and Americanization of the Israeli economy* (Vol. 24, pp. 1–2). Jerusalem Center for Public Affairs.

Khazzoom, A. (2005). Did the Israeli state engineer segregation? On the placement of Jewish immigrants in development towns in the 1950s. *Social Forces, 84*(1), 115–134.

Kymlicka, W. (2015, January). *Solidarity in diverse societies: Beyond neoliberal multiculturalism and welfare chauvinism. Paper given to the IMISCOE and EUI conference 'Mobility in crisis'* (pp. 29–30). Florence: European University Institute.

Lewin-Epstein, N., Semyonov, M., Kogan, I., & Wanner, R. A. (2003). Institutional structure and immigrant integration: A comparative study of immigrants' labor market attainment in Canada and Israel. *International Migration Review, 37*(2), 389–420.

Lior, I. (2016). The immigration of 500 Falashmuras was authorised: Likud MPs did not participate in the plenary vote. (in Hebrew). *Haaretz.co.il*, 7 March. Retrieved from (10/03/2016) http://www.haaretz.co.il/news/education/1.2875253.

Lipshitz, G. (1991). Immigration and internal migration as a mechanism of polarization and dispersion of population and development: The Israeli Case. *Economic Development and Cultural Change, 39*(2), 391–408.

Lipshitz, G. (1998). *Country on the move: Migration to and within Israel, 1948–1995*. Dordrecht: Springer Science & Business Media.

Lis, Y. (2016). The coalition crisis is solved: 1300 Falashmuras will immigrate this year, Amsalem and Negusa will vote again (in Hebrew). *Haaretz.co.il*, 7 April. Retrieved from 11 April 2016 http://www.haaretz.co.il/news/politi/1.2908665.

Penninx, R. (2013). *Research on migration and integration in Europe. Achievements and lessons.* Amsterdam: Vossiuspers UVA.

Ram, U. (1995). *The changing agenda of Israeli sociology : Theory, ideology, and identity*. Albany: State University of New York Press.

Ram, U. (2000). National, ethnic or civic? Contesting paradigms of memory, identity and culture in Israel. *Studies in Philosophy and Education, 19*(5–6), 405–422.

Razin, E. (2003). *Local government reform in Israel: Between centralization and decentralization between traditionalism and modernity*. Jerusalem: The Floersheimer Institute for Policy Studies.

Remennick, L. (2003). What does integration mean? Social insertion of Russian immigrants in Israel. *Journal of International Migration and Integration/Revue de l'Integration et de la Migration Internationale, 4*(1), 23–49.

Rubin, A., Navot, D., & Ghanem, A. (2014). The 2013 Israeli general election: Travails of the former king. *The Middle East Journal, 68*(2), 248–267.

Samuk, Ş. (2020). Can integration be temporary? The (Dis)Integration of Temporary Migrant Workers in Canada and the UK. In S. Hinger & R. Schweitzer (Eds.), *Politics of (Dis)Integration* (pp. 61–79). Cham: Springer VS.

Sassen, S. (2005). The repositioning of citizenship and alienage: Emergent subjects and spaces for politics. *Globalizations, 2*(1), 79–94.

Shafir, Y., & Peled, G. (2004). Citizenship and stratification in an ethnic democracy. In M. Semyonov & N. Lewin-Epstein (Eds.), *Stratification in Israel: Class, ethnicity, and gender* (pp. 365–384). New Brunswick: Transaction.

Shama, A., & Iris, M. (1977). *Immigration without integration: Third world Jews in Israel*. New Brunswick: Transaction.

Shilo, M. (1994). The immigration policy of the Zionist institutions 1882–1914. *Middle Eastern Studies, 30*(3), 597–617.

Sitton, S. (1962). *Israël Immigration et Croissance*. Paris: Cujas.

Smooha, S., & Peretz, D. (1982). The Arabs in Israel. *Journal of Conflict Resolution, 26*(3), 451–484.

Soysal, Y. N. (2012). Citizenship, immigration, and the European social project: Rights and obligations of individuality. *British Journal of Sociology, 63*(1), 1–21.

Storper-Perez, D. (1998). *L'Intelligentsia' Russe en Israël: Rassurante Etrangeté*. Paris: CNRS.

Tzfadia, E. (2005). Local autonomy and immigration: Mayoral policy-making in peripheral towns in Israel. *Space and Polity, 9*(2), 167–184.

Tzfadia, E. (2006). Public housing as control: Spatial policy of settling immigrants in Israeli development towns. *Housing Studies, 21*(4), 523–537.

Tzfadia, E., & Yacobi, H. (2011). *Rethinking Israeli space: Periphery and identity*. Abingdon: Routledge.

Varsanyi, M. (2008). Rescaling the 'alien', rescaling personhood: Neoliberalism, immigration, and the state. *Annals of the Association of American Geographers, 98*(4), 877–896.

Yacobi, H., & Tzfadia, E. (2009). Multiculturalism, nationalism, and the politics of the Israeli city. *International Journal of Middle East Studies, 41*(02), 289–307.

Yiftachel, O. (2000). 'Ethnocracy' and its discontents: Minorities, protests, and the Israeli polity. *Critical Inquiry, 26*(4), 725–756.

Yonah, Y. (2005). Israel as a multicultural democracy: Challenges and obstacles. *Israel Affairs, 11*(1), 95–116.

Chapter 9
Denying, While Demanding Integration: An Analysis of the Integration Paradox in Malta and Refugees' Coping Strategies

Sarah Nimführ, Laura Otto, and Gabriel Samateh

9.1   Introduction

'Integration is a late bloomer in Malta'. This is what a representative of a ministry in Malta entrusted with family matters, as well as questions of care and solidarity, told Laura in an interview on 06 July 2015. Why is this statement remarkable? In 2015, the arrival of refugees[1] was not a new phenomenon in the island-state: people had been seeking refuge on the island since the 1970s (Pisani 2011, p. 27) and the number of refugee boats crossing the Mediterranean was still significant in 2015. With Malta being located along the route between Africa and Europe, almost 20,000 people reached the island-state between 2002 and 2016 (NSO 2018). Even though this was a well-known fact, an Integration Policy was not passed until late 2017. This lack of official and governmental integration measures was also addressed during a demonstration organised by migrant organisations in the summer of 2015 in Malta's capital, Valletta.

When the representative of the ministry stated that integration is a late bloomer he mainly referred to questions of social inclusion as well as access to specific welfare programs; however, integration had not actually been fully absent in previous

---

[1] The term 'refugee' is not used here according to its legal definition. In this chapter it refers to the experience, the process and the involuntariness of the migrated individual. The term 'asylum-seeker' is only used when we refer to persons whose asylum application was rejected.

S. Nimführ (✉)
University of Vienna, Vienna, Austria
e-mail: sarah.nimfuehr@univie.ac.at

L. Otto
Goethe-University Frankfurt, Frankfurt am Main, Germany

G. Samateh
Independent Researcher, Valletta, Malta

© The Author(s) 2020
S. Hinger, R. Schweitzer (eds.), *Politics of (Dis)Integration*,
IMISCOE Research Series, https://doi.org/10.1007/978-3-030-25089-8_9

years. With Malta acceding to European Union (EU) membership in 2004, its government was obliged to conform to certain duties derived from EU policies. The Maltese Military Rescue Unit (MRU) became part of Search and Rescue Missions (SAR) at sea, Malta's government had to accept the Dublin Regulation,[2] and refugees' fingerprints were saved in the EURODAC system.[3] Thus, refugees were integrated into a bureaucratic system; social integration, however, was not promoted.

We address this discrepancy of social exclusion and bureaucratic inclusion in this chapter, by analysing two fields of tension: (1) saving refugees at sea versus questions of border control, and (2) demanding the integration of refugees whilst denying them access to mechanisms leading to (social) integration. The chapter is structured as follows: first, we outline our methodological and analytical framework before, secondly, presenting reactions toward boat migration to Malta and revealing local understandings of integration, mainly communicated by governing actors. Third, we explain the field of tension between rescuing refugees at sea and border securitisation. This is, fourth, followed by an 'intermedium', written by Gabriel who was born in the Gambia and has lived in Malta as a refugee since 2014. In the penultimate fifth section, we engage with practices of (dis)integration, focusing on refugees' reception, allocation of status, access to education and the labour market to highlight these dynamics. Finally we present refugees' coping strategies developed against the backdrop of the situations they (inevitably) found themselves in, concluding that (dis)integration does not only depend on legal frameworks but that social interactions and individually denied access are equally efficacious. Throughout the chapter, we refer to refugees' and institutional actors' agency to highlight that legal frameworks must not be viewed as deterministic but are, rather, an arena within which (dis)integration is negotiated.

9.2   Methods and Analytical Framework

This chapter is based on ethnographic fieldwork carried out by the cultural anthropologists Laura and Sarah between 2013 and 2018 in Malta. Sarah focuses on refugees whose asylum applications were rejected and are non-deportable; Laura's research focuses on the situation for young refugees categorised as Unaccompanied Minors (UAMs; see Otto and Kaufmann 2018). Laura was in contact with 48 refugees classified as UAMs and 17 young refugees who were not categorised as such; she also interviewed 12 institutional actors. Sarah interacted with 22 refugees classified as rejected asylum-seekers, interviewed 27 officials and held informal talks.

---

[2] The Dublin Regulation was adopted in 2003 to determine that the EU member-state in which refugees first entered the EU is responsible for examining the asylum application.

[3] European Dactyloscopy (EURODAC) is the EU's fingerprint database for identifying both refugees and the member-state responsible for examining their asylum application.

Following the ethnographic tradition, both also conducted participant observation in refugee housing centres and refugees' flats, in ministries and non-governmental organisations' (NGO) offices as well as in public. In the course of a revisit in 2018, we had further joint talks with three institutional actors. We complemented our data with policy documents, newspaper articles and NGO reports.

In line with the overall aim of this book, the border regime analysis which is applied here and which was coined by Sabine Hess and Vassilis Tsianos (2010) following earlier discussions by *Transit Migration Forschungsgruppe* (2007) also emphasises that regimes are not to be understood as totalising but that processes such as (dis)integration are negotiated *in situ* and by migrating and non-migrating, governing and non-governing actors (see Collyer et al. 2020; Rass and Wolff 2018). Our understanding of *how* it is possible to research (dis)integration processes and practices derives from this multi-actor approach including various forms of data. Contradictory logics, conflicting interests, facets of agency and shifting positions can thus be taken into account (Collyer et al. 2020; Hess and Tsianos 2010). However, to research these dynamics also means being sensitive.

The highly politicised field of the border regime raises questions of research ethics concerning both non-refugees and refugees. Conducting research with vulnerabilised persons – such as young or rejected refugees – presents a unique set of conundrums, contradictions, and conflicts (Chase et al. 2019). Especially when research partners find themselves in institutionalised surroundings, the question of *how* to approach them for research is vital. It was our concern to translate and communicate our research interests in the best possible way, and we obtained the informed consent (von Unger et al. 2014) of the refugees. In our research-ethical positioning we did not orient ourselves along the categories set by the institutionalised border regime, such as the fixation in the category of a minor, in order to decide whether or not persons could participate in our research. We rather looked for 'person-friendly' (Punch 2002) approaches. Our long-term relationships made it possible to reflect the reserach process with the refugees, and we have discussed interpretations and research outcomes with them. As a result, our research partners often encouraged us to write our articles and monographs, as they communicated the wish to share their experiences with a broader audience. This practice felt better to us than excluding people from research in the first place because of their classification by the border regime, and consequently excluding certain perspectives.

For the protection of the research partners pseudonymisation took place. We decided against a simple anonymisation by numbering or initials, as otherwise important information about the respective persons would be lost. Conclusions about the habitus can still be drawn if a pseudonym is used. Furthermore, we decided on pseudonyms because these facilitate the spontaneous perception of the individual (see Reckinger 2010). Often, our research partners decided on their pseudonym themselves. We were asked to pseudonymise the respective interviewees, but received permission from representatives of institutions to name the institutions. Despite their consent, we have decided to also anonymise the institutions as much as possible without rendering their function unrecognisable. This said, the pseud-onymisation of institutions proved difficult. Given that the island-state of Malta is relatively small, many institutions and above all certain positions which are repre-sented are unique in the country. Even with ambitious pseudonymisation attempts, the respective institution can possibly be identified in certain cases, which is why we are always dependent on the discretion of the readers.

To address issues of representation and analysis of the integration paradox in Malta – not merely from a White perspective (Eggers et al. 2005) – we argue that it is necessary to engage with these issues collaboratively. As researchers, we are involved in (dis)integration processes and might even reproduce these powerful dynamics. By working together with Gabriel we wish to extend knowledge produc-tion beyond 'academic limitations'[4] (Fontanari et al. 2014, p. 111), thereby tran-scending the divide between researchers and researched, theory and practise, academic scholarship and active participation (*ibid.*, p. 118, see also Nimführ and Sesay 2019). Gabriel thus wrote an 'intermedium' that allows us to gain insights from a person who 'lived the disaster' (Khosravi 2010, p. 6). We aimed at presenting an account which does not suggest that researchers who did not go through the same experiences as refugees are claiming to represent the experiences of others (Rodgers 2004, p. 49).

The practices highlighted in this chapter are frequently dependent on the status which refugees receive in Malta. Simultaneously, their integration is nevertheless demanded. This illustrates that (dis)integration is the intertwining of integration and disintegration, created by both legal frameworks and individuals' action, producing various forms of differentiated in- and exclusion (De Genova et al. 2015, p. 79). Ethnographic accounts, as applied here, offer the methodological tools with which to grasp these dynamics. Consequently, what we understand as both the method-ological and the analytical value of this approach is that it highlights how local understandings displayed by governmental actors influence the (dis)integration of refugees within and beyond legal frameworks. Narratives and practices of (dis)inte-gration in relation to legal frameworks build the core of this analysis. Like Nina Sahraoui (2020), we do not further engage with theoretical concepts of integration that are diverse and sometimes contradictory but show how (dis)integration is per-formed and practiced in daily encounters. We do not understand (dis)integration as something which primarily refugees are engaged in but, rather, as a form of inclu-sion and exclusion acted out by governing actors and through which the distribution of and access to resources is decided. This understanding means that we are pursu-ing a structural analysis wherein the refugees in question are not in a positon in which they produce disintegration, but are necessarily respondents to the exclusion-ary conditions they involuntarily encounter. Nevertheless, structure and agency can never be entirely separated and the following empirical analysis also highlights gov-erning and non-governing actors' agency, highlighting that the conditions the refu-

---

[4] All references that are originally not English were translated by the authors.

gees encounter do not lead to a situation of their non-agency. Our account thus reveals that the structural analysis we undertake is itself limited and that actors constantly reinforce or circumvent the structures they encounter. This may take the form of volitional action – i.e. intentionally preventing or enabling access – or it may be unintentional, such as when actions nevertheless lead to outcomes where inclusion and exclusion emerge.

9.3   Political and Societal Reactions to Boat Migration and Integration in Malta[5]

Located in the Mediterranean Sea, the Maltese island-state is the smallest member-state of the EU. Although so-called 'boat refugees' had already arrived on Malta's shores in the late 1990s, records of arrivals only date back to 2002 (Pisani 2011). From the beginning, refugees were represented as the 'others' (Klepp 2011). In political terms, border securitisation and the need of protection against 'dangerous/unwanted intruders' (Pisani 2013, p. 78) were emphasised by governmental actors:

> Given Malta's size you cannot expect the government to release illegal immigrants into the streets, (…). This would send the wrong message and spell disaster for the country (…). As a minister I am responsible, first and foremost, for the protection of Maltese citizens (Minister of Home Affairs and National Security, quoted in Calleja 2009).

Malta's small size was constantly used by various actors to legitimise an exceptional Detention Policy applicable to all refugees who arrived in unregulated manners.[6] According to the former Ministry of Justice and Home Affairs, detention is necessary in the interests of 'national security and public order' (MFFS and MJHA 2005, p. 11), Since Malta joined the EU, its government has constantly called on other member-states to assist in 'burden-sharing' and has argued for a revision of the Dublin Regulation (Mainwaring 2008), as the Maltese government and society do not allegedly possess resources to deal with large numbers of new arrivals and with refugees who already live in Malta (Sansone 2011). Meanwhile, significantly fewer refugees have arrived by boat since 2015.[7] The MRU of Malta argues that this is caused by the geographical shift of rescue operations: 'The nature of the operations has shifted southwards. (…) The rescue and distress [now] starts inside the Libyan territories', claimed a MRU representative in Malta in an interview on 26 April 2016.

---

[5] Parts of this section are based on Nimführ et al. (2017). We thank Assoziation A. for the publishing rights.

[6] Since January 2016 refugees who entered in unregulated manners are firstly accommodated in the Initial Reception Centre, followed by a detention centre or an open centre. Refugees can leave the latter during opening hours. Prior to 2016, refugees were housed in an open centre after detainment.

[7] To compare: 2015–2017: 150 people, 2014: 569 people, 2013: 2008 people (NSO 2018, 2).

These 'politics of defence' materialise in both juridical and social practices – for example withholding legal rights on different levels, thereby placing refugees in a permanent state of insecurity, as a human-rights lawyer of an international charitable NGO in Malta, reflected in an interview on 23 July 2015:

> Their well-being is extremely (…) threatened all the time (…) because [if] you lose your job, everything goes. You get sick so you can't work anymore, everything goes. You have an accident crossing the street and a car runs you over. (…) In one minute (…) everything collapses.

Even though refugees have been reaching Malta for more than a decade, an Integration Policy was not passed until 2017. Looking at the narratives of governmental actors charged with implementing 'integration' prior to this policy reveals that integration was broadly understood as a waste of resources, as refugees would want to leave Malta anyway. To legitimise this ignorance, integration was framed as 'harmful' to refugees as it would force them to stay in a place where they did not want to be. This was also reflected by the representative of a Maltese ministry quoted on integration in the introductory part:

> For a good part of the last ten to 15 years, the thinking was that migrants come, they stay a bit, (…) and then they go and we will live like we used to live before. (…) And therefore there was no investment at all in integration. (…) when some work started to happen it was mostly preparation for the migrants to leave.

What also becomes evident here is that it appears to have been important to maintain a particular lifestyle which was seen as being in jeopardy through the integration of refugees. A representative from a governmental agency also concurred with this assessment in an interview on 25 February 2015:

> It is very obvious that no asylum seeker (…) wants to stay in Malta. And I think the more we are making people stay (…) by integration, the more we are doing harm to these people.

In the following section we discuss whether, in spite of this unwelcoming attitude articulated by our research partners holding vocational positions within the border regime, people nonetheless continue to arrive in Malta, whether by choice or by chance.

9.4 Arriving in Malta?

Even though Malta is comparatively small in size, the island-state plays an important role in SAR missions as the Maltese SAR region is with about 251,000 km^2 relatively broad. The majority of refugees who reached its shores did not intend to reach Malta (Falzon 2012). Due to bad weather conditions or other unpredictable circumstances, however, most did not reach their intended destination – Italy. 'We never planned to come here. I heard about Malta for the first time when we were rescued', stated Blaze, a Nigerian refugee. Several thousand more people were saved in joint SAR missions in which Italian coastguards supported the MRU. Whether these joint missions are even initiated also depends on the local coastguards' reactions. If the MRU sights and contacts refugees at sea who do not want to be rescued, they escort them and let them continue with their journey, provided no perilous conditions are forecast as the MRU representative further explained:

> So they refuse [their rescue] and in that case everyone has still the duty of care (…). They keep close to the boat, monitoring in case the situation changes, weather changes or they will request to be rescued (…) The same mechanism takes place no matter if the distress call was made or not.

Bilal, a young Somali, described a case in which the refugees he shared the boat with asked to be rescued while at sea. Even though the MRU had offered to accompany them on their passage to Italy – in line with guidelines of the International Maritime Organisation (IMO)[8] – the refugees made use of the 'request to be rescued', as Bilal explains:

> When they [MRU] came they told us that they give us fuel and that we can go directly to Italy. And then the adults said that there are children inside the boat and that we cannot go any further. (…) they rescued us from there.

These processes and negotiations of sea rescues are time-consuming and labour-intensive, thereby entailing long waiting times at sea. According to a MRU representative, the long waiting times may be explained by the assumption that refugees communicate inaccurate positions, leading the authorities to then 'start to localise the position through satellites'. To respond to emergencies on board, the MRU cooperates with Malta's Air Force. Mahad, a young man from Mogadishu, was rescued during an air operation: 'I came by helicopter. Because I was very, very sick on the boat and everybody thought I am dead'. While he was taken to Malta, his boat continued the passage to Italy. But who is saved by whom at sea remains the ultimate decision of the Maritime Rescue Coordination Centre (MRCC) in Rome (Leurs 2014), that also decides in which EU state the refugees may disembark from the rescue vessel. What the different SAR actors share is the perspective that, as we have shown, rescues are charged with technical feasibily, issues of coordination and disembarkation as well as assumptions about responsibility. Whilst the governing actors exclusively focus on sea rescue and the sea border, the refugees' perspective on the issue of being saved is ultimately also tied to legal status and practices of (dis)integration during and following arrival, as illustrated by Gabriel Samateh in the next section.

---

[8] The IMO resolution (2004) states that refugees have to be taken to a 'place of safety'. It is not stipulated that this must be a port.

9.5   Journey of Hope and Misfortunes: Gabriel's Account

The night of 06 June 2014 was a distracting one for me, boarding the deadly dangerous, rackety boats in the Mediterranean Sea, searching for a safe destination and a better life. In my boat, there were more than a hundred on board. During the night, the smugglers were beating us and emphasising their power to get us on the boat and then tell one person to drive us. Only God was our guide in this risk of dying. We started moving on Thursday night with everyone thinking about his or her own life and what could happen during this journey of dangerous misfortune because of lots of fighting and quarrels on the boat. The following morning, Friday 07 June 2014 at 2:00 pm, we saw the aircrafts USS Bataan and USS Elrod – on marine patrol looking for boats with problems and in danger of sinking. After 30 minutes we again saw another five migrant boats arriving at the same juncture. One of the boats was damaged and sinking and all the others were leaking and starting to take on water. Then there was an emergency rescue by USS Bataan and USS Elrod (FFG-55), offering rapid assistance to persons in distress for at least 1 h till 3:30 pm. Many died in that sinking boat so we were there waiting for our rescue but it took too long and the day turned into night. All the rescue workers left us and went away. Then everybody else started to go crazy because we thought that we were all going to die because no one was there to rescue us, while our boat was taking on water and other boats ran out of petrol. Then we continued our run without lights or a single directive device to see or know where we were going. We were following the lights we saw from big ships in the very dark Mediterranean Sea until 9:30 pm. Suddenly we saw an airplane giving us a signal light indicating a direction to follow but, due to a termination of contact, we continued our run to an unknown destination for 30 minutes. Then an American soldier with a torch came on a rescue boat, shouting at us to follow them for rescue. When we reached the ship, they took us on boad and provided us with food, water, medical attention and temporary shelter until the following morning, Saturday 08 June. In Malta, a few of us, including myself, where brought to hospital for health care emergency. I spent a few days receiving medical treatment there before I was evacuated from hospital to the detention centre. Arriving in detention was another life-devastating experience due to the violations of human rights and the disrespect for my skin colour. I felt uncomfortable asking to be treated as a human being. So there I was detained for 8 months – others for up to 18 months – with security forces on duty 24/7 and all doors locked. We were handcuffed when we went to the hospital or for the asylum interview. I applied for asylum and got rejected after 3 months. The worry of a miserable life prevails. In this situation, freedom was the most important word of wisdom. Everybody in detention wants to hear 'freedom' and some people went mad just for the word 'freedom'. Now, out of detention, still being in limbo as a rejected asylum-seeker, the fear exists of being

(continued)

> sent back home, your life in the society is disclosed, you will be not respected, no social benefits even if you work and pay all your taxes, applications are rejected unlawfully. So, finally, I can say that human rights in Malta are zero and, due to this, our lives continue to be destabilised in all ways.

9.6 Life in Limbo

As Reinhard Schweitzer (2020) also highlights in his chapter on irregularised migrants living in Britain, it is not the case that refugees are totally deprived of access to EU territory but that processes of excluding 'newcomers' take place *after* they have entered. Keeping refugees at bay thus does not exclusively occur at the sea border but also takes the form of institutional and individual exclusion within Malta. This can be explained by the fact that rescue at sea is still embedded in both refugee and international sea law. These procedures are intensely monitored while, despite intensified processes of harmonisation, the actual treatment of refugees remains under the auspices of the individual member-states (Klepp 2011). As Schweitzer demonstrates, there is a 'policy trend towards a selective prevention of integration' (2020, p. 121). Consequently, 'violence against migrants no longer takes place exclusively at the geographical space between two sovereign territories. Instead border violence today has become much more normalized and diffused into society itself' (Nail 2012, p. 241). The border, thus, has changed: the traditional nation-state border has turned into a boundary, a less visible, inner-state border, comprising socio-cultural, legal and economic dimensions (Fassin 2011, p. 117).[9] Refugees are confronted with these dimensions on a daily basis. In the following sections, we focus on four central aspects that highlight these dynamics. We also illustrate how refugees deal with (denied) access and their different legal positionings.

9.6.1 Reception

The arrival of refugees is a frequent topic in Maltese media in which portrayals of demark refugees as undesirable; this feeling of being unwelcome was often also mentioned by the refugees we talked to. The first people they encounter after the boat ride across the Mediterranean are MRU employees in military attire, the immigration police and medical doctors. When an arrival is documented in the Maltese media, people in uniform, handcuffed refugees or doctors in white overalls are displayed (Falzon 2012) marking the arrival of refugees as a 'border spectacle'

---

[9] Here, border is understood as a flexible arena negotiated by different actors.

(Cantat 2020; De Genova 2013) and creating the idea that refugees are potentially sick and threatening.

The majority of refugees does not possess the papers required by the authorities in order to enter the territory. This discrepancy between the lack of documents and the state's bureaucracy is always stressed. In an interview on 15 June 2018, the Vice Director of a local NGO told us that, as refugees declare their nationality whilst simultaneously not possessing the required documents, a powerful homogenisation as so-called '*il-illegali*' or as '*is-suwed* [the Blacks]' is efficacious. As the refugees have come from a continent often associated with exotic diseases, they are repeatedly perceived as a health risk (Falzon 2012, p. 1669). A government representative described people's first reactions towards boat migration as follows:

> In 2002 people were shocked. That was the reaction of the Maltese society. (…) because we weren't used to have so many immigrants. And African immigrants. (…) (…) Then, just right about last year [2014] things were like settling in. (…) Maltese people then got the feeling that we are a transit country. So it calmed a bit down, because we are like a bus stop.

Mark-Anthony Falzon contends that this 'bus stop' phenomenon is not caused by the refugees but is, rather, grounded in how the Maltese government and society deal with refugees. As he argues the Maltese government creates a transit zone to react to the threat that refugees supposedly represent:

> In contemporary Malta, sub-Saharan 'boat' immigrants are imagined and represented as transients and sojourners rather than as settlers (…). Transience is a product actively and agentively produced by the state and other actors in response to a perceived threat from immigration (Falzon 2012, p. 1661).

This state of transit is especially apparent in the practice of detaining refugees after their arrival. Accessing the detention centres is almost impossible for the public and is highly restricted for NGOs, too. Consequently, refugees are initially 'invisibilised'. When they become visible to the public while detained, then this visibility often goes hand in hand with practices that further criminalise them: 'For my age assessment they took me to (…) hospital. (…) And I was handcuffed also and guarded by policemen. Everybody in the hospital was looking at me', Geelo, a young refugee, told us. After detention, refugees are accommodated in so-called open centres, a form of accommodation where refugees can live after release from detention for up to 12 months. Depending on their allocated status of protection, they also receive a per diem. The Vice Director of a local NGO told us in his interview of 15 June 2018 that the Maltese government did not inform local (non-refugee) residents prior to opening these camps in the respective neighbourhoods:

> Balbi is likely to be the city in Malta who was hit hardest when refugees came. (…) Shortly after the big arrival of refugees, the so-called Balbi open centre has been established in Balbi, a centre for single refugee men. At that time Balbi had a population of 5000 and the centre accommodated 1500 refugees. This has never been discussed or publicized before. In other words, suddenly, people were surrounded by 1,500 single, dark and strong men.

Only a few open centres are located in urban places like Balbi. The Tal Gebel open centre, in particular, lacks infrastructure, as Elais from Mogadishu told us:

> In Tal Gebel there is no life. (…) There is nothing, only eat and sleep. (…) The bus does not
> come often (…) Sometimes we walk to town, but that takes more than two hours. So how
> can I go to work from there?

These centres are often fenced in and can only be accessed through security doors, even though they are declared to be 'open'. According to the security staff of an open centre the fences and security measures supposedly serve to protect the refugees, supposedly from unwanted guests. Being accommodated in an open centre yet again reinforced the refugees' invisibility and/or criminalisation. Rather, it appeared that reasons for protection were instead used to keep refugees at distance.

This relative inaccessibility of the open centres is consistent with the Maltese government's reluctance to develop integration policies – which were not passed until 2017. Before that, the Maltese government had not made much effort to invest in structured integration measures, as the Maltese Asylum Status Agent confirmed on 29 May 2013: 'We cannot really integrate long term all the people that are coming'. Only volunteers offered free English language courses in the centres, as a representative of a governmental authority also stated on 25 February 2015:

> We also have independent volunteers who come here, for example, for long holidays and
> would like to do something fruitful while they are here. It is amazing how many people are
> willing to help (…) it would be a waste if the state would offer that.

At the same time, she argued that the majority of refugees would in any case not want to stay in Malta, thus making integration measures obsolete:

> We are trying to help but nobody wants our help. So it's useless telling us [to] emphasise on
> integration (…) integration is not a win when people don't want to stay (…) We do get cases
> that do integrate but they are very few.

9.6.2 Allocation of Status

Obtaining a status entailed different hurdles for refugees in Malta. Dereje from Ethiopia reported translation problems at court. He was assigned a translator but this person did not speak his language. Dereje tried to explain this to the court staff but they misunderstood him and assumed that he was not grateful enough for the support provided. 'They told me 'Alright, you don't want an interpreter, so here is your reject''. Dereje felt treated badly. That Ethiopia is a country with many languages went unnoticed by the court staff. They just assumed Dereje's language affiliation and hired the wrong interpreter which ultimately led to the rejection of his request. Admitting that they lacked political or geographical knowledge about their country of origin often undermined refugees' trustworthiness, too: 'I have two rejects now. (…) They were asking me 100 questions about Somalia, but I only know Mogadishu. What shall I tell them?' reported Samia, who came to Malta as a single woman. These practices often entailed the result that refugees did not receive the legal status they were entitled to. The asylum procedure in Malta can have four different outcomes: (1) refugee status, (2) subsidiary protection (SP), (3) Temporary Humanitarian Protection (THP) and (4) rejection of the asylum request.

The different legal statuses imply variations in refugees' freedom of movement, access to the welfare system, and the labour market. The most privileged status, that of a refugee, was only granted to 4 per cent of all applicants between 2004 and 2015 (UNHCR 2016). As Tina Magazzini (2020) also highlights with regard to Roma in Italy and Spain, citizenship – the foundation of integration as defined by Ager and Strang (2008) – is not addressed but all asylum outcomes are temporary; in fact, *all* statuses must be understood as temporary solutions. Holders of refugee status can travel freely with a convention pass to all countries, except to the country of origin. Beneficiaries of SP and THP, both international forms of protection, can only travel with a three-month EU visa within the Schengen area. Holders of SP or THP obtain personal documents and a renewable residence permit for 1 year. In contrast to recognised refugees, they have no access to family reunification or citizenship (Aditus and UNHCR 2013). All have access to employment and to core social welfare benefits. To receive an employment licence, the refugee's employer has to file the application before the documents are issued to the refugee, making the latter dependent on the former (Bijl and Nimführ 2019).

A notice of rejection implies the impossibility of having a regular residence permit and any travel documents due to a pending deportation order. The majority of rejected asylum-seekers in Malta are non-deportable[10] and are usually placed in a perpetual 'in-between' situation due to their lack of a legal status (see Hinger 2020). This in-between status is also sanctioned by the EU Return Directive, which does not provide a 'mechanism to put an end to situations of legal limbo that derive from protracted situations of non-removability' (EU Agency for Fundamental Rights 2011, p. 11). To avoid destitution, the Maltese government adopted a policy equipping non-deportable refugees with a so-called 'permit to work'. This 'permit to work' differs from a work permit in that it is only issued for 3 months and must frequently be applied for by the employer to be renewed. Thus, non-deportable refugees are especially affected by (dis)integration practices which are also efficacious over and above their access to social services and the labour market, unless they were eligible for Temporary Humanitarian Protection New (THPN).[11] THPN was a non-asylum-linked, national form of protection which was not contained in any law. It was – until the end of 2018 – granted to persons whose application for international protection had been rejected but who could not be deported for medical or other humanitarian reasons (European Migration Network 2009, p. 10). To be considered for THPN,

---

[10] Usually a notice of rejection is followed by deportation. However, there is a clear gap between the issued notices of returns and effective deportations, caused by various legal and practical factors. These can be a refusal of certificates from the country of origin or transit or human-rights-based decisions, and forms of protest and resistance.

[11] To distinguish THP from THPN, it is important to note that the latter was only granted to individuals who had received a final decision of rejection, whereas the former is granted to those who are not eligible for refugee status or SP.

failed asylum seekers (…) need to present documentary evidence in relation to their integration efforts and their employment history in Malta. Other mandatory criteria for eligibility include living in a private residence in Malta and keeping a clean police conduct (Government of Malta 2016).

Holders of THPN have access to employment and to core social-welfare benefits. When a new Asylum Status Agent took office at the end of 2016, THPN was suspended due to a review process (MHAS 2016). Since the end of November 2018 THPN has been replaced with the Specific Residence Authorisation Policy (SRA) administered by the Identity Malta Agency. The policy addresses former THPN certificate holders and other individuals who do not have international protection and are cannot be deported to their country of origin through no fault of their own. However, not all rejected and non-deportable refugees are entitled to benefit from SRA. The conditions of eligibility for application are 'subject to the fulfillment of a number of integration measures' (Grech 2018).

9.6.3   Participation in Education

Access to education depends on the refugees' status as well as on their assigned age, as school attendance is only obligatory until 16 years of age. However, young refugees who were considered to be under 16 often did not attend school. This should not be understood as their lack of willingness but rather as an outcome of the lack of support they received. Elais, who was considered to be younger than 16 years when he first arrived, reported that he received no support to find a school in Malta, even though he asked his social worker to help him:

> I thought that I can go to school. (…) When I asked the social worker for help to find a school, she said 'You came here alone from Somalia and now you tell me you need help? I think you are able to find one yourself'. I didn't find a school.

Whilst most of the UAMs we talked to did not attend school, it was different for the children of refugee families, who were often much younger than the UAMs. At school, these young children learned English – a language which their parents often did not understand. Furthermore, cultural habits were also taught which irritated the parents and caused conflicts, as Urbi, president and founder of a local migrant NGO, reported on 22 July 2015:

> The children, they go to the school and the mums they don't know English at all. So she [mother] don't know what they give him [child] at school and she tries her best to put her culture on him and when he talks to his mum 'No, no this is not right' (…) some of the women they feel desperate, they think they have to stop their children to go to the school, because they think now their children are becoming rebel against her.

Whilst it was understood by most refugees that receiving an education would be good for children, the parents often felt overwhelmed and feared that they would lose their connection with their children at the same time. Even though many told us that they were also interested in further education for themselves, they often depended on volunteers' offers, as no free English classes were accessible to them. The English courses offered by NGOs are only available to refugees having a protected status, as they receive financial grants from the different EU funding bodies that clearly state the target group – rejected asylum-seekers are not eligible. This example again highlights that integration policies obviously do not aim at the integration of *all* refugees (see Hinger 2020), but that (dis)integration is negotiated via categorisations such as status, as well as understandings of deservingness and undeservingness or age, as Urbi highlighted.

9.6.4 Access to the Labour Market

The labour market presents its own challenges entailing precarious life situations for some refugees. Irregular refugees, in particular, face a higher risk of ending up poor despite having a job. The Vice President of a local NGO explained in an interview on 21 July 2015 that:

> The policies allow a broad scope of exploitation for potential employers. Particularly for rejected cases (…) because they [refugees] need an approval of the future employer to obtain their employment licence (…) But there are also a lot of exploitation in the informal sector – many people are waiting as day labourers at the roadside. I've heard of people who were working a whole day for a bottle of coke and a *ftira* [Maltese bread].

Accessing the labour market is especially difficult for refugees with children. Since 2014, child day care for those less than 2 years of age is free of charge but to get a place for their offspring, parents have to present a long-term contract of employment. The day-care centres often do not cover the times of the working shifts and are, furthermore, not easily accessible due to bad transport connections. Refugees themselves addressed this gap in childcare and took care of each other's children but also charged five to ten euros per day, per child. This amount is not affordable for many. Hana talked about her difficult situation. She was a single mum and her son was 4 years old. The child's father paid her 120 euros per month, which was her only income. As she could not provide a regularised working contract, she was not entitled to free public childcare and private childcare was not affordable. The 120 euros she received every month was not enough to feed the two of them. This is why Hana felt compelled to give her son to a foster family in August 2015:

> This decision wasn't easy. I can go without much food but not my son (…) Working in the hotel without having childcare is not possible. So I asked the Welfare Office to find a foster family for my son (…). But I'm afraid that he won't want to come back to me (…). They can offer him so much more (…) But I have no choice, it will be better for him, that's what I'm always thinking.

9.7   Refugees Between Agency and Vulnerabilisation[12]

Most of the refugees we talked to were united in their wish to leave Malta because, as noted by Ebrima, a non-deportable refugee from Gambia, 'I really like Malta, [b]ut being in Malta without documents is like walking in a roundabout all the time'. Even though some refugees actually received refugee status after a couple of years in Malta, they still felt unwelcome and insecure, like Yasmine from Syria, who was granted refugee status in 2015 after she had lived in Malta for 14 years under the conditions of holding a 'double reject':

> This piece of paper [refugee recognition] does not mean anything to me. After living 14 years with a double reject, I'm still feeling rejected. There is always the fear of deportation. Only citizenship would give me security.

Refugees developed different ways of exiting the 'roundabout' mentioned by Ebrima. We consequently observed different forms of agency – those wanting to leave Malta either participated in the regularised Relocation Programme[13] or left the island-state in a self-organised, unregulated manner. The latter path often entailed a Dublin deportation back to Malta – and being returned meant that they would be punished again, as Ahmed, a young refugee, reported:

> I also got punishment. (…) I have to go every day and do community work. You know in Paola [town] I cut the trees now. It is very hard work. And I only get 80 euros instead of 130 euros per month from the government.

These measures discourage refugees who are still in Malta. Thus, some of them hope to be accepted for Relocation although only those granted international protection can participate in these programmes while those who have been rejected cannot do so.

Nevertheless, we also met refugees who planned their future in Malta despite the apparent and efficacious practices of (dis)integration. To avoid discrimination in their everyday life, some developed new identities so that their social surrounding did not realise that they had entered Malta by boat, as Elais told us:

> At work I don't tell them that I came from the sea because (…) the people they make jokes about that. Because they don't know what we have experienced. (…) I say I came for studying that's it. I don't want to be boat people or immigrant.

---

[12] This term is used to emphasise our understanding of vulnerability as a process. The attribution of a need for assistance and protection culminates in portrayals of refugees as apolitical victims, passive beneficiaries and homogenious masses under the guise of humanitarian protection. The representation of refugees as needy collectives trivialises their integration practices and denies their agency and their ability to act. Nevertheless, we do not generally deny refugees their vulnerability, but place them between agency and vulnerability depending on the context they (inevitably) find themselves in (Nyers 2013). By arguing that refugees would per vulnerable per se, one risks to overlook the processes, regulations and political decision that render refugees as vulnerable.

[13] Relocation merely refers to regulated relocations within the EU.

These practices of 'keeping quiet' and 'laying low' resulted from their fear of being further stigmatised. We were also told about another fear – people whose asylum cases were still pending were afraid of accepting the support of others as they assumed that the authorities might decide negatively on their cases. Nevertheless, some refugees founded their own migrant associations. These organisations are well networked and call attention to the situation for refugees in Malta. Being well connected was one of the most important social pillars in their everyday lives. We observed during our field work that refugees cooked together, shared their money, helped each other out with SIM cards or offered a place to sleep – 'We share life', concluded Bilal. These 'acts of integration' (Collyer et al. 2020) began soon after their arrival in Malta. Refugees took over practices of integration as they supported each other financially, socially and emotionally and also shared important information on the asylum procedure and the bureaucratic rules in Malta.

9.8   Preserving the Imagined 'Maltese Mix'

We were repeatedly told that the Maltese were always able to borrow from and adapt to new dynamics, habits and peoples that have come to the island over the past hundreds of years – usually across the sea – which can best be seen when looking at the Maltese language. 'Over the years and over the centuries we have come to adopt words that come from different other languages', a highly ranked Maltese politician explained during an interview on 13 June 2018. This willingness to adapt did not seem to apply to the integration of refugees and what changes their presence might bring along over recent years. The refugees we met felt unwelcome due to both juridical and social (dis)integration practices: 'In Malta they want you to be stupid, they don't want you to be with their community, (…). Here, they don't like people from the sea', Bilal summarised. This is a key message, as he points out that refugees do not appear to belong to the 'mix' that would make up Maltese identity in the first place. This materialises in hardened barriers between Maltese citizens and refugees, as Absimil, from Somalia observed:

> What has changed over the time is that more refugees think that all Maltese are racists, and more and more Maltese think that refugees are bad people. There is not much interaction, both live in their own worlds. I wish there was more dialogue.

The non-existence of dialogue has became apparent throughout this chapter and is efficacious on different levels regarding disintegration. Between refugee and non-refugee society, between ministries charged with immigration control versus those focusing on their care-taking, and between the government and non-refugee society when, for example, 1500 refugees were placed overnight in Balbi without informing the non-refugee residents.

9.9 Conclusion

We have shown in this chapter that the status assigned to people greatly influences their agency and the (dis)integration they experienced. Whilst they are integrated into the EU's and the Maltese asylum bureaucracy, they are also officially disintegrated from support services and rights, thereby highlighting that integration is misunderstood when it is only equated with a positive experience. The dynamics of (dis)integration are also powerful beyond legal frameworks. As a result, (dis)integration is not only and always organised, but also 'non-organised' behaviour creates these dynamics, and non-governmental actors are also involved in the underlying practices. Thus, (dis)integration not only follows from legal frameworks but also affects the refugees' daily lives and occurs due to unintentional behaviour.

The facets of both the field of tension between sea rescue and keeping refugees at bay and the subsequent dynamics of (dis)integration we analysed clarified our understanding of Malta as a 'bus stop' from the governmental perspective. The processes of security and asylum policies which refugees encounter prevent a safe life (Ralser 2014, p. 282) and are aimed at making manifest the Maltese government's desire to prohibit permanent integration. As we have shown, inclusion and exclusion or (dis)integration do not merely take place at the nation-state's border: instead, the border is permanently and daily negotiated *in* the territory and *between* different actors. Striking examples are the exclusionary forms of accommodating refugees, their non-entitlement to certain rights and services, as well as the various processes of powerful ascriptions and criminalisation. Not only governmental actors but also some refugees understood Malta as a 'bus stop'. However, this understanding of Malta falls short as other refugees try to establish a more or less normal life, despite the many hurdles they face.

These 'acts of integration', however, face limitations: many refugees lack a safe status enabling them to actively criticise and position themselves against judicalised or individual mechanisms of exclusion. Negative public reactions (Carabott 2015) towards the migrant demonstration, for example, fostered fear among the refugees that they would be treated negatively if associated with these activities. Thus, the agency displayed by refugees must usually be understood as both a reaction towards and interplay of the power structures produced by the state's bureaucracy and society's reactions. Referring again to citizenship and equal rights as the core factors enabling integration, as defined by Ager and Strang (2008), illustrates that legal frameworks have a high impact on (dis)integration. Being granted (temporary) refugee protection, however, does not automatically mean that people *feel* 'integrated', as Yasmine's case has shown. Thus, states can limit rights by granting them only to certain categories of people *and* by limiting access to these categorisations. Yasmine's fear of being deported would only dissolve if she were granted citizenship allowing her full rights of participation. Again, this chapter has shown not only that disintegration occurs when integration measures are absent but also that integration measures can, indeed, be the source of exclusion.

Furthermore, refugees still depend on the discretion of individuals. Passing integration policies can be understood as a change in how refugees and their presence are understood, but a full assessment of whether these policies are implemented requires further research. What we were told during our research trip to Malta in June 2018 was that, until now, 'the Integration Policy exists on paper but not in practice'. An NGO employee explained that the Integration Policy merely states that refugees are obliged to integrate themselves; the local authorities charged with the task of integration, however, were not given instructions and are still unaware of how to actually implement this policy.

In summary, we would like to emphasise that we understand (dis)integration as a relational concept. Who or what produces (dis)integration? Who (re)acts how? (Dis) integration practices should be seen as an enmeshment of legal provisions, social relationships, individual and collective experiences and actions. These can relate directly to each other, but do not have to follow a common logic. Therefore, (dis) integration is contextual and contingent, and should not be understood as a timeless or consistent phenomenon. To explore these dynamics, we proposed an ethnographic approach that allowed us to take into account different perspectives to incorporate legal documents and to look at how (dis)integration manifests itself in the daily lives of refugee- and non-refugee, institutionalised and non-institutionalised actors.

As argued in the introduction to this volume (Collyer et al. 2020) and demonstrated in Schweitzer's (2020) contribution, practices of (dis)integration also have an impact on society as a whole. Zygmunt Bauman (2005, p. 11ff.) has already argued that the privileged who produce the 'excluded' in the first place should make use of their responsibilities in another fashion by *guaranteeing* human rights instead of circumventing them. In line with Bauman, Busra Fouad (cited in Diacono 2015), head of the Migrant Association, claimed: '[P]rotect the lives you have saved by respecting our rights (…) so that we can truly become a part of Maltese society'.

References

Aditus & UNHCR. (2013). *Nitkellmu? Refugee Integration Perspectives in Malta*. Retrieved in August 2018 from http://aditus.org.mt/Publications/nitkellmu.pdf.

Ager, A., & Strang, A. (2008). Understanding integration: A conceptual framework. *Journal of Refugee Studies, 21*(2), 166–191.

Bauman, Z. (2005). *Verworfenes Leben. Die Ausgegrenzten der Moderne*. Hamburg: Hamburger Edition.

Bijl, J., & Nimführ, S. (2019). Contesting profit structures in Malta: Rejected asylum seekers between modern slavery and autonomy. In S. Guirk & A. Pine (Eds.), *Profit, protest, and the asylum industry*. Oakland: PM Press. In press.

Calleja, C. (2009). Doing away with detention would spell disaster, *Times of Malta*, 18 April. Retrieved in August 2018 from http://www.timesofmalta.com/articles/view/20090418/local/doing-away-with-detention-would-spell-disaster.253274.

Cantat, C. (2020). The politics of negligence and spectacle in the government of migrants in Hungary. In S. Hinger, & R. Schweitzer (Eds.), *Politics of (Dis)Integration* (pp. 183–199). Cham: Springer VS.

Carabott, S. (2015). Uphold our basic human rights, African Community tells authorities. *Times of Malta*, 19 July 2015. Retrieved in August 2018 from https://www.timesofmalta.com/articles/view/20150719/local/uphold-our-basic-human-rights-african-community-tells-authorities.577270

Chase, E., Otto, L., Belloni, M., Lems, A., & Wernesjö, U. (2019). Methodological innovations, reflections and dilemmas: The hidden sides of research with migrant young people classified as unaccompanied minors. *Journal of Ethnic and Migration Studies*. https://doi.org/10.1080/1369183X.2019.1584705

Collyer, M., Hinger, S., & Schweitzer, R. (2020). Politics of (Dis)Integration – An introduction. In S. Hinger, & R. Schweitzer (Eds.), *Politics of (Dis)Integration* (pp. 1–18). Cham: Springer VS.

De Genova, N. (2013). Spectacles of migrant 'illegality': The scene of exclusion, the obscene of inclusion. *Ethnic and Racial Studies, 36*(7), 1180–1198.

De Genova, N., Mezzadra, S., & Pickles, J. (2015). New keywords: Migration and borders. *Cultural Studies, 29*(1), 55–87.

Diacono, T. (2015). 'Protect the lives you've saved' – migrants in racism protest. *Malta Today*, 19 July. Retrieved in August 2018 from http://www.maltatoday.com.mt/news/national/55263/protect_the_lives_youve_saved__migrants_in_racism_protest#.VsCtkcfVX4w.

Eggers, M., Kilomba, G., Piersche, P., & Arndt, S. (2005). Konzeptionelle Überlegungen. In M. Eggers, G. Kilomba, P. Piersche, & S. Arndt (Eds.), *Mythen, Masken und Subjekte. Weißseinsforschung in Deutschland* (pp. 11–13). Münster: Unrast.

EU Agency for Fundamental Rights (2011). *Fundamental rights of migrants in an irregular situation in the European Union*. Retrieved in August 2018 from http://fra.europa.eu/en/publication/2012/fundamental-rights-migrants-irregular-situation-european-union.

European Migration Network (EMN). (2009). *Unaccompanied Minors in Malta. The Numbers and the Policies and Arrangements for their Reception, Return and Integration*. Valletta. Retrieved in August from https://ec.europa.eu/home-affairs/sites/homeaffairs/files/what-we-do/networks/european_migration_network/reports/docs/emn-studies/unaccompanied-minors/18._malta_national_report_on_unaccompanied_minors_final_version_8dec09_en.pdf

Falzon, M.-A. (2012). Immigration, rituals and transitoriness in the Mediterranean island of Malta. *Journal of Ethnic and Migration Studies, 38*(10), 1661–1680.

Fassin, D. (2011). The social construction of otherness. In S. Bonjour, A. Rea, & D. Jacobs (Eds.), The others in Europe (pp. 117–126). Brussels: Editions de l'Université de Bruxelles.

Fontanari, E., Karpenstein, J., Schwarz, N. V., & Sulimma, S. (2014). Kollaboratives Forschen' als Methode im Handlungsfeld Flucht und Migration. In B. Blätter (Ed.), *Vom Rand ins Zentrum. Perspektiven einer kritischen Migrationsforschung* (pp. 111–129). Berlin: Panama Verlag.

Government of Malta. (2016). *Humanitarian protection*. Retrieved in August 2018 from https://integration.gov.mt/en/ResidenceAndVisas/Pages/Humanitarian-Other-Reasons.aspx.

Grech, D. (2018). Rejected asylum seekers will not need annual certificate to remain in Malta. First step in mending 'system that has been broken for far too long', *Times of Malta*, 15 November. Retrieved in July 2019 from https://timesofmalta.com/articles/view/rejected-asylum-seekers-will-not-need-annual-certificate-toremain-in.694391.

Hess, S., & Tsianos, V. (2010). Ethnographische Grenzregimeanalyse. Eine Methodologie der Autonomie der Migration. In S. Hess & B. Kasparek (Eds.), *Grenzregime. Diskurse, Praktiken, Institutionen in Europa* (pp. 243–264). Berlin: Assoziation A.

Hinger, S. (2020). Integration through disintegration? The Distinction between deserving and undeserving refugees in national and local integration policies in Germany. In S. Hinger, & R. Schweitzer (Eds.), *Politics of (Dis)Integration* (pp. 19–39). Cham: Springer VS.

IMO. (2004). *Guidelines on the treatment of persons rescued at Sea*. London: International Maritime Organization, Annex 34, Resolution MSC.167(78) paragraph 6.12–6.14. Retrieved in

August 2018 from http://www.imo.org/en/OurWork/Facilitation/personsrescued/Documents/ MSC.167(78).pdf.

Khosravi, S. (2010). *'Illegal' Traveller. An auto-ethnography of Borders*. Basingstoke: Palgrave Macmillan.

Klepp, S. (2011). *Europa zwischen Grenzkontrolle und Flüchtlingsschutz: Eine Ethnographie der Seegrenze auf dem Mittelmeer*. Bielefeld: transcript.

Leurs, R. (2014). Private Seenotretter im Mittelmeer: 'Was wollen Sie tun – die Leute ertrinken lassen?' *Spiegel Online,* 11 November. Retrieved in August 2018 from http://www.spiegel. de/panorama/moas-reiches-paar-rettet-fluechtlinge-mit-phoenix-1-aus-mittelmeer-a-1002230. html.

Magazzini, T. (2020). Roma integration as an essentially contested concept: Questioning the assumptions behind the Roma National Integration Strategies. In S. Hinger, & R. Schweitzer (Eds.), *Politics of (Dis)Integration* (pp. 41–59). Cham: Springer VS.

Mainwaring, C. (2008). On the edge of exclusion: The changing nature of migration in Cyprus and Malta. *The Cyprus Review,* 20(2), 19–49.

MFFS & MHAS. (2005). *Malta: Irregular immigrants, refugees and integration policy document.* Retrieved in August 2018 from http://www.refworld.org/docid/51b197484.html.

MHAS. (2016). *Strategy for the reception of asylum seekers and irregular migrants.* Valletta: Ministry for Home Affairs and National Security. Retrieved in August 2018 from https://0d2d5d19eb0c0d8cc8c6-a655c0f6dcd98e765a68760c407565ae.ssl.cf3.rackcdn.com/ ee87eb6093978ddf835be5759bc86d018724f3a8.pdf.

MOAS. (2016). *Über MOAS*. Retrieved in August 2018 from https://www.moas.eu/de/about.

Nail, T. (2012). Violence at the borders: Nomadic solidarity and non-status migrant resistance. *Radical Philosophy Review,* 15(1), 241–257.

Nimführ, S., & Sesay, B. (2019). Lost in limbo? Navigating (im)mobilities and practices of appropriation of non-deportable refugees in the Mediterranean area. *Comparative Migration Studies Journal,* 7(26). https://doi.org/10.1186/s40878-019-0132-8

Nimführ, S., Otto, L., & Samatch, G. (2017). Gerettet, aber nicht angekommen. Von Geflüchteten in Malta. In S. Hess, B. Kasparek, S. Kron, M. Rodatz, M. Schwertl, & S. Sontowski (Eds.), *Der lange Sommer der Migration. Grenzregime III* (pp. 137–150). Berlin/Hamburg: Assoziation A.

NSO. (2018). *World Refugee Day: 20 June 2018.* Valletta: National Statistics Office Malta. Retrieved in August 2018 from https://nso.gov.mt/en/News_Releases/View_by_Unit/Unit_C5/ Population_and_Migration_Statistics/Documents/2018/News2018_095.pdf

Nyers, P. (2013). *Rethinking refugees: Beyond states of emergency*. New York: Routhledge.

Otto, L., & Kaufmann, M. E. (2018). 'Minderjährig', 'männlich' – 'stark'? Bedeutungsaushandlungen der Selbst- und Fremdzuschreibung junger Geflüchteter in Malta. Eine intersektionelle Leseweise ethnografischer Forschungsausschnitte. *Gender,* 2, 63–78.

Pisani, M. (2011). There is an elephant in the room and she's 'rejected' and black: Observations on rejected female asylum seekers from sub-Saharan Africa in Malta. *Postcolonial Directions in Education,* 2(1), 68–99.

Pisani, M. (2013). We are going to fix your vagina, just the way we like it'. Some reflections on the construction of (sub-Saharan) African female asylum seekers in Malta and their efforts to speak back. *Postcolonial Directions in Education,* 2(1), 68–99.

Punch, S. (2002). Research with children: The same or different from research with adults? *Childhood,* 9(3), 321–341.

Ralser, M. (2014). Die Bio-Politik der Migrationsregime und die Normalität des Rassismus. In P. Mecheril, O. Thomas-Olalde, C. Melter, S. Arens, & E. Romaner (Eds.), *Migrationsforschung als Kritik? Konturen einer Forschungsperspektive* (pp. 277–287). Wiesbaden: Springer.

Rass, C., & Wolff, F. (2018). What is in a migration regime? Genealogical approach and methodological proposal. In A. Pott, C. Rass, & F. Wolff (Eds.), *Was ist ein Migrationsregime?* (pp. 19–64). Wiesbaden: Springer.

Reckinger, G. (2010). *Perspektive Prekarität. Wege benachteiligter Jugendlicher in den transformierten Arbeitsmarkt*. Konstanz: UVK Verlagsgesellschaft.

Rodgers, G. (2004). Hanging out with forced migrants: Methodological and ethical challenges. *Forced Migration Review, 21*, 48–49.

Sahraoui, N. (2020). From everyday racist incidents at work to institutional racism: migrant and minority-ethnic workers' experiences in older-age care. In S. Hinger, & R. Schweitzer (Eds.), *Politics of (Dis)Integration* (pp. 81–99). Cham: Springer VS.

Sansone, K. (2011). Malta will try to persuade EU of migrant emergency. *Times of Malta*, 03 April. Retrieved in August 2018 from http://www.timesofmalta.com/articles/view/20110403/local/malta-will-try-to-persuade-eu-of-migrant-emergency.357977.

Schweitzer, R. (2020). Mainstream public service provision and the implementation of a 'hostile environment' for irregular migrants living in Britain. How inclusive institutions enforce exclusive immigration rules. In S. Hinger, & R. Schweitzer (Eds.), *Politics of (Dis)Integration* (pp. 121–140). Cham: Springer VS.

Transit Migration Forschungsgruppe. (2007). *Turbulente Ränder. Neue Perspektiven auf Migration an den Grenzen Europas*. Bielefeld: Transcript.

UNHCR. (2016). *Malta Asylum Trends*. Retrieved in August, 2018, from http://www.unhcr.org/mt/charts/.

von Unger, H., Narimani, P., & M'Bayo, R. (2014). *Forschungsethik in der qualitativen Forschung*. Wiesbaden: Springer.

Chapter 10
Governing Migrants and Refugees in Hungary: Politics of Spectacle, Negligence and Solidarity in a Securitising State

Céline Cantat

10.1 An Invitation to the Hungarian Border Spectacle[1]

One early morning in July 2016, I travelled to Szeged with a colleague to meet with one of the organisers of Migszol, the local pro-refugee movement. Tamas[2] had offered to drive us to the border crossing point in Röszke where, in the autumn of 2015, the Hungarian government had established one of the transit zones in which migrants wishing to enter Hungary are systematically detained as they go through the asylum process. We drove through open fields of paprika stretching to the horizon and reached a bumpy road going through a small forest. At the end of the path, we arrived at the border: if it had not been for the barbed wire fence cutting through the grass, I would never have guessed that this was where Hungary stopped and Serbia commenced. There it was: 'the zone'. In the middle of the otherwise deserted countryside, a set of containers surrounded by a wire fence stood incongruously, presenting us with a somewhat surreal scene. After a few kilometres of emptiness, we had suddenly reached a site of intense activity: the Hungarian army and the police were busy surveying the transit zone where fewer than a dozen people had been admitted from the Serbian side that same morning. They were now waiting to hear whether or not they would be allowed into Hungary. A couple of children were running around, looking and smiling at us from behind the wire. On the Serbian side, a makeshift camp of tents and tarpaulins had emerged, as more people arrived on a daily basis than the number let through the transit zone. Tamas told us that the camp had recently reached 600 people and that numbers were expected to keep

---

[1] An earlier version of this chapter was published by the CEU Center for Policy Studies (CPS) as a Working Paper (2017/3).

[2] All names have been changed for reasons of anonymity.

C. Cantat (✉)
Central European University, Budapest, Hungary
e-mail: cantatc@ceu.edu

© The Author(s) 2020
S. Hinger, R. Schweitzer (eds.), *Politics of (Dis)Integration*,
IMISCOE Research Series, https://doi.org/10.1007/978-3-030-25089-8_10

rising. People were camping at the border crossing point, with no access to cooking or proper hygiene facilities, in the hope of being able to cross into Hungary soon. Around the tents, humanitarian workers and volunteers wearing colourful variations of the same vest were busy distributing water or carrying out medical checks. Some of the police on the Hungarian side were staring blankly at the migrants and their humanitarian supporters across the wire.

'Look', said Tamas, 'this is what they have done here. You can take photos if you wish, but do not photograph Hungarian military or police staff'. Since the summer of 2015, Tamas had been relentlessly working to support migrants passing through Szeged and to document the situation at the border. He had brought numerous journalists and researchers to the Röszke transit zone and had played an important role in allowing the media to gain information about the Hungarian government's treatment of refugees. Yet something felt wrong. Not only did I not feel comfortable getting my camera out to take photos of people stranded in such dreadful conditions but the simple fact of being there and gazing at the scene seemed improper. We walked a few metres along the barbed wire border and reached a small hill at the top of which two men were smoking a cigarette. One of them was a member of the military who had been sent to Röszke from Western Hungary, where he usually lived with his family, to reinforce border surveillance operations. However, in the few months that he had been there, he had never caught sight of a single migrant trying to cross irregularly. He just spent his days standing on top of a small hill, looking at the Serbian fields extending ahead.

It struck me that the scene had been carefully staged. Each person at the transit zone had a clear role to play in a scenario with a simple yet efficient plot: the state had sent national servants to defend the border and the nation against the disruption and menace represented by the migrants. It had its protagonists and its villains. There was a desirable order of things which had been brought into crisis by the movement of unwanted people and which had to be protected. Like other researchers, activists and journalists, I also had a role in this script – I may have felt little sympathy towards the narrative, yet I was part of the public that made the spectacle possible. The Röszke transit zone told a particular story, with its own morals, in which the Hungarian national community was in need of protection and the state was the protector. The production of refugee vulnerability and muteness is central for this staging to proceed: as silenced subjects, refugees can be attributed whichever role is the most convenient to the government's narrative. As such, the narrative requires two simultaneous operations: the systematic silencing of refugees through processes of vulnerabilisation taking away the possibility of self-expression, coupled with the hyper-visibilisation of their vulnerabilised presence.

This was what felt wrong: the simple fact of attending the show, of providing it with a public, made me complicit in this obscene border spectacle. The concept of 'spectacle' has been usefully mobilised by critical migration and border studies scholars to refer to dominant representations surrounding migration and their instrumental role in the consolidation of statist and territorialised politics. De Genova (2015) speaks of the 'border spectacle' in reference to the way in which states stage dramatic scenes of enforcement at/of the border. This, of course, has a purpose: that of displaying the power of the state to enforce the politics of exclusion and control on which national authority and sovereignty rely. Rajaram (2003) also examines the 'spectacle of detention' of asylum-seekers in the Australian context and argues that such a performance is designed for a public, identified and cohered through the consumption of such a spectacle and that it hence plays a central role in the drawing of the moral and ethical limits of the political community.

This visit to the Röszke transit zone stayed with me as I continued researching migration and pro-migrant solidarity in Hungary over the next few months. The uncomfortable feeling of being an unwilling accomplice in the production of a narrative about a 'migrant threat' or a 'migration crisis' in the country was as powerful as it was paralytic. The issue bore some questions: what was the Hungarian government attempting to achieve through this hyper-visibilisation of borders and migration? Moreover, besides what it tried to show, what did this spectacular moment also relegate to less visible spaces? What else was quietly happening backstage as the public's attention was focused on the show? What other practices of exclusion and 'disintegration' might be employed by the Hungarian authorities?

In this chapter, I reflect on the politics of in/visibility that underpin the government of migrants and refugees by the Hungarian authorities. I explore how an ongoing process of disintegration of the already narrow social, political and economic space navigated by migrants and refugees in the country is produced through both spectacular practices of marginalisation and quiet forms of neglect. Unlike 'exclusion', which implies the casting out of particular individuals and groups from an already established community, the notion of (dis)integration insists on the dialectical relation between, on the one hand, preventing the emergence of socialities that bring together, in this instance, 'nationals' and 'non nationals' and, on the other hand, the reinforcement and indeed integration of a particular, and highly exclusionary, interpretation of the 'nation' and the legitimate public (Collyer et al. 2020).

I first examine the various spectacularisation practices deployed by the Hungarian state and reflect on the representations of migrants, migration and the Hungarian national community that the government puts forward. I then look at what may be called 'the other side' of the migration spectacle – that is, the more discreet yet equally corrosive practices that become quietly authorised and banalised in this context. The final part offers some reflections on the effects of this double politics of hyper-visibilisation and quiet neglect in regard to the social space available to migrants in Hungary. I argue that one of the intended consequences of this politics of visibility is to sap the conditions allowing the emergence of alternative communities and ways of being together beyond racialised differences. I also examine examples of pro-migrant mobilisation in Hungary to assess whether and how these can, even temporarily, subvert the conditions created through the spectacularisation of migration. Due in particular to the largely transitory nature of migration in/through Hungary in 2015, the focus of the chapter is primarily on the way in which Hungarian citizens attempt to challenge the politics of difference and separation enforced by the government in relation to migration as well as to other social processes.

10.2   Reinforcing the National Community and Its Others

At the end of November 2016, still in Szeged, the local district court gave a Syrian man known as Ahmed H. a 10-year prison sentence on charges of 'illegal entry' and 'acts of terror'. The acts behind these charges dated from 16 September 2015, a day after Hungary closed its borders to migrants and refugees on their way to Western and Northern European countries. Hundreds of walkers, stranded at the Röszke/Horgoš crossing, where the transit zone mentioned above currently stands, attempted to break through the border fence that had been erected by the Hungarian authorities. The response of the police consisted in the brutal use of force, including tear gas and water cannons, to contain people. Ahmed seized a megaphone to try to call on both refugees and the police to remain calm. As clashes intensified, Ahmed was involved in stone throwing, together with dozens of exhausted refugees. He was arrested in Budapest a couple of months later and held in detention until his trial. Ten other people present at the border that day were also arrested: they were put on trial over the summer of 2016 and received a range of actual and suspended sentences for illegal entry and public disorder. The fact that these people aimed to enter European territory in order to claim asylum which, under international conventions related to refugee protection, should protect them from charges of 'illegal entry' did not make a difference, a testimony to the Hungarian government's voluntary disqualification of all border crossers as 'illegal migrants'. Ahmed was heard separately due to the terrorist charges levelled on him, based on the argument that he had been involved in attempts to intimidate the Hungarian police.

These trials took place in March 2016, a few months after the Hungarian authorities had declared a 'state of emergency' across the country. The measure had officially been taken because of the 'migrant crisis', yet it was passed at a time when the number of people transiting through Hungary had drastically declined, due in particular to the barbed wire fences at the borders with Serbia and Croatia. In June of the same year, the government passed a draconian counter-terrorism package, which included a constitutional amendment[3] and changes to the laws governing the police, national security services and defence forces. The aim of the package was to simplify the process to establish a state of emergency in the country and to grant the executive stronger 'counter-terrorism' powers, with wide scope for restricting rights and increasing surveillance. The package also established Hungary's new Counter-Terrorism Intelligence and Criminal Analysis Centre (TIBEK). In the name of protecting the national community against an imagined migrant threat, the Hungarian government has thus justified a series of repressive and restrictive laws with consequences for all residents.

The passing of this so-called 'anti-terrorism' package is, to a certain extent, in line with developments at the European level, notably since the Paris and Brussels attacks. Yet it is also an element of Hungary's ruling party *Fidesz*'s political strategy

---

[3] To *Magyarország Alaptörvénye*, the Fundamental Law of Hungary.

(Fidesz or *Magyar Polgári Szövetség* means 'Hungarian Civic Alliance'). Since the spring of 2015, the 'safety of Hungarian citizens' has emerged as a key issue in the public and political debate. Fidesz has deployed a range of tactics aimed at asserting a connection between migration and migrants on the one hand and the destabilisation of public order and terrorism on the other. An important element of this strategy was the 2 October 2016 referendum calling for people to vote against the EU's mechanism of refugee relocation. The campaign leading up to the referendum was overwhelmingly focused on affirming a link between migration and terrorism, with billboards across the country displaying messages such as 'Did you know that the Paris attacks were carried out by migrants?' or the distribution of a booklet to over four million Hungarian households containing sentences such as 'Illegal immigration increases the threat of terror'. Previously, in April/May 2015, the government had orchestrated a 'national consultation', as a part of which virtually all Hungarian households received a questionnaire featuring 'leading questions' of a xenophobic ('Do you agree with the Hungarian government that, instead of supporting immigrants, the support of Hungarian families and future babies is needed?') and nationalistically anti-EU ('Would you support the Hungarian government in the introduction of stricter immigration laws as opposed to the permissive policies of Brussels?') nature (Migszol 2015). These moves have been instrumental to Fidesz in order to maintain its levels of support in spite of corruption scandals, protests from various social groups (including teachers and workers) and growing dissatisfaction from segments of the population due to the concentration of power and the long-term rule of the party. In this context, 'security' issues remained one of the key arguments used by Fidesz to attract voters in advance of the spring 2018 parliamentary election. PM Orbán, in fact, claimed that migration was 'the Number One issue' of the election, which would determine whether or not Hungary became an 'immigration country' (*Daily News Hungary* 2018).

Appealing to a fabricated need to secure the nation against the migrant Other has become a key tool of power for the Hungarian government. This process has been recently furthered by the introduction of a legislative package soberly entitled 'Stop Soros', which criminalises a wide range of activities in support of asylum-seekers (including legal and material assistance) and has been presented as a 'national security' measure by the Hungarian government (Cabinet Office of the Prime Minister 2018). The new laws render extremely difficult the work of a number of local and international organisations concerned with the respect of human and migrants' rights. In this sense, the securitisation of migration is a process with broader implications for the country and one that participates in the alienation of parts of its society and civil sector. In other words, beside the production of disintegrating conditions for migrants and refugees, discourses against migration have had a far-reaching disintegration effect in the country as a whole.

Ahmed's trial was a particularly striking example of 'the border spectacle'. It produced a moment of hyper-visibility of both illegalised migration – thereby acting as confirmation of the Hungarian government's discourse of crisis and threat – and of the authority of the state to enforce exclusion, thereby affirming its ability to provide 'safety' for the Hungarian public against an imagined menace. The spectacle portrays a national community whose primary concern consists in the control of 'illegal' migration. It also works to invisibilise the very processes through which this illegality is produced. As noted by De Genova, while some migrants are deemed 'illegal' because they have violated the law, 'in most depictions of these migrants, there is little if any account of what the law truly is, or of how it came to be so" (De Genova 2015). Yet the law has a history. This history is deeply politicised: it reflects a particular reading of reality, which, in most cases, echoes the interests of the powerful. Migrants become illegal when legislative arrangements make certain forms of mobility illegal – in other words, illegalise them. In the Hungarian case, the criminalisation of so-called illegal entry is a recent phenomenon, dating back to September 2015 as part of a series of measures aimed at terminating the so-called migration crisis. Ahmed, and the ten other people arrested and sent to trial alongside him, were all made illegal by recent Hungarian legislative measures which, in turn, provided the state with the perfect scene for the demonstration of its ability to enforce the law, punish those who break it and exclude those deemed as illegitimate.

Those who lack the means to impact on or contest the making of the law and of legality and illegality – among which migrants feature prominently alongside other marginalised groups – typically become irresistible targets over whom states exercise and demonstrate their authority. Structural silencing makes such vulnerable groups ideologically profitable canvasses on which state power can be projected and displayed. This is not unique to Hungary: the 'migrant' has emerged as a key image of otherness globally and states around the world have mobilised this figure of threat to justify security-oriented and authoritarian measures (Cantat 2015). These restrictive measures are often aimed at neutralising domestic social and political tensions and discontent, including those emerging from the mutation of the local state into a manager of global neoliberal capital. At times, this also translates into disagreements regarding the way to approach migration management across different levels of government (see Desille 2020; Hinger 2020).

The borders at which this 'spectacle' has been unfolding are not only the Hungarian borders; they also are the external borders of the European Union (EU), of which Hungary has become a 'guard' in the context of the Europeanisation of immigration control (Cantat 2015). While Hungary has been at times pilloried for its ill-treatment of migrants by other European leaders (*Euractiv* 2015), it is worth highlighting that the process of border securitisation in the country has been actively encouraged and supported financially by EU institutions. Indeed, since at least the mid-1990s and the harmonisation of migration policy at the European level, the increasingly deterritorialised and securitised borders of the EU have been a key location for the production of the forced migrant as a figure of fear (Cetti 2012). It is also important to note that the use of a rhetoric that mixes security and humanitarian concerns in order to justify further border control has also become a feature of the EU border regime at large (Vaughan-Williams 2015).

In Hungary, the most recent moves towards further securitisation and authoritarianism have been justified in relation both to this global figure of the migrant Other and in the name of preserving the country from 'outsiders' and particularly 'Muslims'. Yet the processes of militarisation, securitisation and criminalisation of

Hungarian society, which have targeted primarily Hungary's minorities and poor, including Hungarian Roma and homeless people, must be located in longer-term dynamics. Since his arrival to power in 2010, Prime Minister Viktor Orbán has rewritten the constitution, curtailed the powers of the Constitutional Court, eroded welfare in favour of an enforced workfare targeting primarily Roma and the poor (Szöke 2015) and actively participated in the establishment of an environment within which racist speech and supposedly prohibited far-right paramilitary activities are tolerated, particularly in the villages where the Roma live (Fekete 2016). These developments constitute a redrawing along increasingly discriminatory lines of the boundaries of the legitimate public – a form of 'exclusionary integration' that works in a dialectic relation with attempts at disintegrating alternative spaces and discourses. This must also be analysed in the framework of the so-called Europeanisation of Hungary and Central Europe which has unfolded in the context of a brutal transition from communism to capitalism (from a command economy to a market economy) under the auspices of the World Bank and the IMF. This transition paved the way and indeed was a prerequisite to Hungary entering the EU in 2004. In the next part, I examine how the production of the migrant as a new figure of fear in Hungary has translated into what I call practices of 'banal marginalisation'.

10.3 Quiet Neglect and Banal Marginalisation

The spectacularisation of migration and of border confrontation is thus a process with important implications. Not only does it allow the reassertion of the legitimacy and authority of the state and the conjuring up of a particular image of the national community, it also enables a process of blame displacement. This reorients the popular discontent and hostility triggered by economic and political difficulties towards those produced as illegitimate in the narratives underpinning border spectacles. This process, which manifests itself at national and regional levels, is a global phenomenon, which has worked toward the emergence of the migrant as a global figure of unwanted Otherness (Cetti 2012; Cantat 2015).

Arguably, there is a paradox in migrants and refugees being simultaneously produced as not belonging to and outside the realm of the (nationalised) economy and politics and yet as responsible for the ills of contemporary societies. This is perhaps particularly striking in Central and Eastern European member-states of the EU, where political discourses towards migration are characterised by extreme levels of violence, while the numbers of people actually obtaining asylum and residency (and thus living in these countries) are actually very low.[4] The inconsistency of this

[4] According to statistics produced by the Hungarian Helsinki Committee, in 2016 only 154 people were granted asylum status, while 271 people received subsidiary protection and seven humanitarian protection. Moreover, according to amendments made in June 2016 to the Hungarian legislation concerned with international protection, people who received protection have to review their

double discourse seems, however, to go unnoticed. This is in large part rendered possible through the structural vulnerabilisation and silencing of migrants and refugees, who are systematically denied access to means of political expression. In turn, this has direct consequences on the space available to people produced as both outsiders to the social, political and economic order and as responsible for its erosion or disintegration.

An important way in which this can be illustrated is by reflecting on the way in which the border spectacle staged by the state allows and legitimises a range of racialising and othering practices against migrants and refugees. The hypervisibilised events to which I referred in the first part of this chapter are only one side of the story. The other side of this mediatised discourse, and its more discreet continuity, is the way in which a series of measures of neglect and destitution becomes authorised and normalised.

In the Hungarian context, such examples of active negligence and the violence they entail are plentiful. Some of the most shocking examples illustrate powerfully the extent to which dehumanising representations may in turn authorise inhuman treatment. In the winter of 2016, the Hungarian government quietly closed Bicske camp, one of the oldest open reception camps for asylum-seekers. While such open asylum detention facilities are far from desirable, what came to replace Bicske proved to be even worse. Indeed, as an alternative, the government displaced Bicske residents to containers or tent camps close to the borders of the country. This episode took place quite discreetly, in the heart of a draconian winter with temperatures reaching $-20°$. People found themselves isolated from their previous connections, including those they had established in Budapest – where many of the pro-migrant associations are based and activities of the country take place – and in conditions barely suitable for human beings. A few months later, in April 2017, the Hungarian government decided to stop providing food to asylum-seekers detained in one of the reception camps, which primarily hosts people going through an asylum appeal process. This series of destitution measures was adopted about a year after the Hungarian government drastically reduced support to asylum-seekers (who are simultaneously prevented from working) and cut all benefits specific to refugees on the grounds that there should be no differential treatment compared to Hungarian people.

Acts of everyday destitution – including, among others, the longevity of asylum procedures and the fact that migrants are often implicitly encouraged to leave the country and to continue their travel westward – are also visible in practices of quiet brutality exercised against asylum-seekers in the camps. These practices differ from the hyper-visible spectacle in that they are either unacknowledged or are quite often framed in administrative rather than political terms. They are about the routine and banal way in which mistreatment, neglect and marginalisation are organised, enacted and reinforced.

---

status every 3 years – essentially meaning that even those granted refugee status only benefit from a three-year secured residency permit.

The neglect here is thus not of a benign form. It may amount to forms of physical violence or torture being inflicted onto the bodies of people, yet it is activated through a deliberate *lack* of care rather than through acts of violence. In spite of a tendency to frame this in terms of administrative efficiency (or the lack thereof in the case of long asylum processes), this neglect is political. It is not the mere result of a lack of resources or structural conditions – it is politicised insofar as it is imposed on particular people or groups of people in particular ways. Here, it is articulated through the production of the figure of the migrant as one of national threat, which relies on a dehumanising set of practices and discourses that not only justifies but fully banalises extreme forms of mistreatment towards migrants.

In the next part, I assess the consequences of this double politics of hyper-visibilisation and quiet neglect on the social space available to migrants in Hungary. I argue that, beyond the immediate experience of brutality and its many consequences on people's lives, these discourses, images and practices also have a perhaps less visible but equally pernicious effect. Indeed, they attempt to sap the conditions allowing the emergence of communities based on alternative socialities between Hungarians and migrants, and of ways of being together beyond racialised differences. Against this context, however, I present two solidarity initiatives that have emerged in support of migrants in the country and examine their structure and meaning in the context of the Hungarian 'border spectacle'.

10.4 Migrant Solidarity in Szeged and Pécs

Another expression of the politics of neglect and (dis)integration enacted actively by the Hungarian government, as elsewhere in Europe, has been the criminalisation of a range of acts of solidarity – or their framing as smuggling. When, albeit under restrictive conditions, spaces of relative autonomy and self-organisation – forms of what I call 'vernacular integration', that is, popular practices by citizens and non-citizens that produce social, political and economic relational and/or productive spaces regardless (often in spite) of state's policies – have arisen, they have been systematically dismantled. This is partly how we could understand the closure of the Bicske camp, which had been a space where social relations between residents, both past and current, had developed and around which a certain number of activities were emerging. The disintegration process imposed on migrants in Hungary thus consists in ongoing attempts to prevent the emergence of links with a national public that the government simultaneously tries to define and delineate as it spectacularises exclusion and its putative protection of the national community.

This hypothesis might be particularly true in the light of the mass mobilisation in support of people on the move in the summer of 2015. Despite active government campaigns against migrants, involving billboards and a national consultation since spring 2015, impressive numbers of people throughout the country came out in support of those who attempted to travel through Hungary and found themselves stranded in various sites due to the government's strategy of migrant immobilisation.

Some of the most poignant images of the summer of 2015 perhaps are those of hundreds of volunteers and activists supporting migrants in some of Budapest's central parks and stations. Yet this wave of solidarity extended beyond the more visible Budapest-based mobilisation and also emerged in other cities of the country, primarily those located close to the borders.

I now turn to the examples of two Hungarian border cities that were the stages of relatively significant pro-migrant movements in the summer of 2015 and examine the relation between these solidarity initiatives and official representations of migration and of the national community deployed by the government.

Over the course of the summer of 2015, over 100,000 people transited through Szeged, next to the Serbian border, while up to 5000 people passed through Pécs, close to the border with Croatia. These border cities constituted some of the first places that refugees encountered as they entered the country. Refugees who passed through Pécs were driven by the Hungarian police from other border towns to the city's train station for reasons that remain unclear. Once fingerprinted and provided with a registration number, they were set free in the city with no information as to how to continue their journey. While some claim that people were relocated to Pécs in order to decongest other cities (in particular Szeged), volunteers from Migszol Pécs considered this to be a deliberate, orchestrated move on the part of the Hungarian authorities which, they claim, aimed to provoke hostility towards migrants and refugees by having large numbers of unassisted migrants in the streets of Pécs. In response, however, a significant number of people came together to provide assistance to those on the move, including overseeing transportation to Budapest and coordinating with groups operating there, as well as providing food, clothing and medical support when necessary.

In both places, refugees would just be arriving into Hungary and trying to make their way to Budapest, where they hoped to board a train that would take them to Austria, Germany and beyond. They would be lacking food, water, sometimes clothes and medication as well as, importantly, information. While, as I will comment on below, the local authorities in Szeged and Pécs differed in their approach to the situation of refugees, in both contexts there was no organised and systematic effort by them or by the national authorities to either assist people locally or facilitate the continuation of their journey. In both cases, a group of local residents came together under the name of *Migszol* (respectively *Migszol Szeged* and *Migzsol Pécs*) in order to 'fill the gap' left by the lack of intervention on the part of the local and national authorities. The number of volunteers involved on a regular basis in Migszol Szeged was about 150 people, while the core group of Migszol Pécs consisted of around 40–50 volunteers. Pro-migrant activities in Szeged were, to some extent, facilitated by the local authorities, which provided a storage and distribution place – in the form of a wooden cabin located next to the station where the majority of Migzsol activities were taking place. This was possible insofar as Szeged is distinctive in the Hungarian context and has a Socialist mayor who stands as a declared opponent of governmental party Fidesz. In Pécs, the local authorities did not provide any form of support to the civilian group and their rapport was extremely tense.

What were these groups' politics and how did they relate to governmental discourses regarding migration and the Hungarian 'national community'? Speaking with representatives of both groups quickly indicated an insistence on presenting their initiatives as apolitical and driven purely by humanitarian and solidarity concerns. In particular, they showed strong defiance towards any form of party politics, as the following two anecdotes illustrate. During a group interview on 16 June 2016, two of the key coordinators of Migszol Szeged told us:

> *Interviewee 1*: At some point, we had the opportunity to get a donation from the European Socialists. A large amount. (…)
> *Interviewee 2*: Seven million HUF. That is a really big sum, not something you flush down the drain (…).
> *Interviewee 1*: It was a very big dilemma. If it had just been a truck of mineral water, we could have said 'No' easily, but this is such a sum … So we talked (with other groups) and we said that, if they get out in the media that we get money from the Socialists… (pause) so we said 'Thanks' and recommended giving the money to the Greeks. We don't want to receive money from any political organisation.

In Pécs, the initiator of Migszol explained not only how the local Socialist party had helped them by providing a small storage room and some tents but also how he was worried that this would affect the reputation of Migszol Pécs. One volunteer commented, in an interview on 16 July 2016, on how this was dealt with by the coordinators of Migszol:

> One of the tents … clearly belonged to the Socialist party because it had the flower on it – the emblem of the Hungarian Socialist Party. And A. and the leaders of this little camp, they were always telling us to put that tent on the bar inside out, so as not to show that this belongs to the Socialist Party, because this is not a political venture, this is not a political activity. They were trying to make it as apolitical as possible.

This distancing from party politics, sometimes framed as a reluctance to be political in general, is not unique to the initiatives under consideration. The so-called democratic transition of Hungary has been marked by forms of political and economic instability that often resulted in strong popular disillusion with political parties. Between 1990 and 2002, Hungary saw three different governing coalitions. At the end of each term, the vote swung in the opposite direction. The pattern was interrupted in 2006 with the re-election of the Hungarian Socialist Party but, only a few months after the elections, the uncovering of the Party's alleged lies during the election campaign and of various corruption scandals led to a series of protests and to the repudiation of the government. Since 2010, the nationalist conservative party Fidesz has dominated the Hungarian political scene, leaving little room for opposition. In a context of increasing authoritarianism by the party in power, Fidesz, repeated disappointment with party politics sometimes seems to translate into a refusal to associate themselves with any political party by people engaging in social or oppositional activities.

Yet, in spite of this insistence on distancing themselves from any political party and specific political identity as a group, interviews with the key people (initiators and coordinators) of both Migszol groups clearly showed that they held marked political opinions and that their activities have been shaped in particular by a conflicting relation to the Fidesz-led Hungarian government. In addition to their genuine objection to the mistreatment of people on the move by the Hungarian authorities, the Migszol groups' involvement was influenced and structured by a broader and longer-term opposition to the Hungarian authorities and the social, economic and political relational modalities they encourage. Hence, while insisting on the civilian, non-political nature of the overall group, many individual volunteers were moved by anti-government positions and imaginations of a different society and alternative modes of sociality in Hungary. In other words, these groups actively rejected the (dis)integrating practices of the authorities, refusing to 'integrate' into a fully exclusionary imagination of the national body and rather enacting a form of popular or vernacular integration by engaging with people deemed Others in official discourses.

10.5   Recovering the Politics

The core group who established Migszol Szeged and coordinated its activities throughout the summer was composed of long-term acquaintances with relatively well-known positions as socially engaged people in the city. For years, they had run a local alternative radio station, which had to shut down following the Hungarian government's passing of restrictive broadcasting laws in 2010 (CMCS n.d.). In previous years, they had been key organisers of a number of protests, including the Internet tax protest and the teachers' strike. Volunteers to whom I spoke in Szeged had often been in contact with them prior to the summer of 2015 and their credibility as socially engaged and reliable people was central to bringing people into Migszol Szeged and building relationships of trust.

Experience of previous joint actions and struggles was also key to the establishment of Migszol Pécs. Again, the group was consolidated by previous encounters and relationships. One of its central members whom I met in Pécs declared that she had been involved in workers' struggles and trade unionism for the last four decades. At a time when large numbers of migrants passed through Pécs, she was able to solicit support from the local police union, with whom Migszol could establish a functional working relationship, at least at the beginning. The local police would let Migszol volunteers know every time new people were brought into the city, allowing the group to organise support accordingly. The core Migszol group had also been heavily involved in defending other cohorts of people marginalised and illegalised by the Hungarian authorities. A few years ago, as in other Hungarian municipalities, Mayor Zsolt Pava criminalised homelessness in Pécs. This provoked outrage among some of the local residents, who quickly organised a group to coordinate support for the homeless and poor of the city. The group has been organising food and clothes distribution, as well as solidarity events such as Christmas celebrations, and many group members have been key figures in Migszol Pécs. Here, again, common opposition to the government and local authorities, a shared understanding and rejection of the process through which vulnerable groups are targeted, and previous experience of collective protest, were central to building the initiatives that emerged over the summer.

This is important for several reasons. First, it allows a more complex reading of the solidarity initiatives that took place in favour of migrants in the summer of 2015, on which there has been precious little research in Hungary.[5] In what *has* been published, scholars have, at times, deemed the forms of volunteerism that emerged in Hungary in 2015 as limited or apolitical (Kallius et al. 2016). I suggest that looking at the case of Szeged and Pécs can both challenge and complement such analysis in important ways. It can help us to develop a better understanding of pro-refugee solidarity in Hungary and encourages us to exercise caution when criticising support initiatives towards refugees by deeming them forms of humanitarian or charitable volunteerism with no political awareness.

In both cities, opposition to Fidesz and its attempts to capitalise on the suffering of migrants and other vulnerable groups for political purposes and for promoting a particular idea of the national public, were repetitively referred to as key motives for involvement. This conflicting – and, to an extent, dialectical – relationship to Fidesz *preceded* the so-called migrant 'crisis'. It had been built up over many years in opposition to the multiple ways in which the Hungarian government has produced internal and external enemies with the aim of stabilising its power and creating a climate of social fear and a disintegration of social ties that do not fit into the official narration of the Hungarian 'nation'. It is therefore not coincidental that many of the interviewees recounted that they had previously assisted other vulnerable groups. These latter include, prominently, the Roma, as the national figure of internal Otherness whom Viktor Orbán has relentlessly evoked over the last few years as a counterpoint to his vision of an ordered and desirable Hungarian public. However, it also extends to groups – such as the elderly, the disabled, the poor and the homeless – who have been vulnerabilised in various ways through the neoliberal transition in Hungary. The connection between these conditions and struggles was most forcefully advanced by one of the coordinators of Migszol Pécs, who said:

> I hold Viktor Orbán responsible for the death of my mother. She had cancer, and had her leg and breast amputated. They operated on her and after the operation … they threw her out on the street... Now it is the same thing with my wife: she had a serious brain operation and they have taken away her 'pension for disabled people'. We got into such a serious situation, by the way, that officially I am now homeless. I don't have a flat... But even with all of these events, we have to keep doing things, because there are people who are in the same boat as

---

[5] Though limited, scholarly attention has been paid to pro-migrant initiatives in Hungary, including to volunteers' motivations for engaging in support activities and the effects of 'helping encounters' on their understanding of migration (Feischmidt and Zakaria 2016). Questions regarding the tensions and contradictions between the different humanitarian and solidarity actors active in Budapest in 2015 have also been raised (Kallius et al. 2016). However, up to now little research has been conducted on pro-migrant solidarity in the Hungarian context beyond the city of Budapest.

us and we try to help them. I can give the example of how, on a daily basis, they push the homeless out of the city centre. They can't even be there. The police harass them (Interview 18 July 2016).

The connections recognised between the different forms of marginalisation and inequality in this excerpt sketch out forms of identity and solidarity that go beyond charity and humanitarianism. They speak to the recognition of shared material conditions and of comparable positions in the face of the state and of capital. The forms of exclusion referred to here concern the violent discursive and physical segregation faced by migrants and refugees, as much as forms of economic relegation leading to situations of poverty, hardship and exploitation. This also highlights forms of belonging that could work towards the expansion of the space available to migrants so that they can form connections to other groups in the country. In other words, against a process of marginalisation and alienation of certain social groups orchestrated by the Hungarian government, the volunteers in this research engage in actions which one could call 'acts of integration' (see Collyer et al. 2020) or, as proposed, of 'vernacular integration'.

This must also be assessed in light of the history of the city of Pécs. As explained, Pécs was an old industrial and mining centre which experienced the brutal closure of it industries and mines over the last two to three decades, followed by a brief period of foreign investment that has largely come to a halt, leading to high levels of unemployment and social misery. The interviewee previously quoted explained that he came from a working-class family of 14 children, marked by poverty and economic hardship. He positioned himself in material terms and articulated a discourse close to a class positioning that frames and makes intelligible the actions he carries out in solidarity with various groups, including, but not restricted to, refugees. For instance, at the end of my first day of fieldwork in Pécs in July 2016, a number of Migszol Pécs volunteers explained that they were driving to deliver clothes and food to impoverished Roma communities living in villages around Pécs.

Activists who made up the core group of Migszol Szeged came from somewhat different class positions. They were mostly university-educated people working in higher education or non-governmental organisations. The motivation they put forward for engaging in solidarity initiatives towards refugees was not about the sharing of material conditions, yet they also articulated ideas of a common struggle in opposition to the vision of society and of the national community imposed by the Hungarian government. One of the key organisers of the movement explained in an interview on 17 July 2016:

> This is not only about supporting people in need, this is about the sort of people we want to be, the sort of countries we want to live in, the sort of social relations we want to imagine. We do not want this narrow nationalism, we never did; ever since Orbán has come up with this way of speaking of Hungary and its history I have fought against it.

Here again, the position articulated is one of solidarity, where concepts of reciprocity and commonality are strongly emphasised. The interviewee mentions motivation that may be understood as humanitarian ('supporting people in need') yet he frames such concerns in a way that insists on the mutual interests embedded in pro-refugee actions, in the sense that supporting refugees and migrants is also about producing integrated socialities that reflect more closely his vision of a desirable society. He understands these initiatives as part of a larger struggle against particular political visions of Hungarian society that were mobilised to justify the mistreatment of refugees in the summer of 2015 and beyond, but that also existed before and were previously employed by the Hungarian authorities to redraw the boundaries of the national community along narrow socio-cultural lines and to target vulnerable groups.

I would like to argue that it is precisely because such political positionings and reflections existed before the arrival of refugees and migrants in Hungary that large-scale initiatives could be promptly established in cities like Szeged and Pécs. A number of the volunteers who participated in this research understood their pro-migrant stance as a moral and political necessity in relation to the broader context of authoritarianism in Hungary. While the forms of morality involved might have underlying humanitarian tones, they were also articulated politically. Volunteers' and activists' actions were triggered by a wider outrage towards the national and local authorities' ongoing criminalisation and Othering of different groups. In other words, these were forms of opposition to the official dialectics of (dis)integration that attempts to prevent socialities with those identified as not belonging to the nation. They were, at times, sustained by powerful forms of identification with the circumstances faced by people on the move.

10.6   Conclusion

As seen, the Hungarian state has deployed a series of mechanisms and measures aimed at marginalising refugees and migrants, and at preventing their integration within Hungarian society and socialities. This process relies on the production of a legitimate and desirable Hungarian public, which excludes not only migrants but also a number of citizens and civil organisations engaged in supporting those framed as Others in the dominant national narrative put forward by the Hungarian authorities. The related disintegration of certain socialities and reinforcement of a particular image of the nation can be usefully conceptualised through the notion of (dis)integration, which forces us to reflect on the dialectic between the integration of certain social groups and the prevention of others from entering the symbolic, discursive but also social and political space of national belonging. The shift to a securitising and authoritarian mode of government in the country has led to both a spectacular rise in xenophobic discourses and practices and to a narrowing of the public sphere underpinning a process of alienation and an experience of disintegration for an increasing number of members of Hungarian society.

In spite of and against this repressive environment, a series of pro-migrant initiatives emerged in the country throughout 2015. This chapter has focused more particularly on the cases of Migszol Szeged and Migszol Pécs, two independent civil initiatives in support of and solidarity with migrants and refugees that were established at the borders with Serbia and Croatia respectively. As seen, volunteers engaged in Migszol groups often refer to their activities in terms that would be broadly understood as humanitarian. This chapter, however, shows that their work has a political dimension, especially thanks to the long-term involvement of core volunteers in both Migszol Szeged and Migszol Pécs in practices of mutual support and solidarity that challenge not only the discourses of crisis and exceptionalism deployed in relation to the mobilities of summer 2015 but also the ongoing process of nation-building along various exclusionary lines deployed by the Hungarian authorities.

Since the 'crisis' was terminated through the deployment of aggressive bordering strategies, some of the Migszol volunteers in both Szeged and Pécs have remained socially and politically active or have resumed their previous activities. In Szeged, the initiators of Migszol have been key in allowing the monitoring and documentation of the situation at the border and in particular at the Röszke transit zone. Some of them have changed career to become involved as professional aid workers with local or international NGOs. In Pécs, Migszol members are continuing their activities in support of the homeless and poor people from the city and neighbouring villages. They have also been providing support to the Roma inhabitants of nearby towns.

In conclusion, despite difficult circumstances and the ongoing closure of spaces where solidarity can be practiced, these initiatives keep rejecting the restrictive representations of a moralised Hungarian public and start imagining alternative communities. In so doing, they enact acts of integration that directly challenge the official discourses of belonging of the Hungarian government.

References

Cabinet Office of the Prime Minister. (2018, February 21). *'Stop Soros' legislative package is an important step*. Retrieved May 5, 2018, from http://www.kormany.hu/en/news/stop-soros-legislative-package-is-an-important-step

Cantat, C. (2015). The ideology or Europeanism and Europe's migrant other. *International Socialism Journal, 152*. Retrieved May 5, 2018, from http://isj.org.uk/the-ideology-of-europeanism-and-europes-migrant-other

Cetti, F. (2012). *'Europeanity', the 'other' and the discourse of fear: The centrality of the forced migrant as 'global alien' to an emerging European national identity*. Unpublished PhD thesis, University of East London, London.

CMCS. (n.d.). *Public service media*. Retrieved May 5, 2018, from http://medialaws.ceu.hu/public_service_media_more.html

Collyer, M., Hinger, S., & Schweitzer, R. (2020). Politics of (dis)integration – An introduction. In S. Hinger & R. Schweitzer (Eds.), *Politics of (dis)integration* (pp. 1–18). Cham: Springer VS.

Daily News Hungary. (2018, March 26). Election 2018 – Orbán: Migration number one issue. *Daily News Hungary.* Retrieved May 5, 2018, from https://dailynewshungary.com/election-2018-orban-migration-number-one-issue/

De Genova, N. (2015, May 20). The border spectacle of migrant 'victimisation'. *Open Democracy.* Retrieved May 5, 2018, from https://www.opendemocracy.net/beyondslavery/nicholas-de-genova/border-spectacle-of-migrant-%E2%80%98victimisation%E2%80%99

Desille, A. (2020). Jewish immigrants in Israel: Disintegration within integration? In S. Hinger & R. Schweitzer (Eds.), *Politics of (dis)integration* (pp. 141–159). Cham: Springer VS.

Euractiv. (2015, August 31). Fabius calls Eastern Europe's reluctance to receive migrants 'scandalous'. *Euractiv.* Retrieved May 5, 2018, from https://www.euractiv.com/section/justice-home-affairs/news/fabius-calls-eastern-europe-s-reluctance-to-receive-migrants-scandalous/

Feischmidt, M. & Zakaria, I. (2016, November 17–18). *Identity-based politics and solidarity beyond and across borders. Case study on Hungarian civic activists effected by refugees.* Budapest: Central European University, paper given to a workshop entitled Challenging the political beyond and across borders.

Fekete, L. (2016). Hungary: Power, punishment and the 'Christian-national idea'. *Race and Class, 57*(4), 39–53.

Hinger, S. (2020). Integration through disintegration? The distinction between deserving and undeserving refugees in national and local integration policies in Germany. In S. Hinger, R. Schweitzer, *Politics of (dis)integration* (pp. 19–39). Cham: Springer VS.

Kallius, A., Monterescu, D., & Rajaram, P. K. (2016). Immobilizing mobility: Border ethnography, illiberal democracy, and the politics of the 'refugee crisis' in Hungary. *American Ethnologist, 43*(1), 25–37.

Migszol. (2015, May 5). *Fidesz's 'National Consultation' is no consultation at all. It is a shameless piece of propaganda – A Migszol commentary.* Retrieved May 5, 2018, from http://www.migszol.com/blog/fideszs-national-consultation-is-no-consultation-at-all-it-is-a-shameless-piece-of-propaganda-a-migszol-commentary

Rajaram, P. K. (2003). *The spectacle of detention: Theatre, poetry and imagery in the context over identity, security and responsibility in contemporary Australia* (Asia Research Institute Working Paper No. 7). Singapore: National University of Singapore. Retrieved May 5, 2018, from http://www.ari.nus.edu.sg/wps/wps03_007.pdf

Sözke, A. (2015). A 'road to work'? The reworking of deservedness, social citizenship and public work programmes in rural Hungary. *Citizenship Studies, 19*(6–7), 734–750.

Vaughan-Williams, N. (2015). *Europe's border crisis. Biopolitical security and beyond.* Oxford: Oxford University Press.

Chapter 11
Conclusions: Perspectives and Puzzles in Researching Politics of (Dis)Integration

Violetta Zentai

Much has been written in academia about integration following migration to and within Europe in the post-WW II era. Integration has served as a central term in political, policy and scholarly debates to denote principles, discourses, interventions and social practices which ensure sustained interactions and cooperation across different groups or parts of society, including those who were born within and outside of particular, typically state, borders. The ideal of integration has mastered both the feared and the cherished aspects of social difference. Disintegration, in turn, has been posited as a concept referring to processes that neglect, diminish, dilute or deliberately deconstruct what liberal political systems have promoted through the idea of integration. (*Dis)integration* is investigated in this volume to examine the complex interactions and controversies of the twin processes of integration and disintegration by which societies and policies respond to people moving across (nation-state) borders and contribute to redrawing the social landscapes where they arrive. A European perspective is extended to other migrant destinations in the global North, more precisely to Israel and Canada, in order to offer insights into diverse domestic social and political practices as well as cross-national debates on the politics of human mobility.

The authors in this volume have originally contemplated to explore the politics of integration by engaging in multi-layered investigations into how migrants and refugees are defined, placed or moved by policies, institutions, and administrative protocols, yet deliberately, tacitly or inadvertently affecting institutions and relations in society at large. As highlighted in the introduction, the contributing authors have explored a whole continuum of practices producing integration and disintegration, often simultaneously or interlaced. The exchanges, cross-readings, and horizontal conversations across the authors' collective have helped the editors acknowledge that the nuanced attention to the processes of integration and

V. Zentai (✉)
Central European University, Budapest, Hungary
e-mail: zentaiv@ceu.edu

© The Author(s) 2020
S. Hinger, R. Schweitzer (eds.), *Politics of (Dis)Integration,*
IMISCOE Research Series, https://doi.org/10.1007/978-3-030-25089-8_11

disintegration mechanisms can be best captured by the master concept of *politics of (dis)integration*. This concept, at first sight, embodies a tension, if not a contradiction: it implies that something systemic is coming together through changes that detach, distance or deconstruct what should or could be parts of a whole. The notion of politics refers to a plethora of actors who participate in dynamic acts of integration and disintegration, the outcomes of which are partly fluid and ambiguous, but in other cases controversial and harsh. The authors of this volume are scholars of migration accompanied by others who study Roma and other minorities. The scholarly endeavours behind the chapters have dwelt on recent or contemporary transformations in cognisance of wider and longer-term changes in European political and policy scenes, juxtaposed with Canadian and Israeli contexts of distinctive immigration and integration traditions.

In this concluding chapter, I reflect on some of the coalescing and occasionally diverging experiences and arguments that the authors of the volume have presented. This will be embedded in a review of key messages that the volume as a whole articulates regarding the conceptual, political and policy formations that tailor relations between people on the move and other members of society amidst weakening mechanisms for protecting human dignity, rights and equal citizenship in Europe and beyond.

11.1 What Is Changing in Europe and Beyond?

In the introduction to this volume Collyer, Hinger and Schweitzer propose that a European integration regime has been functioning for 50 years on shifting conceptual foundations but within a wider liberal consensus which has now become challenged. The regime on the wane emerged in post-WW II (Western) Europe in response to the arrival of guest workers from Southern Europe and later from the former colonies joining with the post-war economies. At that time, globalising economic relations attracted new labour migrants from all over the world to Europe from the 1980s (Favell 2014). Later, the internal borders in Europe got opened to the newly admitted member-states to the European Union (EU) in the 2000s. The enlarged EU generated hopes for managing migration practices by reducing internal boundaries and providing safe protection of its external borders. This migration regime, split between immigration and integration, is promoted by an 'embedded liberalism' favouring the interests of national economies (Rass and Wolff 2018, p. 29). The EU has retained major responsibility for security and border control, the least progressive aspect of immigration management (Favell 2014). The European scope of action, freed from nation-state confinement, has been left with a policy task largely distanced from the goals of social integration and the expansion of citizenship rights. Other sharper voices in the literature, inspired by Mezzadra and Nielson (2013), emphasise how objectives and imaginaries of immigration regimes have moved to dominate the concept of integration in Europe by bringing the state's border onto the state's territory and undermining integration policies way beyond the explicit targets of these policies.

The current volume encourages an understanding that migration is always conceived and managed in a wider complexity of visions, ideologies and policy paradigms aiming to respond to various differences, belongings and disparities in society. Therefore, it is important to note that the enduring integration regime in Europe has been underscored by the acknowledgment that the liberal order cannot solve all structural inequalities and smooth out all tensions of diversity understood beyond migration affairs. The recognition of historically accumulated disadvantages, the formation of legal and institutional safeguards against discrimination and further steps to ensure power-sharing between the disadvantaged and the privileged were strengthened across Europe in the 1980s and the 1990s (Shaw 2005). The advancement of the concept of multiculturalism enriched and partly rethought the human rights paradigm by advocating the recognition of collective identities and belonging, in particular along ethnicity, religion and language within nation-state-bound societies. However, not even the heyday of multiculturalism eliminated certain hierarchies among groups in society that integration concepts tacitly or deliberately accepted.

The chapters of the volume have intensively commented on how the European regimes of 'migrant integration' started to change markedly from the mid-1990s. In view of the milestones in this process, contributing authors have referred to the post-Cold War start of the massive migration of Russian Jews to Israel in 1989–2000 which further hierarchised the citizenship regime of the country (Desille), the EU Roma integration strategic framework announced in 2011 by marking the Roma as the most vulnerable minority in Europe (Magazzini), the official announcement of a deliberately hostile environment for undocumented migrants in the UK in 2013 (Schweitzer), a 'refugee crisis' in 2015 involving a number of European polities (Cantat) and the passing of a new Integration Law in Germany in 2016 to define which refugees are (not) 'likely to stay' in the country (Hinger). Most of the scholarly voices in the volume resonate with interpretations that reveal a gradual shift to principles and goals of tighter population control, labour-force-driven social engineering and selective inclusion in the core through exclusions on the margins of society. These approaches had not been completely alien from European policy practices under the former integration regimes yet did not coalesce into a dominant scheme.

The broader literature also highlights paramount inequities in the European migration system and shrinking opportunities for inclusion for marked groups of migrants. The free movement of European citizens is accompanied by the tightening control of mobility from outside the European borders. The demands of labour markets are openly promoted, together with the noble goal of circulation of human capital and the belief in the entrepreneurial spirit of migration. However, belief in cooperation and solidarity between people of different or multiple group belongings and of varying mobility and placement conditions is diminishing (Favell 2014; Scholten and van Breugel 2018). Increasingly resistant or hostile attitudes have developed toward specific recipients in welfare provisions. Among these 'groups of suspicion', immigrants usually stand out (Banting and Kymlicka 2015; Lafleur and Mescoli 2018). Political statements demonstrating tight (or, at least, tightening) control still endorse a political economy which perpetuates the flow of foreign-born labour supply, wherever needed. Within this duality – one might even call it hypocrisy – deep European racist convictions and everyday routines of racialising exclusion also surface. Not restricted to newly arriving migrants, this often concerns populations of colonial origin and, most recently, the Roma, the stigmatised subjects of East–West migration within Europe. In recent extremist imagination and discourses, the ideological nexus of 'non-European'-ness increasingly conjoins the figures of 'Roma' with 'migrant', with 'Muslim', with 'terrorist', with 'criminal', with racialised Blackness (Yildiz and De Genova 2017). Even in less-antagonised political contexts, a negative integration spiral is often observed: social groups move away from each other even if mixed identities and increasing diversity within the immigrant groups, particularly in larger cities, soften the boundaries between majority and minority groups in society (Crul 2016).

Parallel to capturing the limiting and disconcerting transformation, the portrayal offered in this volume of contemporary European, Canadian and Israeli integration practices should also be seen within the state of the art in wider social justice struggles. More precisely, I propose to evoke the visions and platforms against racial/ethnic exclusion and marginalisation in recent histories of European equality thinking. Group differences enacted along ethnic, racial and religious lines, including the position of migrants and the marginalised Roma, have been elevated to a protected ground in European politics and policy making by the EU's 'Race Directive' of 2000. Nonetheless, the politics of recognition of these groups and their conditions has always been more contentious than that of women, sexual minorities or people with disabilities, just to name few other protected grounds. Furthermore, socio-economic (class) distinction has not become subject to transformative equality thinking in Europe, except in some Nordic countries, even if enduring poverty has been seen as violating human dignity. Notwithstanding, the European political and policy infrastructure for anti-discrimination, likewise the Canadian one, is perhaps more significant and transformative in its potential and partial effects, than assessed in this volume. This infrastructure has become constitutive of the wider European integration landscape in the last five decades, appearing the most prosperous in the 1990s and early 2000s (O'Cinneide 2013). Since then, it has become contested, or even weakened, due to mutating consequences of global capitalism, competing states within the enlarging Europe, inward looking welfare regimes, and populist electoral politics, to name some of the forces behind debasing the norms of human rights and equal citizenship practices. The volume has presented a compelling call for critical inquiries to relate more systematically the agendas of migration research with a comparative historical account of various European social justice struggles and tangible policy changes over the last five decades.

11.2   (Dis)Integration Politics and Policies

The chapters in this volume have uncovered considerable variation in contemporary integration governance across localities and their recent histories. The authors believe in that the multi-scalar configurations of integration and disintegration practices can be examined through the interfaces and linkages between international, national and sub-national actors and domains. Cities with diverse populations linked to global economic and cultural exchanges and nation-state power structures are examined as multiscalar place-making configurations resonating with important recent trends in migration research (Çağlar and Schiller 2018). With due respect to the risk of methodological nationalism, the authors have also put the nation-state policy machinery under their magnifying glass in cognisance of its power, institutions and resources in shaping politics of (dis)integration. It is acknowledged that civil society actors and citizens also become constitutive of (dis)integration processes through their solidarity actions with and for migrants on the one hand, and xenophobic mobilization on the other. As Collyer et al. proposed in the introduction of the book, in the contact zones of authorities, migrants and host society and in various policy domains, contradictory processes embracing exclusionary and inclusionary drives and instances contribute to co-producing (dis)integration effects in society.

The individual chapters have shed light on different balances and tipping points between scales of action, frictions between politics and policy practices, and operations of policy or social sub-systems. For example, the chapters have revealed how immigration policies and integration measures may embrace saliently different paradigms, like in Malta with a more lenient former and more restrictive latter system. The recent refugee legislation in Germany constrains integration yet allows laxer border control. Other contributions have uncovered that national-level policy framings get contested or bent by sub-national actors such as some German cities and street-level bureaucrats in the UK. By the example of the Spanish and Italian Roma inclusion strategies, it has also been explained that the wide-spread policy jargon of social inclusion enables both difference and equality-based interventions and can usher in disintegrating moves and outcomes. Disjointed principles and practices are pursued and assembled together in the UK social services to help preventing 'illegal' immigration yet to respect the ethics of service provision, and in the Canadian regulatory regime concerning temporary migrant status.

In addition to portraying and explaining complexities, and transient or enduring properties or modalities of (dis)integration, the chapters together have contributed to sharpening knowledge on three essential components of (dis)integration practices: framing the organising principles of policy (non-)interventions, categorisation and hierarchisation of people, and everyday acts of exclusion and inclusion.

11.2.1 Framing

Political and policy frames built and promoted by state or civil society actors targeting public issues encompass a problem statement, name the problem-holders, articulate a need for interventions or change and outline the direction of the latter. All
this is glued together in a meaningful reasoning. The volume has mapped these
frames and frame-making acts as domains of fight, change and contestation, rather
than as sheer state machinery to legitimise and perpetuate population control.

Maintaining the foundations of the nation is an old but still paramount rationale
for domestic policy regimes' interest in integration measures. Hinger, in her chapter,
has revealed that the Integration Law of 2016 in Germany envisions the maintenance of a peaceful, liberal and communal society and, to this end, public policies
will regulate the privileges and duties of asylum-seekers. In contrast, municipalities
often consider the asylum-seekers as potential resources in a heterogeneous urban
society. Magazzini has argued that the National Roma Integration Strategies – compulsory policy tools for multi-year actions in the EU member-states – in fact articulate what constitutes the idea of being 'national'. Of the two Roma integration
strategies closely observed, the Spanish one defines the regular citizens' living conditions and expects the Roma to assimilate to them. The Italian strategy identifies
separated social groups, the relations of which it intends to mediate. In Israel, contemporary immigration is supported to enable general socio-economic development, to balance out-migration, to enrich cultural diversity and also to provide new
channels of public funds for municipalities, as Desille has argued. Thus, immigrants
boost the resources of the host society and compensate for certain shortages that it
may face. The well-being and sustainability of the nation is again a prime objective.

In other cases, the framing of integration actions is conceptualised around the
in-betweenness of the refugees and other migrants. The study on Malta by Nimführ
et al. has uncovered how transience and permanent temporariness are purposefully
produced and institutionalised, thus showing an interesting analogy with the Polish
state's perception of the returning migrants, which Karolak discussed in his chapter.
Temporariness seems to justify minimum interventions and leaves in limbo the status, potential citizenship and recognition of those considered as temporary. In contrast, the framing of the status of temporary migrants in Canada and the UK by
perpetuating the language of temporariness does not seem to strongly shape or limit
the depth and intensity of integration effort in these contexts, as Samuk's chapter
has shown. This might indicate that, in current political contexts, strategic framing,
i.e. articulating less 'progressive' vocabulary, may tame political and popular resistance to hosting migrants and enable more supportive actual integration measures.

The volume has eloquently revealed that forms of disintegration are also produced by non-action or willful and justified negligence by state or other responsible
authorities. As Cantat has shown in her chapter, the current Hungarian refugee management system turns its back on the needs of asylum-seekers. The dominant immigration policy frame aggrandises the role of the Hungarian state to defend the
Schengen borders. The refugees' needs and humanity are erased from the policy

vision. Karolak has examined how the Polish state has had a lukewarm reaction to the problem of large numbers of returning migrants in a belief in their increased skills and employability. The deployed integration frame overvalues the assets of the returning migrants and turns a blind eye to the context of the growing precarisation of work. More closely, some kind of involvement in the labour market, regardless of its quality and stability, is viewed as integration by default. Further, as Karolak suggests, this approach to return migrants valorise a flexible, docile and politically abstinent global workforce and distracts the attention from the vulnerable, typically low-skilled migrant workers. Sahraoui has found that it is the dominant frame of direct discrimination and the individual complaint principle that are posited against the racialising employer practices concerning migrant care workers in larger European cities. In fact, structural discriminations are produced on a massive scale by the intersections of migration, employment and care regimes. The preferred anti-discrimination principle with its restricted attention to equal treatment and individual scope neglects the duty to protect the vulnerable and to prevent institutional discrimination. This restrictive policy lens bleaches the existing European equality norms which have moved beyond the sheer prohibition of discrimination and individual legal actions.

Several chapters in this book have touched upon the hidden references to or more tangible imaginaries of racial hierarchy in European societies, one of the most stubborn and controversial forces of disintegration. Racial oppression has been explained as a wicked form of inequality and exclusion in the norms and vocabulary of liberal democratic politics. In spite of the major international human rights treaty mechanisms and the hard law provision in the European Union (Race Directive), racialised ethnic 'othering' is still part of social imagination, politics and social relations in Europe. Racist discrimination can result from policies and practices, which might or might not be imbued with explicit racist ideology, as Sahraoui's chapter has discussed. Institutional practices effectively transform the experience of individual prejudice into forms of institutional racism. Against these institutional practices, standard liberal anti-discrimination frames appear as feeble and unsubstantial: they allow integrating various migrants in the labour market of larger European cities at the cost of regular maltreatment and abuse in which racial hierarchising can be captured.

11.2.2   Categorisation and Hierarchisation

Contemporary migration governance systems enact hierarchical integration opportunities for various groups of people on the move. A closer look shows that earlier state interventions had also been prone to use this practice. A wide array of policy analyses portrays the fact that states tend to hierarchise people to ensure control and rationalise divisible and indivisible resources (Mügge and Van der Haar 2016; Yanow et al. 2016). Categories are used to separate people and to rank their worth, their needs and the respect which they can be given, in order to justify differential degrees of deservingness. Inclusion-driven civic actors may also rely on categories for building solidarity, support and empowerment, but their intention is rarely to solidify social hierarchies. Hierarchies of people in European migration processes frequently resonate with a colonial imagination but without colonial powers. As several authors in this volume (Hinger, Samuk and Schweitzer) have argued, the categories that immigration regulations define set the (dis)integration paths that are available to migrants.

The divide between European and non-European migrants saliently structures public discourses and affairs in Europe and Israel but in a less obvious way in Canada as well. Desille's chapter has described the situation in which immigrants gain the attention of policy-makers when their economic performance is positive and when they fall into the category of vulnerability. This polarised practice is constructed by the interplay of Israeli nation-building, migration governance and integration policy. At the beginning, the line was drawn between Jewish immigrants of European and those of other origin. Today, the country of origin still plays a decisive role but has become enmeshed in a neoliberal discourse around un/deservingness based on perceived economic utility and the ability to actively participate in society. The 'Russians' are idealised as 'active, participatory and productive individuals', whereas groups from the Global South are accepted due to their potential vulnerability. This still strongly racialised distinction is translated into a dual (dis)integration regime: as Desille has shown, the resourceful ones are granted individual freedom and choices while the vulnerable ones are limited in their freedom and choices. The property of resourcefulness measured by a degree of fit to actual labour market needs is further differentiated by the skill capacities of the migrants. This neatly resonates with Samuk's finding that migrant workers categorised as low-skilled might very well have high(er) skills but refrain from claiming them in order to fit the host countries' labour market and/or visa regimes.

The most drastic practice of labelling people emerged in the recent European 'refugee crisis' in 2015. Some immigration regimes, with the disconcerting lead of the government of Hungary, disqualified all border-crossing refugees as 'illegal migrants'. This radical message was endorsed by the treatment of these refugees at the entry point to the country and at the point of their departure for their continued journey. Cantat warns in her chapter that migrants become illegal when legal provisions define certain forms of mobility as illegal. By promulgating the notion of illegality, the respective government normalises its indifference to suffering and its denial of solidarity in the name of the security of Hungarian society. This disqualifies any liaison between migrants and members of the host society, other than feelings of fear or suspicion. Although Germany emerged as the most inclusive and welcoming society in the milestone year of 2015 in European refugee politics, its 2016 law on integration introduced unambiguously restrictive measures. More closely, as Hinger has revealed, it defines a legal division between genuine and bogus asylum-seekers by assigning strong or weak 'likelihood of staying' and rendering their treatment and access to services accordingly. The significance of the distinction based on the notion 'likely (or not) to stay' is powerfully illustrated by the Bavarian 'special camps' for refugees who are 'not likely to stay'. The two cases illuminate that categorisation often becomes not only the effect, but part and parcel of the fundamental principles respected or denied in the dominant integration frames.

All these examples reveal that the categories that underlie integration policies are imbued with powerful classifications by simplifying complex narratives and biographies of human lives with the purpose of creating and endorsing order and hierarchy. These classifications reflect and endorse bureaucratic operations which always look indispensable, consequential, and neutral, thus detached from political controversies and struggles. The actual categories, such as 'refugees', migrants', 'illegal', 'legal', 'temporary', etc. function as empty vessels into which human beings can be placed by inducing a one-dimensional status embracing a specific moment in time and crafting the individual as being ahistorical and neutral in relationship to state authority (Sajjad 2018).

11.2.3   Everyday Acts of (Dis)Integration

State and market forces and their cooperation are seen as the most powerful actors to influence the conditions of integration and disintegration practices. This volume offers a number of important observations to refine this argument. Even in the most favourable institutional and framing constellations, in which state administration is mandated to care about equal access to citizenship, bureaucratic procedures often differ from the official policy ideals and frames. In reverse, as already mentioned, bureaucratic practices can, to some extent, resist restrictive paradigms enforced from above. The ways in which bureaucracies operate are embedded within broader cultural patterns of conduct and sociality (Rozakou 2017). This implies that bureaucracies could perform above and below the quality of their protocols and could be either devoted or reluctant supporters of equal citizenship ideals. In some cases, state authorities enact irregularity and disorder when organising their integration services. In other cases, routinised practices of security and control override any other principles of public service. In the contemporary political climate prone to sorting out un-welcome immigrants, one can expect bureaucracies, service providers and local authorities resonating with the expectation to perform restricted services to those who are marked as 'undeserving'. However, this is not always the case.

Several chapters in this volume have explored the behaviour and everyday practices of state at the nodal points of social-service provision (e.g. borders and cities). They have revealed how particular sites operate where the exclusionary logic of immigration law intersects with the different inclusionary practices of public service provision, including health care, education and social assistance in the UK, and services for newly arrived immigrants to help in their integration offered by the municipalities in Malta and Israel. Where the major divide is drawn between regular and irregular migrants, in order to effectively constrain the latters' access to various rights and services, the spirit of immigration law penetrates ever more spheres of everyday life and social interaction, as highlighted in the chapters by Schweitzer, Nimführ et al. and Desille. Consequently, control and surveillance are not only intensified but also gradually extended from the external boundaries to the interior of the state and society, as Mezzadra and Neilson (2013) indicate. This impacts fundamentally on how street-level bureaucrats handle irregularities in their daily encounters with service-users. They generate institutional innovations to maintain a firewall for the regular operation of public administration and to comply with the task of criminalising interaction with unlawful citizens, as Schweitzer notes in his chapter. This complicity, although incorporating some resilience, appears to disintegrate the classical ethos of social services and public administration.

The role of state authorities is also complex and contradictory in Israel and Malta. In the former, they have to develop two different modalities of operation: one for the resourceful migrants deemed to be productive and of high utility, another one for the discounted ones limited in their freedom and closely managed in their integration. In Malta, as opposed to several other countries in Europe, the authorities, in their first encounters with migrants, are mobilised by the norms of rescuing at sea. The authorities then treat migrants as transients and sojourners who only deserve to stay in inaccessible open centres equipped with temporary arrangements. By linking the modalities of framing, the hierarchical clustering of migrants and the everyday operation of state institutions, the chapters by Desille, Nimführ et al., and Samuk have all revealed that transience is not the property of the migrants: it is produced by the integrating state and its institutions.

It is worth acknowledging a particular tension in the political and conceptual views of the authors regarding the sub-national and local actors of state authorities. It is argued that, at the sub-national and local levels, the practicality of inclusion often reconfigures or neutralises the ethno-nationalist rhetoric and thus enables local actors be rid of the evils of exclusion or instrumental inclusion, as Magazzini discussed. An explicit clash between central and local policy-makers was captured by Hinger when discussing recent integration policy trends in Germany. She shows that local actors are still prepared to consider asylum-seekers – regardless of their status – as having rights to equal access to the welfare system and social institutions. Quite the opposite potential for local acts of integration is stressed by other authors. Nation-states often rely on local governments to struggle with the messy and costly details of servicing and policing the expanding non-citizen populations – Desille cites Varsanyi (2008) in her chapter. Other authors in the book also refer to migration scholars such as Glick Schiller and Çağlar (2011) who highlight that immigrants are seen as potential members of the 'creative class' acting as neoliberal agents of urban restructuring. In sum, the local domains of social interaction are more open and fluid than the national ones but often at the expense of further hierarchisation and selective support. The volume stresses that local policy-making appears more willing to consider different forms of migration as part of regular urban life in which inclusion is based on dynamic reactions to changes, rather than on restrictive formations of life conditions for migrants in the belief that authorities protect the majority.

In other contexts, everyday acts of negligence or destitution towards refugees and asylum-seekers are produced behind hyper-visible spectacles of scrutiny and control at the country borders. These acts contribute, as Cantat has indicated, to the 'un-weaving of the social, economic and political ties' which migrants and refugees may build in society. It is proposed that border spectacles stage dramatic scenes of enforcement and demonstrate a state's ability to enforce the law, punish those who break it and exclude those deemed as illegitimate. These acts set the moral and ethical limits of the political community. Parallel to this, state-sponsored and complicit media discourses stigmatising migration have far-reaching disintegration effects in society writ large. Notwithstanding, this negligence also provokes everyday acts of solidarity which complicate the dynamics of producing and reducing integration. Authorities try to delegitimise and, most recently, to vilify the refugee solidarity actions of the host society and thus prevent the emergence of links with a national public, as Cantat has shown.

Another salient political economy configuration is that migrants accept jobs that are not taken by ordinary citizens in exchange for some degree of welcome. A regular form of unambiguous exclusion of migrant workers from within and outside Europe is to employ them in completely unregulated and separated time–space constellations. As a recently completed ethnography uncovers, the low skilled night-shift workers in global cities of Europe are at the mercy of their employers, who are rarely subject to labour inspections. These workers not only suffer from a lack of labour protection, but they are also barely able to develop any social and human ties, let alone seek political support outside their workplace. They not only have limited rights compared to ordinary citizens or highly skilled migrant workers, but they live outside the social spaces populated by regular citizens. They have never been integrated and nothing they do conveys the hope that they ever will be. Non-action for integration is normalised by the invisibility of these patterns of separated human lives and punctuated spaces between migrant and main society (MacQuarie 2018).

By lacing together observations on framing strategies, hierarchical categorisation and everyday acts of organisations and administration, the volume reveals that, with few exceptions, European nation-states (as well as Israel and Canada) are not withdrawing fully and noisily from the ideals of social integration or inclusion. However, many of them circumvent or undermine the integration of certain individuals or groups who are identified as undeserving, resourceless or illegal. As Collyer et al. have argued in their introduction, the increasing exclusion of irregular residents from public welfare affects not only the excluded, but also the institutions providing such services and ultimately societal relations more broadly. Equally importantly, the norms, pronounced frames and practices of integration policies become constitutive of a broader social imagination which renders particular experiences acceptable, disturbing or unacceptable. Normalising racial hierarchies, non-action amidst perceived disparities and destitution and getting rid of the duty to protect, are all making their way in public affairs and discourses in contemporary Europe and Israel, whereas they are still resisted or neutralised in Canada.

11.3   Conceptual and Methodological Puzzles

The volume also deserves acknowledgement for experimenting on three major conceptual and methodological puzzles. First, it has ventured to translate the concept of (dis)integration into an analytical device by teasing out the relations between migration and other societal affairs. Second, it has acted upon the critique of methodological nationalism yet continues to view the nation-state as a centre of politics and operational mechanisms that shape integration and disintegration debates, practices, and regimes. Third, it has instigated discussions on separating normative and critical positions seen to differentiate policy actions and reflexive social research.

The scholars contributing to this volume respect scholarly traditions that delve into politics of integration as a complex phenomenon combining discursive, administrative and institutional acts across scales that are not only given but shaped by these acts. They all share a conviction that integration and disintegration practices should be examined through relational approaches: even if a power group, typically a social majority or the 'mainstream', is devising paths for those who want to be part of particular social, economic and political spaces, the institutions and relations of the power group do not remain unaffected. Moreover, the majority or the mainstream is not necessarily composed within the structures of the nation-state.

The analytical frames applied in this book resonate with recent noteworthy proposals to pursue complex integration studies. Garcés-Mascareñas and Penninx (2016) offer a composite analytical scheme and holistic tool for comparative studies on integration policies. Beyond disaggregating different dimensions, social parties (migrants and the mainstream) and levels of analysis, it is proposed to dwell on policy frames, concrete measures and the horizontal and vertical processes in different policy domains, including those that specifically target migrants and those regulating broader societal institutions. Rass and Wolff (2018) have also drawn up a complex analytical frame to examine migration governance which has obvious overlaps with integration research. Their multi-layered scheme takes further steps to investigate regime formations without searching pre-analytical nation-state-framed domestic regimes. They sort out specific analytical tasks in relation to all constituting factors of a regime captured on three layers. The key tenets that the authors in this volume hold also correspond with the core arguments of the introduction to another recent and inspiring thematic journal issue. Hamann and Yurdakul (2018) suggest that traditional integration research viewed migration as a peripheral phenomenon on the margins of society, whereas contemporary critical inquiries conceive migration as a constituting force within societies. This shift enables scholars to look at society as 'inevitably and irrevocably shaped by migration' (ibid. p. 111).

One of the biggest challenges for the researchers in this volume has been to open up the box of wider societal structures beyond migration management and integration. The chapters offer rich insights into streams of collective imagination, governance practices and social-service institutions beyond migration management that all contribute to shaping (dis)integration acts. This richness does not eliminate the methodological puzzle of identifying the most relevant societal interactions that reveal how integration regimes are embraced and conditioned by broader structures and movements in society. It is fair to argue that the volume as a whole portrays a wide set of the mutations and the controversies of (dis)integration formations which is not yet a systemic account yet more than a colourful picture to which individual chapters offer context specific experiences and enunciations. The volume also presents a compelling invitation to investigate how politics of migrant (dis)integration generates effects beyond its scope, and as recent trends show, even game-changers in broader citizenship relations.

The chapters have all offered important insights into how politics of (dis)integration are shaped by a variety of actors who engage in migration and integration affairs, with their intentions, rules, values, distinctive power positions and aspirations. The chapters by Cantat, Karolak, and Sahraoui have offered particularly refined accounts of citizens' encounters as subjects and agents of various immigration and integration measures. It is noteworthy that the majority of the authors have examined those subjects of policy measures who are marginalised, placed at the bottom of the societal hierarchy and face precarious working and living conditions. The conceptual and empirical links to approaches in the broader literature which articulate the notion of common marginalisation should be acknowledged here. These approaches investigate the economic, political and ideological forces that generate surplus populations – such as undocumented migrants, refugees, the deportables, precarious night-workers, the Roma and other racialised poor (Rajaram 2015).

Notable exceptions to marginality have been captured by Karolak in the lives of 'successful' Polish return labour migrants and by Desille in those of the new Russian immigrants in Israel. These migrants are posited as norm groups whose aspirations and assets contribute to social integration. The portrayal of the resourceful and welcome migrants is an important stepping stone to expanding the complexity of integration research. The experiences presented in the volume endorse the analytical attention stressed by Glick Schiller and Çağlar (2011, p. 12) about migrants' multiple pathways, diversified engagements in transnational connections and participation in generating alternative social visions. Karolak and Sahraoui have also revealed in their respective chapters, however, that not all agential positions among mobile people and concerned citizens end up in empowerment and capacities to resist disintegration.

The reader will notice that the authors of the volume have not been captured by the epistemological cage of the nation-state. The nation-state 'burden' is carried through the book in a reflexive manner. The investigations explicitly target configurations that frequently take the most powerful shape and claim authority within nation-state structures. Instead of seeing through state structures, the authors have advocated for seeing within and across state structures through observing multiple actors' perspectives – including people on the move, second- and third-generation migrants, sub-national/local service providers, official policy-makers, opinion-makers and citizens of various identity constructions. As several streams in migration research, the volume considers sub-national and local policy measures, economies and civil society actions and their supporting frames through their contributions to integration politics and policies, and their frequently enacted defiance of higher-level policy paradigms. Space has been left to further investigate the conditions under which governance and bottom-up citizens' actions not only tolerate but *do* support solidarity and equality-driven interactions in local settings.

The volume's sharpened attention to what is imagined, referred to and organised within the nation-state context creates noteworthy intellectual linkages with other scholarly efforts to capture political and social changes that may debase the static, demobilising or self-enacting energies of nation-state structures. In the contemporary world of nation-states, nationhood is the default boundary of social membership (Banting and Kymlicka 2015), yet various utterances, reflections and acts regarding collective belongings do question the principle of bounded nation-states protected by membership privileges. It would be an enticing opportunity for the authors to investigate whether the dominant, dissecting or resistant framing and practices described in this volume encourage any alternative articulations of belonging and structures of integration by enhancing rather than restricting equal citizenship. It is also with the aim of furthering scholarly efforts to explore how collisions and collusions of global capitalism and nation-state practices co-produce regimes with their differential relations to boundaries and bounded belongings. An inspiring track in the literature is composed of scholarly contemplations at the intersections of migration and labour studies, exemplified in a recent collection of studies to which several authors of the current volume have also contributed (Fedyuk and Stewart 2018). Governed localities with distinctive identities and representations, like socially diverse cities, are at the centre of another stream in the literature which also offers composite observations on these collisions and collusions (Çağlar and Glick Schiller 2018).

The final set of reflections concerns the difference between scholarly and policy reasoning which intrigues several authors in the volume. They harness open and non-normative analytical positions to identify the main dimensions, levels and forces in politics of (dis)integration. With such an approach, they intend, in the first place, to distance themselves from the regular reasoning of integration policies in which a legitimate distinction is made between migrants and non-migrants, and duties and entitlements, and in which it is usually those born outside the borders, who have to conform to the norms of the host society. The non-normative principle is strictly observed even against some progressive moments and trends in post WW II history when the relations between moving and 'hosting' social groups has been envisioned as largely mutual and the mainstream societal norms, positions, and practices have also been doomed to change. With due respect to the scholarly drive to position research as non-normative, the notion of (dis)integration still connects the horizons and the vocabularies of policy-making and scholarly thinking. The authors in this volume have made prominent efforts to engage with the field of 'critical policy studies' without explicitly claiming it, in which the production of power positions and the articulation of policy paradigms and measures are discussed in a joint analytical framework (Clarke et al. 2015). Policy frames, categories and regulatory acts are always products of contentious relations of power holders, the subjects and commentators of policies. Resonating with this approach, scholars in this volume seem to be ready and well prepared to conduct inquiries on the multiplicity and heterogeneity of the ways in which policies are done and policy effects are demonstrated and interpreted.

Non-normative positions regarding policy-making, however, cannot be fully detached from normative assumptions on wider political and moral grounds. The chapters in this volume do not refer directly to any elaborate theories of justice but their reasoning is unambiguously normative. The authors' choice to dwell on the powerless, the neglected and the undeserving, their critical attitude to preventive and restrictive power structures – in particular for maintaining borders and limiting welfare provisions – enacts and endorses positions on social injustices. They address humanity, solidarity and the extension of citizenship rights when formulating critical insights into (dis)integration policies and practices. The researchers in this volume have been ready to tease out the embodied controversies, negligence and cracks in the theorems and governance infrastructure of (neo)liberal political and social systems, increasing disparities and selectivity in allocating resources and opportunities, even if neoliberalism is not used as an all-encompassing explanatory scheme. All these properties of the intellectual space generated in this volume are unquestionably normative in a broader political and ethical sense. The tensions and consequences of critically reading integration policy formations, as critical policy studies suggest, and commenting on the normative justice arguments within those policy formations, often with the same conceptual repertoire, could be the subject to further scholarly cooperation within the authors' immediate or wider circle.

The young academics involved in this volume seem to stand between two diverging viewpoints regarding the wider questions of the nature and potential of migration and integration research. One is imbued with a belief that integration policies are able, at least in principle, to produce public good. A credible voice of this sort is articulated by those who seek reforms or paradigmatic changes in European integration policies, which are both possible and desirable, and use critical social research to assess progress towards these changes. A fresh volume edited by Scholten and Van Breugel (2018) argues that a new policy paradigm is in the making, inspired by an understanding that migrant groups are becoming heterogeneous, often cultivate multiple identities and incorporate generational difference within ethnic belonging. Therefore, mainstreaming ideas which link the specificities of a particular social group to structures and institutions of society as a whole are potentially more prepared to respond to the heterogeneity of migrant groups (*ibid.*). The assessment of mainstreaming experiments offers a less than moderately optimistic account, yet the trust in public policies to deliver virtuous social outcomes remains tangible. The other account on policy-making describes integration interventions as regularising and concealing exclusions. Policy and law-enforcement practices produce illegality and irregularity among migrants, which inclusion policies then strive to mitigate. The tandem process results in the collapse of the dichotomy of exclusion and inclusion and fosters disintegration through selective and limited integration. The most salient form of this lapse – border control – reveals the 'obscenity of power'. Public policy in this theorem in fact produces minority citizens and naturalises a chasm of social difference (De Genova 2013). The authors of this volume possess a great deal of intellectual autonomy and have a substantial body of own research that protect them from quickly choosing between these opposing views. They are on their way to positioning themselves in the wider spectrum of theories concerning the interfaces between critical policy thinking and critical scholarship. And it will be absolutely credible if they still end up with allying with one of these intellectual positions by continued efforts to explore politics of (dis)integration.

To conclude with the most far reaching theoretical puzzle, the notion of migrant integration as a research agenda is contested by several authors due to its inherent assumption that there is a society out there with its reified inside to which the migrants and refugees as outsiders shall be related and positioned (Schinkel 2018). To embrace the notion of integration entails that scholars dock their analytical instruments to the dominant products of political imagination. The most critical move to explore exclusions endorses the underlying patterns of societies' inner and outer spaces, positions, and entitlements in an unwanted way. To imagine what happens when 'migrants' move against the grain of today's 'immigrant integration' discourse, it is important to undo the existing imagination about what happens when people move and settle in another country (ibid. pp. 8–9). I propose that critical scrutiny to the exploitative and separating processes and citizenship practices in the present shall not be weakened or beaten by drives to imagine radically different social conditions and human relations. Social collectives do produce inner and outer worlds and actors, which the vocabulary of inclusion and exclusion, or in this volume, integration and disintegration tries to capture and unpack. Conceptual and framing proposals for critical research are not neutral instruments but may not be the main culprits in generating exploitations and separation between various groups and spaces in society. Critical alertness, however, is essential to the social and political lives of our key concepts as exemplified by the authors of this volume.

References

Banting, K., & Kymlicka, W. (2015). *The political sources of solidarity in diverse societies* (Working Paper RSCAS 2015/73). Florence: European University Institute.

Çağlar, A., & Glick Schiller, N. (Eds.). (2018). *Migrants and city-making: Dispossession, displacement, and urban regeneration.* Durham: Duke University Press.

Clarke, J., Bainton, D., Lendvai, N., & Stubbs, P. (2015). *Making policy move. Towards a politics of translation and assemblage.* Bristol/Chicago: Policy Press.

Crul, M. (2016). Super-diversity vs assimilation: How complex diversity in majority–minority cities challenges the assumptions of assimilation. *Journal of Ethnic and Migration Studies, 42*(1), 54–68.

De Genova, N. (2013). Spectacles of migrant 'illegality': The scene of exclusion, the obscene of inclusion. *Ethnic and Racial Studies, 36*(7), 1180–1198.

Favell, A. (2014). *Immigration, integration and mobility. New agendas in migration studies.* Colchester: ECPR Press.

Fedyuk, O., & Stewart, P. (2018). Introduction. In O. Fedyuk & P. Stewart (Eds.), *Inclusion and exclusion in Europe* (pp. 1–14). Colchester: ECPR Press.

Garcés-Mascareñas, B., & Penninx, R. (2016). The concept of integration as an analytical tool and as a policy concept. In B. Garcés-Mascareñas & R. Penninx (Eds.), *Integration processes and policies in Europe* (pp. 11–30). Cham: Springer Open.

Glick Schiller, N., & Çağlar, A. (Eds.). (2011). *Locating migration. Rescaling cities and migrants.* Ithaca/London: Cornell University Press.

Hamann, U., & Yurdakul, G. (2018). The transformative forces of migration: Refugees and the re-configuration of migration societies. *Inclusion, 6*(1), 110–114.

Lafleur, J.-M., & Mescoli, E. (2018). Creating undocumented EU migrants through welfare: A conceptualization of undeserving and precarious citizenship. *Sociology, 52*(3), 480–496.

MacQuarie, J-C. (2018). *Invisible migrants: Glocturnal cities' 'other workers' in the post-circadian capitalist era*. PhD thesis, Central European University, Budapest. Retrieved April 1, 2019, from https://bit.ly/2FCMkFX

Mezzadra, S., & Neilson, B. (2013). *Border as method*. Durham: Duke University Press.

Mügge, L., & van der Haar, M. (2016). Who is an immigrant and who requires integration? Categorizing in European politics. In B. Garcés-Mascareñas & R. Penninx (Eds.), *Integration processes and policies in Europe* (pp. 77–90). Cham: Springer Open.

O'Cinneide, C. (2013). Completing the picture: The complex relationship between European anti-discrimination law and 'social Europe. In N. Countoris & M. Freedland (Eds.), *Resocialising Europe in a time of crisis* (pp. 119–137). Cambridge: Cambridge University Press.

Rajaram, P. K. (2015). Common marginalisation: Neoliberalism, undocumented migrants and other surplus populations. *Migration, Mobility & Displacement, 1*(1), 67–80.

Rass, C., & Wolff, F. (eds) (2018). What is in a migration regime? Genealogical approach and methodological proposal. In A. Pott, C. Rass & F. Wolff (Eds.), *Was ist ein Migrationsregime? What is a migration regime?* (pp. 19–64). Wiesbaden: Springer.

Rozakou, K. (2017). Nonrecording the 'European refugee crisis' in Greece. *Focaal: Journal of Global and Historical Anthropology, 77*(1), 36–49.

Sajjad, T. (2018). What's in a name? 'Refugees', 'migrants' and the politics of labelling. *Race & Class, 60*(2), 40–62.

Schinkel, W. (2018). Against 'immigrant integration': For an end to neocolonial knowledge production. *Comparative Migration Studies, 6*(31), 2–17.

Scholten, P., & Van Breugel, I. (2018). Introduction. In P. Scholten & I. Van Breugel (Eds.), *Mainstreaming integration governance: New trends in migrant integration policies in Europe* (pp. 3–22). Cham: Palgrave Macmillan.

Shaw, J. (2005). Mainstreaming equality and diversity in European Union law and policy. *Current Legal Problems, 58*(1), 255–312.

Varsanyi, M. (2008). Rescaling the 'alien'. Rescaling personhood: Neoliberalism, immigration, and the state. *Annals of Association of American Geographers, 98*(4), 877–896.

Yanow, D., Van der Haar, M., & Völke, K. (2016). Troubled taxonomies and the calculating state: 'Everyday' categorizing and race-ethnicity'. The Netherland case. *Journal of Race, Ethnicity, and Politics, 1*(2), 187–226.

Yıldız, C., & De Genova, N. (2017). Un/free mobility: Roma migrants in the European Union. *Social Identities*. https://doi.org/10.1080/13504630.2017.1335819.

Printed by Printforce, the Netherlands